Praise for *Waking from the*

"David L. Chappell has long been one of our sharpest and most original historians of civil rights. He confirms that reputation with *Waking from the Dream*. Chappell invites us to reconsider Dr. King's legacy and critically appreciate the efforts of those who carried on in the 1970s and 1980s to keep his unfulfilled agenda before the nation's conscience. This is an important book that will be of tremendous value to anyone interested in the history of race, inequality, and civil rights in modern America."
—Eric Arnesen, George Washington University

"*Waking from the Dream* skillfully traces Martin Luther King, Jr.'s legacy during the two decades following his assassination. The previously untold story of continuing struggle and posthumous inspiration that dominates this compelling and groundbreaking book will forever change the way civil rights historians view this era."
—Raymond Arsenault, author of *Freedom Riders:*
  1961 and the Struggle for Racial Justice

"*Waking from the Dream* offers the kind of clear-eyed analysis of our post–civil rights worlds of politics and memory work that we desperately need. David L. Chappell gets to some essential truths about the costs and benefits of myth-making. It is critical that we know this history so that we can properly contextualize the successes and failures of civil rights politics that brought us to this allegedly post-racial age."
—Jonathan Scott Holloway, author of *Jim Crow Wisdom:*
  Memory and Identity in Black America since 1940

"Beautifully written and thought-provoking. . . . Historians have cast the period after King's death as the New Nadir. The constant invocation of his name by allies, outsiders, and enemies made it appear as if nothing could measure up to his image, memory, or the seminal feats of Montgomery, Birmingham, and Selma. Chappell, however, has uncovered what the bright light of King has blinded so many to—the ongoing work by communities, politicians, and NGOs to build and sustain a more inclusive rights-based nation."
—Carol Anderson, author of *Eyes off the Prize:*
  The United Nations and the African American Struggle
  for Human Rights, 1944–1955

WAKING FROM THE DREAM

WAKING FROM THE DREAM

The Struggle for Civil Rights in the Shadow of Martin Luther King, Jr.

DAVID L. CHAPPELL

DUKE UNIVERSITY PRESS

DURHAM LONDON

2016

Published by arrangement with Random House,

a division of Penguin Random House LLC.

First published as a paperback edition by Duke University Press, 2016

Book design by Victoria Wong

Library of Congress Cataloging-in-Publication Data

Chappell, David L., author.

Waking from the dream : the struggle for civil rights in the
shadow of Martin Luther King, Jr. / David L. Chappell.

pages   cm

Reprint. First edition published: New York : Random House, 2014.

Includes bibliographical references and index.

ISBN 978-0-8223-6172-5 (pbk. : alk. paper)

1. King, Martin Luther, Jr., 1929–1968—Influence. 2. Civil rights
movements—United States—History—20th century. 3. African American
political activists—Biography. 4. African American civil rights
workers—Biography. 5. African Americans—Civil rights—
History—20th century. 6. United States—Race relations—
History—20th century. I. Title.

E185.97.K5C455 2015

323.1196'0730904—dc23

2015034665

Printed in the United States of America on acid-free paper

To my mother, Sally Kitt Chappell,
who taught me to see

Contents

Introduction

Martin Luther King's assassination marks a great turning point in American memory. In retrospect his death often appears to be the tragic, sudden end of the triumphal story of progress in civil rights, a story that Americans associate with King's career. After the major victories of the civil rights movement in the mid-1960s, most Americans remember a dreary story from that point forward: a story of dire rhetoric over incremental bureaucratic and judicial changes in affirmative action and racial redistricting, punctuated by seemingly random flare-ups, such as the Atlanta riot of 1980, the Rodney King beating and subsequent Los Angeles riot of 1992, and the O. J. Simpson trial of 1995. There is no heroic narrative of those post-King years to match the narrative that unfolded in the King years: no tendency of the plot to run from dramatic show-down in the streets to redemptive national legislation. There is no pattern of exposing evils leading to crisis leading to remedial steps. In other words, there is no rhythm like the one that appeared to propel events from Montgomery to Selma in the 1950s and 1960s, a rhythm of long-unrequited hopes of freedom finally resolving in national recognition and substantial fulfillment. After the unraveling of the movement, the times have no trajectory, ever being corrected, toward redemption of the full promise of American life—liberty and justice for all. The post-King years in the history of race, rights, and freedom appear rather to lurch aimlessly—the movement directionless, if not entirely stagnant.

As I attempted to take a fresh look at the post-King era, several episodes emerged as uniquely revealing, misunderstood, and undervalued in our history. These events added up to a richer, more fascinating, and more significant post-King era than has been previously recognized. The episodes in this book show that those years were full of ferment and vital experimentation in civil rights. Though some of the experiments failed, the failures proved as instructive and as important as foundations for future progress as the previous generation's successes.

Many devoted and courageous Americans took up Martin Luther King's unfinished business when he died. Over the next several years, they struggled to complete his work—or the work his name symbolized to them—in creative, often unexpected ways, in response to shifting circumstances. Again and again they invoked King's name as they strove to continue and often to correct the course on which King had led a generally resistant America. Some of them succeeded in extending the principle of desegregation to the private housing market. Others attempted to consolidate and institutionalize the power of new black votes. Others attempted to remedy the economic deprivation of black neighborhoods—and to tap the creativity and energy of a long-suppressed underclass—with full-employment legislation. Others sought to make America recognize and honor King's memory with a national holiday, a remarkable achievement that reflected a greatly weakened opposition to civil rights in an otherwise very conservative age. One of King's most brilliant but most erratic and controversial disciples, Jesse Jackson, tried to parlay black voting power into a more active and independent voice within the Democratic Party in two quixotic presidential campaigns. Through all these episodes, Martin Luther King's memory was put to the test—and finally, when new, damaging evidence about his character was opened up for public discussion in the late 1980s and 1990s, it did not diminish his stature, or that of the cause he symbolized, in any appreciable way.

These episodes do not just lengthen the story of civil rights, but broaden and deepen it: The effort to free America from its historic legacy of slavery and institutionalized racism did not simply devolve into endless bureaucratic trench warfare over affirmative action policies, though it often looked that way, with interest groups and policy makers frozen into irreconcilable positions. Rather, it engaged the creative energies of a wide range of African-American activists, in many cases white allies, and a diverse assortment of the booming new class of black elected officials. In the years after 1968, they rediscovered some old truths and tactics. They tested the limits of equality and black power in modern America. Often, their efforts, even their successes, have been completely forgotten.

The story of the continuing struggle for rights and equality after 1968 is central to the meaning of freedom in America. The struggle of black Americans for full participation in and contribution to the full promise of American life brings to light the contradiction that haunted American history from the start: The degradation and deprivation of an entire "race" of people exaggerated the freedom of white Americans while exposing America's hypocrisy to the world. Black Americans' demand for their freedom raised the question whether a nation conceived in liberty, as Lincoln said at Gettysburg 150 years ago, and dedicated to human equality could endure. The story did not end with the Civil War and Emancipation or with Reconstruction and the granting of civil and political rights to the ex-slaves in the Fourteenth and Fifteenth Amendments. It continued by creative, unpredictable fits and starts. It did not end again with the so-called Second Reconstruction, culminating in the Civil Rights Act and Voting Rights Act of the mid-1960s. Nor could it be contained in the bureaucratic, partisan, and ideological channels that defined politics-as-usual after the 1960s.

Other books on the post-King years have conveyed parts of the story but, in many instances, present them in teleological and piecemeal terms. The story is, in some of these books, one of lawsuits to extend the reach of affirmative action policies, and the representation of black populations with black representatives. In other books it is a story of the undoing of school desegregation by white flight and Supreme Court retreat. What these accounts miss are the more ambitious efforts to claim large-scale public victories. They miss above all the energies expended to expand the reach of freedom and equality, rather than simply flesh out or secure rights already won, in principle and in law, in the 1950s and 1960s. The larger-scale public efforts covered in this book—even when they failed—trace the now-flickering, now-flaring, now-fading-and-flaring-again spirit that persisted after the King years, the heyday of civil rights victories that he symbolizes in national memory.

Some authors say the African-American civil rights movement of the 1950s and 1960s simply evolved into a fuller-blown "rights revolution," which sprouted from the yearnings of other deprived and degraded populations: women, Hispanics and other recent third-world immigrants, American Indians, the disabled, gays and lesbians. That was indeed a real expansion or series of expansions, largely inspired by the African-American movement's dramatic successes and building on the foundation of principles established by it.

But attention to the post-1960s rights revolution tends to eclipse the struggle for more freedom and equality for black America, and for the poor of all races—the populations for which King sacrificed his life. Indeed, to the extent that a declining post-1960s economy allowed aspiring members of other minority groups, the disabled, and many kinds of white women to claim their rights, it did so in some ways at the expense of further rights for the black population and the poor.

By narrating the vast numbers of private grassroots struggles for more opportunity under existing laws, scholars have demonstrated that some kind of freedom movement is always going on. There is always some kind of unorganized resistance to oppression; there are always countless individual evasions and partial escapes from it. But that sort of unorganized struggle is precisely what the civil rights movement, as that term is conventionally understood, rose up to overcome. After the Supreme Court finally banned segregation in the *Brown v. Board of Education* decision of 1954, black southerners did not taste freedom in the day-to-day reality of their lives. On the contrary, the court decision, in practice, appeared to consign them to an endless series of individual lawsuits to make the newly articulated—or, rather, newly restored—principles of equality real in their own lives and the lives of their children. Giant steps were needed. The civil rights movement culminated in two of the greatest leaps of all time, the Civil Rights Act of 1964 and the Voting Rights Act of 1965. That kind of giant leap is what diverse bodies of activists prayed and planned and fought for after King died. Though they struggled on as people always do for improvements in their individual and local lives, the need for fundamental changes in the structure of American society on a national scale would plague King's survivors in the movement over the next several decades. History is the winding, switchbacking trail of their hopes and failures.

They failed more often than they succeeded. But in the depths of their failures they found new determination to keep striving and new paths to strive on. In striving, they gave shape to a spirit that was older and worldlier than King's hopeful dream of a future world where the children of slaves and the children of slave owners would sing old Negro spirituals together. King invoked this worldlier, more mature spirit two years after the "dream" speech, to conclude a speech that spoke of the process, and not just of the distant goal, of the struggle. That speech captured the long-wave motion of social change, the effort to give meaning to history by action as well as words. It reflected the abundance of disappointment in the struggle for freedom, and the sly resilience that hope, tempered by disappointment, can bring. The speech was titled "Remaining Awake Through a Great Revolution," but its concluding lines are perhaps even better suited to the task of remaining awake after an exhausting, though partial, incomplete revolution. King quoted a nameless "old Negro slave preacher," who said:

> Lord, we ain't what we oughta be;
> We ain't what we wanna be;
> We ain't what we gonna be;
> But thank God we ain't what we was!

King's successors would struggle in their own creative and irreversible ways, as previous generations had, to learn and relearn the wisdom of those lines, and to renew their truth.

WAKING FROM
THE DREAM

CHAPTER ONE

King's Last Victory

THE CIVIL RIGHTS ACT OF 1968

Exactly one week after Martin Luther King's murder, President Lyndon Johnson signed the third great civil rights act of the twentieth century, the last of what historians call the civil rights era. Supporters of the Civil Rights Act of 1968, also known as the Fair Housing Act, said that they wished to pay homage to King and to show restive ghetto-dwellers that hope was not lost. Since his strategic shift to northern cities in 1965–66, King had been losing hope of achieving victory with the housing bill. But the bill's prospects changed when King died. The resulting act was not just a symbolic purge of emotion, or a mere show of respect. It was a substantive answer to some of King's most radical demands and his last real victory.

The Civil Rights Act of 1968 has been almost completely forgotten—unlike the previous two major civil rights acts, of 1964 and 1965, which people reflexively attribute to King and the movement he led. Yet many in the black freedom movement saw housing as the final frontier. School desegregation had aimed to undo the *effects* of residential segregation, but white flight from desegregated schools had in fact intensified residential segregation, in a vicious circle that threatened to restore and fortify Jim Crow. Housing was a tough nut to crack, because it was largely a private market of individual transactions.[1]

Before King died, the housing act's supporters, including King, had doubted that any serious civil rights legislation could pass, given the widespread white reaction to the long hot summers of rioting, in 1965, 1966, and 1967. The Johnson administration had conceived the new bill in 1965, to complete the restoration of civil rights in the president's Great Society program. President Johnson announced a major campaign to pass the bill in April 1966, with King and other civil rights leaders at his side at the White House.[2] As the 1964 act guaranteed equal employment and equal access to hotels, cafés, theaters, parks, pools, rinks, and the like, and the 1965 act guaranteed equal access to the ballot, the final act would guarantee equal access to the market for private homes—including the financing that most Americans needed in order to be in that market. If it ever passed, that is.

A home of one's own had become the new version of the American dream when post–World War II subsidies and loan guarantees put a freestanding, single-family house within reach for an expanding middle class. Housing had been a basic civil right since the Civil Rights Act of 1866, which declared that former slaves had the same right as everybody else "to inherit, purchase, lease, sell, hold, and convey real and personal property." The right to housing then expanded, haltingly, in roughly the manner that the elective franchise had previously expanded. Thousands had gained access to housing in Supreme Court decisions, in acts of Congress in 1934, 1938, 1944, and 1949, as well as in minor appropriations for housing and urban development, and in much state legislation. The new bill aimed to complete the picture by banning the discrimination that previous policies had left untouched: in most of the private market.[3]

Moderates like Republican representative Charles Matthias of

Maryland watered down the first version of the bill in 1966. Matthias's amendment, reducing the act's coverage to large-scale apartments and transactions of the biggest real estate firms—only about 40 percent of the nation's yearly housing trade, rather than the 100 percent the administration seemed to envision—had weakened the administration's bill so much that King said it was no longer worth passing. Its passage would only spawn false hopes and ultimately increase urban despair and violence.[4] The amended bill passed the House in 1966. But even that weak version was too strong for the Senate, whose axis of rural northern Republicans and southern Democrats choked it off with a filibuster.[5]

Though it was an omnibus bill, which also sought to integrate federal and state juries and to protect civil rights workers from vigilante attacks, most of the controversy focused on its housing provisions. From Reconstruction on, segregationists held private space to be politically inviolable. This was a central tenet of their ideology. They might concede formal equality in law courts and as an abstract principle or a distant goal. But southern Democrats could rally angry masses to resist encroachments on schools, churches, small businesses—and in the twentieth century, increasingly, urban residential neighborhoods. The tactic often worked by insinuating a motive of sexual predation whenever black citizens violated white southerners' notion of their proper "place." By emphasizing respectable principles of private property, segregationists could also appeal across sectional and party lines. The modern "conservative" ideology of pro-big-business Republicans in the North and West similarly targeted a national government, hellbent on elbowing its way into "private" businesses. Such a government might soon encroach on other "property," such as residences. A man's home is his castle, was an ancient common-law principle.

Early in the next session in 1967, President Johnson urged Congress to try again to complete the civil rights revolution, urging action on his comprehensive bill to end discrimination in housing.

Prospects for passage of the great new act remained dim, however.[6]

Nobody was gloomier about the reintroduced housing bill's prospects, or more ardent about the need to pass it, than King. Against strong resistance within King's organization, the Southern Christian Leadership Conference (SCLC), and outside it, King was already organizing the Poor People's Campaign (PPC). King's ambition was to organize the nation's poor, of all races, to demand action from the federal government, to alleviate their misery and give them hope of a decent life and truly equal opportunity for their children. In addition to testing the patience of that government at a moment when voter sentiment appeared to range from indifferent to fed-up with protests and social problems, the venture took King far from the self-restrained and largely middle-class adult culture of the black churches that had nurtured and disciplined his successful ventures in his southern homeland. King was proposing now to stage massive demonstrations in Washington, D.C., on April 22, 1968, with a broad agenda that named open housing—including nondiscriminatory financing—as one of its most urgent demands. Open housing was the goal that had recently been within Congress's reach. King sometimes made it clear, as he usually had in the past, that he would accept a partial victory, to end the disruption of commerce in return for achievement of some of his goals. But King threatened that if Congress did not act upon the movement's demands in the spring, there would be massive demonstrations at the major party conventions that summer.[7]

King clearly feared that the days of civil rights success were numbered. Internal squabbles and increasingly wily resistance had hobbled the movement since the Voting Rights Act of 1965, and civil rights leaders could not agree on what their next goal should be. Racial discrimination could not compete with the war in Vietnam as a provocation for mass protests. For King that meant he should rally whatever he could salvage of his movement. His well-connected middle-class allies were growing ever fainter at heart. The time had come to muster the forces who had the least to lose and most to gain, those who had been left out of the progress so far: the poor, of all races. To that population he devoted his time—whatever he did not divert to the Vietnam War—with increasing abandon in the last years of his life. Such progress as Congress was making probably resulted from the threat of renewed demonstrations. King knew that his using force made much of white America restless and resentful. The point now was to ensure that the force was not used in vain. He had to stick to his plan, though it sickened him in some ways more than it sickened his fair-weather friends. As one biographer put it, "All of King's previous campaigns had suffered adverse criticism, but none rivaled the nearly universal hostility his Washington project was generating."[8]

Doubts and fears engulfed King in this period, frequently overwhelming him. Many of his own people questioned his tactics and judgment. Bayard Rustin was King's most brilliant tactician—nobody left on King's staff could match his virtuosity in knowing when to launch a surprise first strike and when to beat a strategic retreat. But in anticipation of the 1965 Voting Rights Act, Rustin declared in his famous essay, "From Protest to Politics," that the movement should shift its energies away from the streets, and use its new electoral power to bring concrete changes. To King that was too much of a retreat. He had never believed that political work should cease or diminish just because protests were going on. For King, protest and politics were partners, not rivals. Protest was the military force behind the diplomacy and horse-trading of politics, enabling him to negotiate from a position of strength.

Many in the movement feared that the April march would break out in violence. One of King's friends and most respected board members, Marian Logan of New York, confronted King even more starkly than Rustin had. She doubted "very seriously" that the April protests would yield success on the civil rights bill. "If anything, the demonstrations may well harden congressional resistance and create an atmosphere conducive not only to the victory of reactionary candidates in the coming elections, but also to the defeat of those candidates who are, or would be, friendly to the social and economic objectives of our struggle." Like Rustin, Logan thought King had planned the demonstrations "inadequately," which made her "troubled and unhappy." King called her almost daily, his biographer David Garrow explains, and wrote to her and her husband, trying to get her to withdraw her complaint to the board. He insisted "we are too far gone to turn around. . . . We certainly have nothing to lose."[9]

Even radicals who stayed close to King—James Bevel and Jesse Jackson, in particular—persistently opposed the idea of the Washington demonstrations, and even the PPC itself. King openly began to suspect that Jackson was undermining him, trying to hijack the movement in a direction of his own.[10] The White House was warming up to the tactic of blaming King for the riots, too. Staffer Larry Temple wrote to President Johnson in early February, "When Martin Luther King talks about violating the law by obstructing the flow of traffic . . . he is talking about criminal disobedience. . . . 'Civil disobedience' is a complete misnomer. . . . As the time nears for Dr. King's April activities, I hope the President will publicly unmask this type of conduct for what it really is."[11] The FBI was predicting a "massive bloodbath in the nation's capital" and worked to stir up public indignation against it.

And yet King himself feared the outbreak of April violence. He was increasingly haunted by thoughts of his forces spinning out of control. His new recruits shared none of his rather buttoned-up, Victorian sense of middle-class Christian propriety. As a yet-unformed coalition of diverse groups, they had no common culture or tradition, indeed shared little beyond inexperience, desperation, and perhaps a temptation to grab whatever short-term advantage they could and think about the consequences later. King worried that the plan might have to be called off and said in March that he thought the D.C. demonstration was "doomed."[12]

Mitigating King's pessimism but intensifying his sense of urgency were occasional signs that the public might respond positively to urban despair. On August 21, 1967, *Newsweek* had published a Harris poll showing that white Americans "are ready and willing to pay the price for a massive, Federal onslaught on the root problems of the ghetto." Ultimately, that helped get King over his own hesitations and second thoughts about initiating the April demonstrations in Washington. Dramatizations of that despair—his own or those of unruly rioters—might move or scare enough affluent Americans to demand the legislation he wanted. Speaking to the D.C. Chamber of Commerce in early February 1968, King gave a hint as to why he was not following Rustin's advice to abandon protests in favor of working within the system. If violence broke out in the ghettoes again that summer, he said, "I don't have any faith in the whites in power responding in the right way. . . . They'll throw us into concentration camps. The Wallaces and the Bircherites will take over. The sick people and the fascists will be strengthened." His spring project, launching the Poor People's Crusade in Washington, had to succeed, he believed, to prove that outsiders could still get a hearing by nonviolent means. It was time to go all out, despite the criticisms of his allies. "We're going to plague Congress," he said.[13]

Opponents of the bill mercilessly flung King's name about as a symbol of all that had gone wrong in America. King was fomenting disorder, they said. He claimed to be "nonviolent," but in fact he preached and practiced disrespect for the law. King's call for civil disobedience was the "high-water mark for perfidy against the United States," said Congressman Roman Pucinski of Chicago. It was "inconceivable" to Pucinski "that there can remain any doubt that Martin Luther King is determined to destroy America from within." By choosing to obey the laws he liked and to violate those he disliked, King used his charisma—and the authority conferred on him by congressional attention, a Nobel Prize, and adoring masses—to turn lawlessness into a moral imperative.[14]

Prospects for passage of a housing act were dim, particularly in the House, which had grown more conservative after the 1966 elections.

Established black leaders from older civil rights organizations mobilized to pass some form of the bill and to restore the respectability of the cause.[15] From today's perspective, people across the spectrum tend to exaggerate King's respectability in his own day, when black and white liberals often saw him as a troublemaker and loose cannon. The director of the National Association for the Advancement of Colored People (NAACP), Roy Wilkins, who had often clashed with King, accused King of "bowing to the trend" of black militants and of putting an "alarming twist" on the whole idea of peaceful demonstrations.[16] Wilkins and other black establishment leaders were poised to outflank King and do the visibly effective, old-fashioned work of getting legislation passed. It seemed that many wanted to deny King not only the ability to sabotage the bill's chances with what they saw as his reckless and recalcitrant plan to shut down the capital in a few weeks.[17] They also wanted to deny him the ability to take credit for it.

Prominent religious leaders piled the pressure on Congress. Soon an impressive list of business magnates, including chief executives or chairmen of Allied Chemical, General Motors, Goldman Sachs, and major banks in Chicago—the hometown of Senate Minority Leader Everett Dirksen—gave the bill a jarring flicker of feasibility.[18] White flight may have convinced some of the business leaders that housing desegregation would not impinge on them.

Black home-seekers were a rare sight in high-rent districts and expensive new suburban enclaves.

President Johnson, after some hemming and hawing, threw himself into the battle one last time in late March.[19] The push for open housing was to be his last major domestic initiative before he announced, at the end of March, that he would not seek re-election.

The bill's prospects improved when a powerful group of Republican governors and senators joined forces to break from their conservative coalition with southern Democrats and join the business executives in demanding a serious bill with an open housing provision.[20] The coming presidential election played no small part. Republican senators from the Electoral College's high-yield states calculated that, in 1960, the Republican presidential candidate had *almost* won a sufficient number of big states to clinch the White House. Richard Nixon had lost to John Kennedy in 1960 by margins as low as 0.2 and up to only 2.7 percent in New York, Pennsylvania, Illinois, Texas, Michigan, and New Jersey. Between them, those states had 161 of the necessary 270 electoral votes. With just a small-percentage gain among the huge populations of Negroes, Jews, and ethnic (largely Catholic) urban voters in them, the GOP could tip those states their way in the upcoming election. Senators from those large states were determined to make their congressional Republican colleagues play along.[21]

In the end, big-state Republican senators' eyes-on-the-White-House strategy—along with their desire to pacify their own home-state ghettoes—pulled enough votes together to defeat the conservative minority leader Dirksen in three straight Senate votes on the housing bill in early 1968. In the face of that potentially humiliating resistance, with a presidential election coming in which Nixon—who had had a strong civil rights record in Congress—was likely to be the Republican nominee again, Dirksen retreated and engineered the compromise to snuff the white South's last filibuster against the civil rights movement.[22] He told the liberals in both parties that he would induce his conservative die-hards to let the bill come to a vote, if the liberals would accept amendments to cut the bill's coverage of the nation's housing market back to approximately 68 percent of the units that changed hands every year. That was almost halfway between the watery 40 percent the House had passed in 1966 and what civil rights leaders thought reasonable.

To raise the stakes higher, Senate liberals soon found they had the momentum to make the bill even stronger. They extended coverage another 12 percent—to approximately 80 percent of the nation's residential sales and rentals.[23] Senator Sam Ervin of North Carolina then succeeded in adding an amendment to grant the protections of the Bill of Rights, for the first time, to American Indians living in areas of tribal jurisdiction. Probably the most brilliant segregationist tactician in Congress, Ervin had tried every trick in the book to kill this civil rights bill along with all the previous ones. It is possible that he sought to spread the burden of civil rights to parts of the country beyond the South, hoping to turn more House votes against it. On its face, however, his amendment amounted to a declaration of human rights for America's indigenous peoples. "If we're going to give rights to the black man," Ervin said, "then we ought to give them to the red man, too."[24] The amendment would become law.

There were also sops to conservatives in the final bill, which passed the Senate on March 11, notably a title that made it a federal crime to cross state lines to incite riots.[25] The revised bill would now go back to the House for final passage. Buoyant liberals in the Senate, Democratic and Republican alike, knew that they had come out of the Senate with a confidence-boosting victory. They may have overreached.

———

King said he was pleased by the breakthrough, but as biographer David Garrow observed, "it did not free him from a deepening depression"[26] that stemmed from his general fears and frustrations. Discouraged by the rising backlash, and fretful about the growing temptations to violence and other breakdowns of discipline, King appeared to set his eyes on more distant goals. He seemed to believe that a whole new climate, if not a whole new social and political order, would have to be established before serious reform could even be contemplated. Beset by bad and intrusive press, as well as dissension bordering on rebellion among his staff and many long-term supporters, he was, according to various confidants and associates, "beginning to have self-doubts" about the Poor People's Campaign; "almost despairing"; "really exhausted"; "tired . . . drained"; "sad and depressed"; "troubled and worried . . . frightened"; "discouraged and depressed"; "very unhappy . . . dark, gaunt, and tired"; "spiritually exhausted"; "really emotionally weary, as well as physically tired." Several people, including doctors, counseled him to get more rest and take better care of himself. Quite a few commented that he thought increasingly about death. Gwendolyn Green, for example: "He felt that his time was up. . . . He said he knew that they were going to get him."[27] On the trend, Andrew Young recalled: "In the later years he was given to a kind of depression that he had not had earlier. He talked about death all the time. . . . He couldn't relax, he couldn't sleep. . . . I was afraid."[28]

In the midst of all this, however, the downtrodden black South beckoned King back to his home turf. The cause of striking garbagemen in Memphis would not make King give up on the massive mobilization he had long planned to launch on April 22, on behalf of the poor of all races and regions. Rather, Memphis would give that crusade an auspicious symbolic birth. It would allow King to feel he was rededicating himself to his original purpose—to Jesus' original purpose. In Chicago, in Cleveland, and especially in his lurch into the movement against the Vietnam War, he may have felt out of his depth. Former allies said he was. To go back to Dixie, to a small, underdeveloped city, at the invitation of people who really needed his kind of help: That would ground him again in a mass movement. He would be leading a cohesive local group of people with a clear, achievable goal, as in the beginning.

News about his maneuvers in Memphis and his plans in Washington brought more vituperation than ever: Opponents blamed King for the nationwide breakdown of law and order. With the House under pressure to pass the open housing act, Dan Heflin Kuykendall, a Republican who had taken over a mostly white Memphis district in the "backlash" election of 1966—the seat had been Democratic since 1883—put himself between King and the South that had beckoned him home. Kuykendall objected to the disruption of his home city, especially to King's exhorting youngsters to leave school and march downtown, and then fleeing the scene in fear for his own safety when violence broke out:

> The Negro teenagers of our city are no more and no less impressionable than those of any other city, Negro or white. If a nationally known leader is irresponsible, they will become irresponsible. Very quickly . . . violence erupted, and this so-called national leader . . . tucked his tail like a scared puppy and ran.

John Ashbrook of Ohio outdid Kuykendall and all King's other denouncers, however. One of a rising breed of right-wingers emboldened by the riots, Ashbrook was making a career out of denouncing King, having recently contributed a densely documented thirteen-page report on King to the *Congressional Record*. He seemed delighted to announce on the floor of the House that "Martin Luther King is now doing to himself what many of us have been trying in vain to do for some years. He is finally removing his mask." King was showing, "in his Memphis riot," the "familiar pattern" that keen-eyed observers like Ashbrook had seen all along: "He exhorts others to civil disobedience and then tries to evade the blame himself when the logical result of his disobedience follows: rioting. . . . Having set a pattern of illegal conduct himself . . . it came as no surprise when his nonviolent followers turned violent. Reverend King has the false notion that you can encourage lawlessness while at the same time limiting it."[29]

Few people had heard of Ashbrook, at that stage. But he would come to play a significant role in King's afterlife.[30]

There is no evidence that King's assassin, James Earl Ray, read the daily rushes of criticism of his quarry in the press and the *Congressional Record*. But the media conveyed such damning sentiments about King from congressmen, who sent them home either to placate unrest among their panicky constituents or to gin up anger among them, which might increase voter turnout. Congressional leaders' own statements on the floor were fueled by editorials, columns, and the flood of neutral as well as negative reporting on King.

President Johnson did his part, demanding that Congress pass the housing law: "quit fiddlin' and piddlin'," he said. "The time for excuses has ended. The time for action is here." The bill was "a very good step on a very proud journey."[31] (He was just four days from bowing out of that journey himself.)

Likely GOP nominee Richard Nixon, who had a strong civil rights record in his days as a congressman and vice president, added his considerable weight to the campaign for a strong housing bill before Easter. So did his top rival for the coming GOP presidential nomination, Governor Nelson Rockefeller of New York. But House Minority Leader Gerald Ford, who had recently expressed some willingness to support the bill, refused their pleas.[32] Ford maneuvered to detour the bill into a conference committee, presumably to water it down, rather than force it to a vote before the Easter deadline that so many nervously wanted to meet. Ford's decision was the single biggest disappointment in the whole process since 1966, and he surely knew that the delay might kill the bill.

The correspondent for United Press International summed up the dynamics of the game that was left to play. "The House Rules Committee has agreed to act on the measure April 9. Congress starts its Easter vacation April 1, returning April 22, the day the Rev. Dr. Martin Luther King Jr. begins his 'poor people's crusade' in Washington."[33]

On April 4, King was assassinated on the balcony of the Lorraine Motel in Memphis, Tennessee. Soon after he died, congressional sponsors of the bill began forging the reaction to his death into a lever. They wanted his death to play the role that the violence in the streets of Birmingham, Alabama, had played in 1963. The ugly racist reaction to King's massive demonstration in that city—dogs, fire hoses—had induced Congress to pass the 1964 Civil Rights Act. That logic had played out again the following year, in Selma, Alabama, when the reaction to King's massive demonstration in that city—troopers and mounted sheriff's deputies leaning down like Cossacks to club the women and children who prayed for them on the Edmund Pettus Bridge—induced Congress to pass the 1965 Voting Rights Act.[34]

Would King's death have a similar effect in 1968? It was the last hope for a tribute that might have meant something to him.

The first to speak about King's death on the floor of Congress, Democratic Senate Majority Leader Mike Mansfield, set the new tone for discussion of the leader, on April 5, 1968, the day after he was killed. "Dr. King was a man of moderation and hope." Mansfield prayed that "our people will realize" their responsibility now "to put into effect the rights guaranteed to all our citizens under the Constitution. Only in this way can we overcome the inequities and the injustices which have marked too many of our people for too many centuries. All of us, in a sense, are on trial."[35]

Many members of Congress spoke of taking up King's burden and of Americans' general duty to redeem his death by completing his work.[36] But Democratic senator Joseph Clark of Pennsylvania was the first to tie the death of "the sanest and most persuasive voice of moderation and nonviolence this Nation ever had" to specific action. He tied it first and foremost to the open housing bill that had fallen upon the lower House three weeks earlier.[37] While Clark prayed that moderation and nonviolence had not died with their apostle, he emphasized that "[w]e in this chamber can help to make that so. But we must act now—swiftly—to build for him a lasting monument of law." Republican senator Jacob Javits of New York, another veteran fighter for civil rights, immediately took up Clark's call. The Senate should direct its leadership to "the affirmative actions which are looked for—and which Martin Luther King looked for—as the basis for the justice which he sought and for which he gave his life." That required "the passage by the House of the Senate civil rights bill with relation to segregation in housing" and protection of civil rights workers. "Martin Luther King was a very great man. He would have been the first, if he could speak to us today, to counsel this kind of a living memorial."[38]

King's opponents—who only the previous day had delivered gales of denunciation of King's practices and ridicule of his purposes—generally went on the record to convey the most circumspect sympathy to King's family and to deplore the senseless violence of his death. Virginia segregationist Harry F. Byrd, Jr. (no relation to his West Virginia colleague, Robert Byrd), confined himself to three sentences: "Mr. President, I deeply deplore the assassination of Dr. King. I regard this criminal act—this senseless act—as a tragedy for all Americans. The problems of our Nation cannot be solved by violence."[39] The anticlimactic bromide from the head of the white South's most formidable political machine, and heir to the dynasty of his legendary father and namesake, may have done as much to set the new tone as the suddenly emboldened liberals. Moderate opponents saw the rush for a new civil rights bill as a rash overreaction to tragedy and turmoil. Stronger opponents said a new act would be capitulation to the rioters in the streets, another episode in legislating at the point of a gun. Either way, it was the nation's grandest tribute to the martyred civil rights leader—a far more significant response to his death than any at the time or since.

In the U.S. Senate, most segregationist leaders kept their mouths decorously shut. The most notable exception was Robert Byrd of West Virginia. King's murder did not surprise this Byrd. For "mass protests, mass demonstrations, mass marches and the like—whether labeled nonviolent or otherwise—can only serve to encourage unrest and disorder, and to provoke violence and bloodshed." That logic, so widespread in Congress before King died, had been hanging in the air like an icicle. Byrd was the first to extend it so far as to suggest that King brought his own murder upon himself. Byrd did it cleverly, by invoking a liberal icon, former Supreme Court justice Felix Frankfurter, who rejected the folly of calling certain laws unjust—which King, following Augustine, Aquinas, Henry David Thoreau, and Gandhi, famously did. "One cannot preach nonviolence," Byrd added, glossing Frankfurter's point, "and, at the same time, advocate defiance of the law. . . . For to defy law is to invite violence, especially in a tense atmosphere."[40]

If Byrd's taste and timing were questionable, his logic was hard to fault. There was a kernel of honesty in what he said. King and other nonviolent activists had often made the same rough point in the past. King said he deliberately strove to bring the intrinsic tensions of an unjust society to the surface.[41]

Strom Thurmond of South Carolina had played a far more prominent role than Robert Byrd in segregationism. He had led the Dixiecrats' early flight from the Democratic Party in 1948, when Harry Truman, Hubert Humphrey, and millions of new black voters in northern cities finally began to pull the party away from its 120-year-old commitment to states' rights and white supremacy. Thurmond became the second U.S. senator to take the floor to say that King had it coming.[42] King's death and the rioting "sprang from the same source," Thurmond said: "The philosophy that one need only obey the laws that please him. Both the act of the assailant, and the actions of the rioters were nurtured in an atmosphere of tension and agitated emotion."[43]

The House had its day of grieving on Monday, April 8, four days after the murder, one day before the funeral. There, too, most segregationists kept their counsel. Only Thomas G. Abernethy (Democrat of Mississippi) echoed the Robert Byrd line, and he rather obliquely: Only "outside meddlers" had kept the troubles in Memphis (near Abernethy's home) from peaceful resolution. Marches "create tensions" beyond the intention of the First Amendment. Abernethy blamed the courts more than he blamed King for allowing "people to take to the streets with a design to stir tensions among our people." Riots and shooting resulted. Leaders of both parties worsened matters with their "irresponsible bidding for minority votes." He meant the sudden surge of support for the 1968 civil rights bill.

Five southerners in the House denounced that bill as irrational appeasement of rioters, without blaming King for his own murder.[44] Three emphasized that King's was not the only death of national concern. Innocent bystanders were dying, too: They did not get national rites of sympathy. (After King's assassination Presi-

Rioting in Washington, D.C., and some other cities after King's assassination was an outlet for the anger of some young city dwellers. Opponents of the last civil rights bill that King had supported said that passing the bill would only reward and encourage the rioters. Supporters of the bill saw it as a tribute to King and a way to keep the restive ghettoes from exploding.

AP Images

dent Johnson ordered the lowering of flags, including on bases overseas, to half-mast and called a day of mourning.) But their deaths were as painful to their families as King's was to his.[45]

In any event, no opponent of civil rights could hold back the tide of sympathy—or the political need to express sympathy—with whatever King symbolized.

The House of Representatives, which had been considering the open housing bill and other new civil rights provisions since 1966, finally passed the Senate's relatively strong version of the new civil rights act the day after King was buried. Both supporters and opponents of the act said that its passage was a response to King's death and the mass outpouring of grief and anger that followed it.

The final bill sweepingly outlawed housing discrimination on the basis of race, color, religion, or national origin, in housing transactions *except:* sales or rentals of single-family dwellings without use of a broker or other professional help; rental of living space in an owner-occupied dwelling for four families or fewer; or rental of dwellings operated by religious societies or private clubs for the noncommercial benefit of their members. The act thus covered about 80 percent of the housing market, though some state laws raised the percentage higher, and a Supreme Court decision in June 1968 (which expanded the Civil Rights Act of 1866) curtailed the exemptions nationwide, raising the coverage to nearly 100 percent.[46] Strong enforcement provisions were not added till 1988, but the 1968 law clearly put discrimination outside the bounds of law. The act banned discrimination not only in the sale and rental of housing, but in the making of loans for purchase, renovation, and maintenance of housing, and for professional services of realtors and brokers. A buyer or renter who believed he was subject to discrimination could report it to the Department of Housing and Urban Development, whose secretary would have to investigate and respond within thirty days, though the secretary could defer to state or local fair housing laws where applicable. If the secretary or local agency failed to resolve the dispute, the complainant could file suit in federal court, which could award punitive damages as well as order an end to the discriminatory practice.[47]

Opponents of the bill in Congress had argued that to extend civil rights law into housing would go beyond the revolutionary 1964 Civil Rights Act, which, they claimed, trampled the property rights of those who owned "public accommodations" (restaurants, hotels, skating rinks, and the like) and large employers (of fifteen or more workers). Opponents emphasized those cases that were in fact exempted from the 1968 law's coverage: individual home sellers and little old ladies renting a garage attic or bedroom down their own hallway. Many understood at the time, and scholars have overwhelmingly concluded since, that segregation of residence (typically if not always established by government policies and subsidies) was the keystone of continued discrimination in education and the larger society in general.

The most interesting of the bill's provisions was aimed at people who got rich off racial fears and white flight—a hot topic in 1968 that inexplicably dropped out of civil rights discourse in later years. Real estate agents used the tactic of "blockbusting" to leverage increases in turnover and reap huge profits. They would induce a black family to move into an all-white block. Then they would spread panic, authoritatively assuring residents that the value of homeowners' investments would soon plummet on that block. That typically scared a significant number of white owners to sell, though many were surprised to learn in the end that the upwardly mobile black buyers were willing to pay high, not low, prices. But the more black families who moved in, the more precarious the remaining white families felt about the risk of decreased value. More and more would sell at a discount, and more and more black buyers would pay a significant premium, and segregation would be reestablished, simply in a different place. In fact, as Attorney General Ramsey Clark pointed out in one of the 1967 hearings, the social science research showed that "migration of minorities into an area in an orderly way" did not cause "any depression in real estate values." The tactic was in fact based on the opposite theory—on realtors' knowing full well that they were lying to white homeowners to induce them to sell their houses cheap.[48] As Senator Walter Mondale of Minnesota described it: The realtor gets the sellers to panic, "to drive down real estate values artificially, and then he expects the values to rise, because he is the one who is going to hold this property and resell it . . . so he can profit from the sales of that housing which he expects to rise in value." There was profit in the practice precisely to the extent that the rumors of declining value were false.[49]

It was a toss-up whether Congress was honoring King's memory directly or was responding to the violence and destruction that greeted his death. While some black militants insisted that white America made patsies out of nonviolent Negroes, Bayard Rustin would later complain that America's rich and powerful indeed rewarded violence. American authorities had failed to respond to responsible political action, to collective self-reliance and peaceful efforts to reconstruct their blighted communities. There is thus some perverse justice in America's amnesia over its last great civil rights act, for the act's passage did not unambiguously honor the constructive politics of nonviolence. King wanted and fought for the housing law. But in the event, it looked too much like a reward for the rioting that King's supporters opposed.

The *Pittsburgh Courier,* perhaps the most influential black newspaper, referring to passage of the housing bill as "A King Dream," pointed out that it was nonetheless only a minor step toward the goal of eradicating poverty in America—the goal that King had founded the PPC to accomplish. The *Courier's* editor believed that violence generally increased congressional resistance to civil rights. Before King's death, "a riots-aftermath-angry 1967

Congress and a rock-willed 1968 Congress were almost solidly against passing." Yet action "miraculously" came. Passage was "directly due to Dr. King's assassination, subsequent riotings in 110 cities and more than 150,000 persons of all walks of American life who attended his Memphis [*sic*] funeral services."[50]

The point was not lost on segregationists and other conservatives. The *Charleston News & Courier* scolded Congress for surrendering to "emotional pressure" to create new buyers' rights that sacrificed sellers' established and "more precious" rights, and for raising expectations that "the law cannot fulfill," thus presaging "greater disappointment and more violence." Representative William Colmer of Mississippi, who had held the bill hostage in his Rules Committee for some time, said his committee caved in "under the gun": Only King's murder made it possible to muster the votes to move the bill to the floor. "Needless to say, it was a great disappointment to me." When the bill passed the House, Republican representative H. R. Gross of Iowa suggested flying the flag at half-staff in mourning for "this once great House," which had surrendered to intimidation by rioters.[51]

Republican representative Robert A. Taft, Jr., of Ohio, who had attended King's funeral, was one of Gross's many GOP colleagues who disagreed, saying the bill was a step on "the road back to reason and reality" after the rioting. Republican representative John Anderson of Illinois said, a little defensively, "We are not simply knuckling under. . . . I legislate today not out of fear but out of deep concern. . . . The violence . . . has not blinded us to our responsibility. . . . Rather . . . it has illuminated that responsibility." Several hundred Marines were still on guard around the Capitol on the night of the vote.[52]

Thus America's elected representatives stepped up to vindicate King, at the end of the weeklong process of mourning him. They delivered a civil rights bill that King had been seeking for years but nobody thought he could muster the force to win anymore. But solid congressional majorities in both Houses—from both parties—acted to ensure that future pursuit of black freedom would remain nonviolent, despite the violent death of the last convincing voice for nonviolence. It seems a minimal goal in retrospect, but at the time it was quite an achievement—one that is practically impossible to imagine without King's sacrifice.

The great legislative victory for the civil rights movement in 1968 is the last of the victories of the movement that King symbolizes, and it is more properly his legacy—more a result of his sacrifice—than the others. It may be that the nation's memory has neglected that final act because it did not satisfy the high expectations of its supporters. It was imperfect in its effects: It took a Supreme Court decision in 1969 to remove its major exceptions. Women were not specifically protected by it till 1974. Enforcement was rarely available except via individual lawsuits—cumbersome and expensive for discrimination victims to pursue—until Congress strengthened the enforcement provisions in 1988.[53] And even after 1988, housing remains, with the criminal justice system, probably the greatest living example of the persistence of the old-fashioned racial divide. The continuing gap between black and white in income, wealth, education, and health may result fundamentally from the spatial separation of the two populations, which emerged as the main theme in scholarly study of twentieth-century histories of racial divisions. Spatial separation persists because of zoning laws, persistent steering of clients by housing brokers and real estate agents—including many black ones—redlining by lenders, crime and bad schools, which often follow black migrants to the suburbs, as well as barriers erected by federal, state, and local highways, and other taxpayer-financed projects. Though affluent black home-seekers are now much freer to move where they choose, especially in major metropolitan areas, the poor have become in many ways more isolated and concentrated than ever. Economic barriers, beyond the reach of the law, continue to trap poor people, who are still disproportionately black, in high-crime areas with weak schools. Those barriers feed upon, as well as feed, older racial divisions.[54]

But the act is perhaps more significant as the beginning of the post-King era—above all because it had no memorably singular, decisive, world-changing effect. Achievements of the post-King era will be notable not because they are solid, bedrock achievements that future generations can build on, but rather because they mark the great effort to keep up the struggle for freedom—and thus to recognize that the struggle is eternal. That may be the lesson of the civil rights movement in historical perspective. Revolutionary, history-changing acts like those of 1964 and 1965 are extremely rare—as are world-historical fame and self-sacrificial devotion like King's. Those acts and King's leadership themselves define the nation's memory of the Second Reconstruction, a shining moment in the relatively recent past that reminds us that the great achievements of the first Reconstruction—the Fourteenth and Fifteenth Amendments—were effectively neutered by their determined and often violent opponents in the South. Freedom is not what the movement finally achieved in 1964–65, or what some future movement will achieve. Rather, freedom is the act of regrouping and improvising, with agility and resourcefulness, to keep fighting for freedom. Freedom is the realization that staying awake is just as important after the victory of freedom as after its defeat. It requires conservation and stewardship of freedoms already won, and vigilance about the tendency of freedoms to atrophy.

In building up to this last great victory of the civil rights era, King alienated friends and longtime allies while emboldening and legitimating his enemies. He made mistakes. He was tired, and trembled frequently on the brink of despair. He might have failed to inspire further action, had he not given his life at that moment, and thus snatched victory—even a limited one—from the jaws of anarchy and hopelessness. Never again was the memory of Martin Luther King to pay off in such substantive, and controversial, advancement of his cause. A few times it came close, however, and the resignation to symbolic as opposed to substantive memorialization was still a long way off.

CHAPTER TWO

Can a Movement Be Institutionalized?

THE NATIONAL BLACK POLITICAL CONVENTIONS

C an black unity be achieved without a charismatic leader? That question came to the forefront of black public life in the early 1970s, as black leaders struggled with King's absence and the loss of momentum that his death came to symbolize. Major figures from the black freedom struggle argued that the whole idea of leadership was obsolete: White leaders retained a dehumanizing expectation that a "head nigger in charge" could speak for a population of 25 million. As the unraveling of King's movement made clear, however, there was as much variety and individuality in the black minority as there was in the white majority, which nobody expected to speak with a single voice. Too many black people had, for their part, relied for too long on captivating spokesmen who promised a better day. Even when honest and accountable, such leaders were vulnerable—Medgar Evers and Malcolm X were murdered before Martin Luther King. The freedom movement could no longer risk such crippling blows, which the decade of assassinations had almost made normal. Black people would instead have to build institutions of their own: structures and programs that would outlive and obviate ingenious emissaries to the white power structure.

Whatever they needed to build, black leaders continued to make gains in political office, despite the growing conservatism of white politicians. Since November 1966—a "backlash election," according to the press—conservative candidates appealed successfully to constituencies on whom twentieth-century liberalism had long depended. White southerners, overwhelmingly Democratic since Reconstruction, were ripe for recruitment to the GOP—now that their party and especially their southern president, Lyndon Johnson, had repudiated Democratic traditions of white supremacy and states' rights. Republicans were blaming nationwide disorder on the liberals in power. Northern white voters were angry. Their own sacrifices and deprivations were not recognized in the rush of attention to minorities and the poor. Mass rioting year after year terrorized them, threatening everything from their property values to their day-to-day sense of safety. Most had never personally deprived a black person of opportunity. Their hard-won faith that they were on the winning side of history, after harrowing years of depression and war, was shaken. They did not feel—with prices, taxes, and street crime rising—that their own rights were being respected.

In these shifting political crosswinds, the preservation and the full honoring of the movement's victories—now a conservative project, in the strictest sense, as well as a progressive one—depended on the adequate mobilization, and the full counting, of newly enfranchised black voters. It had never been easy to keep the black masses publicly unified and focused on achievable goals. Making their cause attractive to potential allies and coalition partners was a greater challenge than ever.

The argument that black Americans needed to create structures and programs of their own culminated in the National Black Political Conventions (NBPCs) of 1972 and 1974. The 1972 convention would be the first great test to determine whether politics and protest could do anything more for black freedom and equality—and whether the movement's greatest victory, the right to vote, made a difference—after King's death. The first NBPC appears to have been the largest political gathering in African-American history.[1] In light of the startling gains and losses of the 1960s, it recast the historic debates between coalition politics and self-development, the idea that to realize their full potential, black Americans needed to control their own educational, cultural, economic, and political institutions; and related debates between integrationism and nationalism, the idea that black Americans were a separate people whose only liberation lay in maximum independence from a relentlessly oppressive white America that held them in thrall and often in captivity. But the NBPC has been largely forgotten.[2] Forgotten along with it were the waves of tremendous hope that both conventions raised among intelligent and careful observers of the national scene, including the more than seven thousand who attended, and thousands more associates at home who spent days preparing local nominating conventions and tried to maintain the momentum by sending 427 delegates to an ongoing, national body called the National Black Political Assembly. The NBPC movement had tremendous promise. The thousands of attendees made an unprecedented show of force and generated commensurate optimism about what black power could achieve. "Unity" was the theme under which the convention initially gathered. That theme would soon be greatly qualified and redefined, as the often contentious diversity of black political interests and opinion asserted itself. Charismatic leadership, for all its unreliability, would prove too difficult, too tempting, to overcome. And local and moneyed interests would make a hash of black unity, as had happened in the past. But the attempt to build a unified national black political body—as an alternative to both charisma and to the normal horse-trading of interest-group politics—marked a crucial, formative stage in the consolidation of the civil rights movement's victories, and in the project of restoring the movement's progress. Nothing that happened later can be fully understood without that model and the years of energy that thousands of intelligent black activists put into building and testing it in the early 1970s.

The "Leadership Vacuum"

King's death created what the press called a "leadership vacuum," an expansive and contentious figure of speech that largely set— and often obscured—the nation's understanding of the historical changes in black power that King's life came increasingly to symbolize. Many contenders tried to fill the perceived vacuum. Their very numbers rendered them somewhat unconvincing, however, even when they delivered victories.

Ralph Abernathy had been King's companion and confidant since the beginning of King's public career in Montgomery. King had instructed his followers that Abernathy was to succeed him. "I have taken the mantle of Dr. King," Abernathy told forty-two thousand marchers in Memphis, the day before King's funeral, "and I have become the Joshua who will lead you across this Jordan to the land of promise."[3] Other staffers could not keep the new leader's ineptitude to themselves, however. A month later, *The New York Times Magazine* ran a fretful article, " 'No Man Can Fill Dr. King's Shoes'—but Abernathy Tries."[4] As King's seemingly humble and largely unknown assistant, Abernathy had stood firm against defeatism in the ranks, just like Joshua. His Moses gone, he was now supposed to lead the new Israel's nonviolent armies, call God's wrath down upon their enemies, and reclaim Canaan for His chosen people. Abernathy alone had the qualifications for this role: the private, though highly visible, long-term bond with King; the official position as head of King's Southern Christian

The Rev. Ralph Abernathy said he was the "Joshua" to carry on
the struggle of the now-departed Moses. Abernathy got the
press's attention as King's designated successor. He lacked the
energy, charisma, and skill to hold that attention, however.
The press and much of the public clamored for someone better
suited to fill the "leadership vacuum."

AP Images

Leadership Conference; the quiet maturity that looked, at a distance, like gravitas; and, as soon became evident, the blithe, uncomprehending egotism to claim the dead King's realm. Abernathy had no more head for administration than King had had, however. He was a far less commanding speaker. He showed little interest in writing or publicizing his strategic ideas, which looked more and more like scattered impulses. With these and other disabilities—poor health, fecklessness in relations with the press, sensitivity to criticism, a tendency to cry foul and wolf—King's chosen successor amplified and magnified the emptiness rather than filling it. "Not all [of King's] aides were happy with the choice of the slow-talking man with the new serious air who was always late and seemed compelled to consistently proclaim 'I am the leader,'" United Press International reported in August 1969.[5] In January 1972, Abernathy was still telling people, "I am not a Moses and I know it. I will not try to be Moses." It was far from clear how his self-identification as Joshua showed greater realism, humility, or growth in the job, however.[6]

The institution that King founded, the SCLC, had been shaken by dissension even before King's death turned dissension into the only real news coming out of it. Jesse Jackson's name was nearly always featured in that news. The young upstart had haunted the succession crisis at least since August 1969: "In Chicago, the Rev. Jesse Jackson, a tall, handsome young man with a mustache and a platform delivery challenging the electricity of the late founder, was gaining a following that seemed to challenge that of Abernathy." Many in the movement believed that Jackson would even "challenge Abernathy for leadership of SCLC."[7] Jackson was actually breaking away from Abernathy, and from the southern-based movement altogether. After a suspension from SCLC over Jackson's handling of half a million dollars in receipts from the Black Expo that he organized for black businesses under SCLC auspices in Chicago, Jackson resigned from King's organization and founded his own, on December 18, 1971. He called it, with all due immodesty, People United to Save Humanity, or PUSH.[8] He had inherited King's militant determination, but not his caution and reserve. Raucous crowds of supporters cheered Jackson's independence. Jackson was mastering the art of threatening demonstrations and winning concessions, often in the form of contracts for black-owned businesses, and, later, representation in corporate decision-making. That often meant respectable token jobs for his allies—as much respect for black America as corporate patronage could offer.

King's widow, Coretta Scott King, had been the official leader of the Memphis march where Abernathy declared himself Joshua. Like her husband, and like Moses, she never sought to lead a movement. She would remain uniquely uncontroversial among King's prominent legatees. But she never tried, or presumed, to rally masses or to sacrifice her family further for the cause. She focused increasingly on building a monument to her husband that would carry on the work she had shared with him. She obtained foundation and government grants to build the Martin Luther King Center in Atlanta, which would sponsor research, study, and promotion of King's nonviolent mission. She would surpass all as keeper of King's flame. She was named "honorary" chair of things—such as the national organizing committee of the hospital workers' union, which kept alive an old social democratic activism and, unlike most unions, grew after the 1960s. She gave her blessing to the union's establishing its headquarters in New York: the Martin Luther King Jr. Labor Center.[9] That center would help to launch the National Black Political Convention in 1972.

Bayard Rustin, the great nonviolent strategist who had urged an abandonment of protest in favor of politics, more than any national leader wanted to save the alliance that King had made with the older union movement. When Rustin drew lessons from history on the first anniversary of King's death, he emphasized that

Three days after King's assassination, Coretta Scott King, Ralph Abernathy, and others led forty-two thousand marchers in Memphis, who vowed to carry on King's work. Displays of unity and determination became increasingly difficult to mount as the movement splintered and lost momentum.

AP Images

King "died in a labor struggle." "King's essential insight was that the civil rights struggle had moved beyond the need to desegregate public accommodations and into a period in which the requirements for racial equality were fundamentally economic." To Rustin, that meant political action on behalf of a broad majority coalition—not mobilization of America's most desperate poor people to demand more from the broad majority.[10] This came at a time when Jackson and even Abernathy were meeting with black nationalists and with the jailed revolutionary Angela Davis.[11] For Rustin, to abandon majority coalition-building, even for radical aims, would only reinforce the conservative trend of the country. For that reason, Rustin also dissented from other civil rights leaders' growing support of the Nixon administration's affirmative action initiatives: policies that may have been crafted precisely to make white workers believe that further black gains would come at their expense. But to some nonviolent veterans Rustin, not they, had grown conservative. Electoral majorities showed little interest in further black progress, and Rustin's beloved unions were still part of the established order.[12]

Each of these leaders sought, even if ambivalently, to fill the vacuum in the immediate aftermath of King's assassination. Abernathy, Jackson, and Coretta King had formed a united front in their return to King's work in Memphis just before King's funeral. Other aides and staffers, who had haunted King's last months with their bickering, fell into line as guilt-and-grief-stricken people will. Rustin strikingly overcame his alienation from the SCLC and organized the Memphis march.[13] More than anything, Rustin's return to the fold made the time look propitious for a civil rights revival. His allegiance to the cause and his organizational skills—along with the worldwide spotlight at an unbearably fragile moment of historic transition—proved that King's devotees could still muster, and discipline, a huge crowd.

For the organizers of the 1972 National Black Political Convention, however, the quest for leadership could be a barrier to black unity and a damper upon black political initiative. During the early 1960s, a faction within the Student Nonviolent Coordinating Committee, which often challenged King's leadership, preached more generally that ordinary black citizens needed to empower themselves by taking the initiative to assert their rights— not wait for a leader to come along and lead them to freedom. With King dead, many more activists—and most historians since— concluded that charismatic figureheads were overrated. This was not only because they could be picked off by assassins. The vacuum, to many black leaders, was not a leadership vacuum, but a vacuum of sustainable institutions and ideological programs around which the divided forces of the once and future movement could coalesce.

The idea that black people needed institutions rather than leaders gained memorable expression the year before the convention, at the founding of its forerunner, the Congressional Black Caucus, which turned out to be the most durable new black political institution of the era. According to *The Washington Post,* caucus founders "believed they should fill a leadership void caused by the death of the Rev. Dr. Martin Luther King"[14]—essentially, what individual leaders could not do alone. The rousing sermon by actor-activist Ossie Davis at the caucus's founding captured a different emphasis, however. Davis evoked the disappointments of the 1960s that caucus founders needed to overcome. He voiced their yearning to restore the momentum of that decade's victories. He echoed a growing consensus among black leaders in the wake of the civil rights era that they would have to build lasting structures rather than invoke high ideals and make memorable speeches.[15] Davis used his own charisma to take the emphasis off the charismatic men who had represented black power till then.

Black people, he suggested, should no longer be content with mere representation. Representatives were often just rhetoricians. Masses of ordinary black people had to step up and participate, to stay focused on their urgent common needs, rather than divide and dissipate when their leaders died. "It's not the rap, it's the map," Davis said. "It's not the man, it's the plan."[16]

That line captured the great hopes behind the Congressional Black Caucus, and the more ambitious black political convention that soon followed. Though Davis and others wanted to redefine, rather than fill, the void that King's death had come to symbolize, *The New York Times* introduced the new year in civil rights a few months after the caucus's founding in terms of the void: "The survivors of the Rev. Dr. Martin Luther King are still searching for the answers he died looking for."[17] The next month, the Martin Luther King Jr. Labor Center in New York issued a call to arms, urging people to attend the coming National Black Political Convention, in February 1972.[18]

The 1972 Convention

The chosen venue was Gary, Indiana, where electoral politics had succeeded dramatically in advancing black power: In 1967, Gary and Cleveland became the first major cities to elect black mayors. In Cleveland, which had a white majority, Carl Stokes had won only because he had substantial white support.[19] But in Gary, which had a black majority, Richard Hatcher was able to win without substantial white support. No one knew which would be the working model for future black electoral success. White flight was already creating black majorities in other major cities. And it was not clear that enough white voters would support black candidates in racially balanced or integrated constituencies. Though Gary was associated with reassuring small-town nostalgia in *The Music Man,* and with an upbeat black urban version of postwar

Actor-activist Ossie Davis framed expectations for the
National Black Political Convention in 1972, and for the general
shift in black political organizing, when he expressed the growing
conviction that charismatic leaders were outmoded. Expansion
and preservation of black power would require investment of
energy in programs and institutions. He told the founders
of the Congressional Black Caucus, "It's not the rap, it's
the map. It's not the man, it's the plan."
Bernard Gotfryd/Getty Images

optimism in the young Jackson Five, the choice of Gary symbolized the harder-edged, more nationalistic theory of black politics on its own, coalition-free. According to the political scientist Charles Hamilton—who had embraced black political independence in his bestselling manifesto of 1967, *Black Power,* co-written with Stokely Carmichael—Gary's new black mayor "has the confidence of street gangs in Gary's ghettos as well as the ear of top national political and economic decision-makers." In a foreword to Hatcher's biography, Hamilton prophesied that "black elected officials like Richard Hatcher constitute, in a very real sense, a kind of last hope for the society. As Dr. Martin Luther King Jr. was in the pressure politics arena, so Mayor Hatcher is in the arena of electoral politics."[20]

Delegates to the convention broke down into two categories that illustrated the tensions within the movement: elected officials, whose hands could reach the levers of actual power, and activists, especially nationalist ones, who were allegedly closer to the needs of the people and less beholden to the moneyed interests that threatened to co-opt all black leaders.[21] The two groups had the potential to represent the full range of black America—if they could work together, that is.

As elected officials faced accusations of ignoring their constituents' needs to maintain their own positions at the table, nationalists faced accusations of unrealism: Too few black people lived in the black-majority constituencies that could gain political representation without forming coalitions with parts of the white majority. And even if all black people could be perfectly represented by black officials, they would still only amount to 12 or 13 percent of officeholders, not enough to vindicate the millennial hopes of the civil rights movement, and more to the point, not enough to revive the mass participation that the movement had generated in the 1950s and 1960s. Nationalists responded to these worries by saying that black people had to gain experience in exercising

Richard Hatcher symbolized one version of black power when he was elected mayor of a major black-majority city, Gary, Indiana, in 1967. Organizers of the 1972 National Black Political Convention chose that city as the site for their effort to create a systematic and unified form of black power—perhaps a new black political party. King's somewhat erratic former aide Jesse Jackson, standing here between Hatcher and one of his convention cochairmen, the playwright and music historian Amiri Baraka, drew increasing attention away from such efforts.

AP Images

power. They could do that by controlling domains of their own, where they would not have to compete with entrenched white leaders. A full range of local black businesses and community organizations was within the black masses' grasp for the first time. Controlling those organizations was a necessary first stage, nationalists argued, even if for most black voters that control could not be the ultimate goal. Black people needed to solidify their own power as the basis for meaningful political coalitions with outsiders in the future—coalitions to which their contributions would be vital, and from which they could derive serious benefits.[22] Black elected officials were essential to the nationalists' vision, though often secondary to local black community organizations and businesses.

As the new class of black elected officials (BEOs) grew to critical mass on city councils, in state legislatures, in certain state congressional delegations, and in Democratic Party councils, however, many of the BEOs stole the nationalists' thunder. They had increased access to patronage and other political tools to inspire, or at least to deflect and co-opt, mass support.

Though most successful BEOs were coalition builders in practice, they were not so much ideological integrationists as practical ones. They made allies to get things done. But their coming from black-majority districts and cities, as most of the major ones did,[23] allowed them to lay claim to greater allegiance of the authentically black masses than ideologues of any stripe. Their mass support in the form of votes legitimated their position and by the same token undermined the nationalist activists' own credibility. Nationalist enthusiasm, like integrationist enthusiasm, had already peaked in the streets. To maintain legitimacy and visibility, the activists needed to influence the BEOs or to supplant them.

The call to the convention had gone out to all black political groups of whatever strategic or ideological commitment. The banner under which they gathered, "Unity Without Uniformity," acknowledged the obstacles to coalescence.[24] It was a hedged, even somewhat apologetic slogan: an admission that unqualified unity—unity as most people understood the term—was beyond reach. Pre-convention publicity and planning nonetheless radiated an extraordinary optimism about unity—an optimism that King himself had never dared invest his faith in. Unprecedented numbers—some 3,400 delegates, plus as many as 4,000 observers, including newsmen—responded to the call.[25] That was not the same as unity, though it was a necessary first step.

The national press quoted one of the three convention chairmen, Congressman Charles Diggs of Detroit, saying, "This convention will allow Roy Wilkins (NAACP) to sit next to Huey Newton (Black Panthers) and discuss how both groups can work toward black improvement together."[26]

In the event, neither Wilkins nor Newton, representatives of the two most prominent black political strategies, showed up. All else seemed to depend on the goal Diggs had articulated: reconciliation of the ideological poles of "black" strategy. Most attendees on record echoed Diggs's aim, including Bobby Seale (Newton's elder cofounder of the Panthers) and several minor and local NAACP officials. Diggs's other two cochairmen, Amiri Baraka, known then as a gun-wielding nationalist from the streets of Newark, and Gary's mayor, Richard Hatcher, formed a tripartite version of the reconciliation to come. *E pluribus unum* was the message. The convention was to be the medium.

Conflicts haunted the convention before it even began, however. The local black paper, the *Gary American,* gave top billing on its list of featured speakers to Shirley Chisholm, a congresswoman from Brooklyn, and Julian Bond, a Georgia state legislator.[27] Chisholm, the first black woman elected to Congress and one of the founding members of the Congressional Black Caucus, was perhaps the most visible black leader of the moment because she was running for the Democratic presidential nomination. She was the first black woman to run for the presidential nomination of a major party. When she got news of the coming black political convention in 1972, she said that the delegates came to Gary hoping to live up to Ossie Davis's challenge to agree on a map and a plan. She wanted to go for the same reason. But Chisholm decided not to attend. She later explained that most of the other prominent elected officials headed to Gary had already pledged themselves to Hubert Humphrey or George McGovern: They would never take the independent course that most other delegates were expecting the convention to take.[28] Bond, the smoothest-talking and most self-confident of the young idealists to emerge from the southern black movement, had gained national fame when the Georgia legislature denied him his seat because he had spoken out against the Vietnam War. He had spoken on national TV in favor of the antiwar candidacy of Eugene McCarthy at the Democratic convention in 1968. Bond also found he had better things to do on the weekend of the Gary convention: He had to attend a meeting in Georgia to choose delegates to the Democratic National Convention.[29] Those two newsworthy absences landed as last-minute surprises to the delegates in Gary.

Two celebrated guests offered a picture of unity, however. Coretta King—whom the press had not mentioned in pre-convention publicity—sat on the dais next to Betty Shabazz, Malcolm X's widow. The two widows symbolized the ideological poles of recent African-American history. They also reminded everyone of the reason they had come together: Nationally and internationally inspiring black men get murdered.

During the proceedings, the two widows talked at length with each other. Though the press failed to quote them, or even to note their presence in most cases,[30] the documentary filmmaker William Greaves captured the two exchanging confidences onstage, seeming to be on the most intimate and serious of terms. It is a tantalizing moment. Yet Greaves recorded no soundtrack to go with the scene. Perhaps the most memorable moment in the known convention footage thus remains a wordless one.[31]

Coretta King did not appear to speak to anybody else at Gary, at least not publicly. She just sat there inscrutably on the dais. When Walter Fauntroy, who had run the SCLC branch in Washington, D.C., and now represented D.C. as a nonvoting "delegate" in the House of Representatives, took to the podium to heap praises upon her—mainly by praising her husband—she showed great reluctance even to stand. She finally consented to acknowledge the crowd's raucous expressions of adulation—which evidently embarrassed her a bit. But she refused to speak. She had to take several bows before the crowd accepted her silence.[32]

Betty Shabazz did speak on the record, though only briefly. Her few public words turned out to be a prelude to the most dramatic hour of the convention. Shabazz introduced the other great presence known to the public from his close association with Dr. King. Jesse Jackson had been on the cover of *Time* magazine's special Black America issue, on the second anniversary of King's death in 1970.[33] He had been featured in a *Harper's* profile as King's "true heir," and under similar superlatives in *Ebony* and *Playboy*.[34] He responded to the crowd very differently from King's widow.

For Jackson had a conscience that would not let him leave a hungry crowd unfed. His mission—even if the NBPC was not up to it—was to conjure up a "new black politics" and to rally the crowd around it. He alone dared to revise and outshine Ossie Davis in defining the historical moment.

A seasoned preacher evokes mangers, great stones rolling from freshly vacated graves, and such, sparingly. Now was the time to pour it on, however. Easter, Christmas—something was coming. "When the baby is gonna be born," Jackson hollered ominously, "everybody gets scared." "We are pregnant," he continued, making his echo ring from the walls. "We are ready for change!" He had to shout over the crowd's roar: "And whether the Doctor is

Though organizers of the National Black Political Convention
wanted to break the habit of reliance on charismatic
leaders, Jesse Jackson stole the show, enthralling the crowd
with stirring rhetoric.

Gene Pesek/Chicago Sun-Times/*PARS*

there or not, the water has broke!" His voice cracked, perhaps because his figure of speech, "the Doctor," must have meant Dr. King to many present. The ovation drove away all sounds and thoughts but those of this moment. "The blood has spilled! A new black baby is gonna be born!"[35]

Jackson, at least, appeared reborn.[36] The audience reacted with what looked and sounded like unanimity. They thundered and stomped. Their season of mourning had come to an end, and their minds—for this ecstatic shared moment—fixed on a new hopeful future. The future was not about any particular agenda item or about the need for a comprehensive agenda. It was about something deeper and more exciting. Fear of death and hope for rebirth ran deep enough to be universal. Jackson alone had the intuition and the nerve to tap deep emotional currents in public. It is *not* the plan, Jackson was saying in effect, and I *am* the man.

Jackson had considerable credibility with a wide range in the crowd. His lack of polish, relative to the privileged King, was surely an asset, for some of them. Jackson had shown he could reach out to young militants and nationalists. Though Jackson continued to support King's strategies of nonviolence and economic coercion, he did not devote much time to the discipline of mass action and even seemed at times to repudiate integration. In 1970, he had said "the time for integration is passed." Appearing with the Congress of Racial Equality's Roy Innis at the first Congress of African People, held at Atlanta University, Jackson also said there was a "systematic plan" in America to destroy black people under the guise of integration. White reporters were barred from the meeting. Jackson said he was laying his career on the line to support the Pan-African movement: "black people must reject the myth that there is a gap between the ideologies of Dr. Martin Luther King and Malcolm X. . . . Had they lived and been invited, . . . they would have brought the ideal key to what the Congress is talking about."[37] With King and Shabazz on the dais now in 1972, and Jackson behind the microphone, the hoped-for unity appeared to be possible.

But the next day, Coleman Young, Michigan state senator and future mayor of Detroit, led most of the Michigan delegation—the second largest—out of the convention.[38] Young and his union-allied delegates objected to the nationalist "Agenda" that convention cochairman Amiri Baraka had publicized in the convention's name. Young told the press that most black people came to Gary expecting realistic action on such urgent matters as soaring black unemployment. They wanted "quality integrated education," "quality dispersed housing," and a crackdown on "the increasing drug traffic among Black youth." According to two press accounts, the Illinois delegation came very close to walking out because it, too, felt frustration over the convention's inattention to more substantive matters.[39]

By this point, the convention could not unify on any proposal—or more to the point, present a plausible image of unity. The final declaration was not passed till late on the last day, after many of the delegates had already gone home. With no clear majority endorsement, it contained two controversial resolutions. One condemned busing. The other called for the dismantling of Israel in favor of Palestinian self-determination.[40] Prominent elected officials from the convention quickly convened a post-convention "steering committee," which rewrote the controversial resolutions in an attempt to make them uncontroversial. Rather than condemn busing outright, the revised version instead condemned both "the dishonesty of the Nixon Administration in making busing an issue" and the "false" notion that "Black children are unable to learn unless they are in the same setting with white children." It gave up on dismantling Israel, and settled for condemning Israel's "expansionis[t] policy and forceful occupation of the sovereign territory of another state."[41] But in rejecting the convention's undemocratically proclaimed resolutions, the steering committee did not consult the majority of delegates. Whatever image of consensus the steering committee mustered came at the expense of all claims to representative legitimacy.

Even that much unity among the convention leaders soon collapsed. From New York, Roy Wilkins's NAACP stole the headlines by dramatically withdrawing its support from the convention, just before the release of the final Agenda—which the steering committee had softened partly to appease the NAACP. The NAACP's participation had been slight and grudging from the start, but the official withdrawal showed the old organization's mastery of public relations. Wilkins received a heartbroken letter from Amiri Baraka: "We are not a monolithic people. . . . We should be allowed our diversity, but in generally unifying structures. . . . [T]he NAACP is essential to the legitimacy of the continuing body of the Gary convention." Baraka pleaded with Wilkins to bring the NAACP back into the convention, which he planned to reconvene in two years. Its withdrawal could "destroy" the whole effort.[42]

The watered-down National Black Political Agenda pleased nobody, and Baraka was the only prominent figure to defend it when it was released to the press on May 19, Malcolm X's birthday.[43] Predictably enough, many black elected officials repudiated the resolutions they had tried to water down. Among the officials who joined the "growing number of blacks in rejecting convention resolutions opposed to busing . . . and condemning Israel" were Baraka's cochairmen, Hatcher and Diggs, and King's old friend Walter Fauntroy. The Congressional Black Caucus officially rejected the two resolutions, too.[44]

The project of setting an agenda around which black America could unify, and building a nationwide institution that black people could call their own, had withered—just as the new organizations of King's era had. The yearning for a stable platform on which black America could construct an alternative to charismatic leadership remained a dream.

The Aftermath of 1972

Coretta King did not take the convention's final statement sitting down. Underneath the regal reserve she had shown onstage, she recognized at some point that she was being used. She had publicly lent her image and reputation to the convention effort. Just who was exploiting her and her late husband's aura, and to what ends, took a while to come into focus. But the unraveling of the convention's credibility finally emboldened her to get even. Forty days after Gary, she tore into Baraka's "Agenda" in a withering memo to Walter Fauntroy. She criticized Baraka's strategy to rally black America against a white America that was about to collapse from decadence as an "intentional or unwitting ideological hoax."[45] Baraka deluded himself with the notion that black America would find salvation in white America's teetering "on the brink of chaos," she wrote. "White America is indeed in a crisis and is morally degenerating very rapidly." That was hardly news to her. Her husband had famously written that America was a "sick" society, and she had emphasized that line herself when she talked to the press after his murder. "But if nearly 88% of the nation is on 'the brink of crisis' how can the 12% go on to a glorious future[?] . . . When a ship sinks, it does not leave the ballroom with its dancers floating in safety." According to Coretta King, Baraka and his collaborators wasted time on chimeras like "Black unity, pride & conscience." Their childlike habit of "demanding" justice from an unwilling society was obsolete. To expect what Baraka's resolution called "a monolithic structure of racism and militarism" to yield to protesters who had no allies inside white America was, she wrote, "worse than Utopian[,] it is inherently false." She sensed that it was also insincere. Could the writers really expect white America just to hand equality over, "out of the[ir] goodness of heart or sense of justice or fear of Black wrath"? Mrs. King had no patience for impracticality. "We have the obligation to Black people not merely to recite evils nor merely [to] paint a picture of social justice to replace it." Baraka's Agenda "offer[ed] no hint" of means to its ends. "This is the stuff of poetry and dreams."[46]

She had her own ideas for filling the gap left by her husband's death. But she could not begin to raise a substantial coalition for another two years.

The convention provided great opportunities for those who wanted to impede the progress of racial equality—or at least to thwart the most controversial strategy for progress. Right in the middle of the convention, Richard Nixon made his great reversal on busing, announcing a "moratorium" of court-ordered busing by executive order. The controversial practice of busing—the only way to achieve school integration that had been proposed for the most recalcitrant school districts—was halted just in time for the presidential election in the fall. Nixon worried about challenges from the right. Black anti-busing sentiment, publicized in Gary, not only emboldened Nixon but gave him cover—as it did to millions of liberal and moderate voters who recoiled from what they saw as an extreme and often counterproductive way to desegregate. Coleman Young accused anti-busing nationalists of naïve or cynical cooperation with Nixon's plans, and there is some evidence that the administration did try to influence the convention.[47] Supporters of busing insisted that opposition to busing was racism, pure and simple. But the more black voices who sounded off against the practice, the harder such claims were to credit.[48] The shift of millions of voters away from the Democratic New Deal consensus (which gave Lyndon Johnson a landslide in 1964) involved a great psychological leap for people who associated national salvation with modern liberalism. Self-doubts were easier to overcome when appreciable numbers of black people—the symbols of liberalism's most recent and most satisfying act of liberation—opposed the most recent thrust of the liberal state.

One major conservative newspaper, the *Chicago Tribune,* also the major daily paper that served Chicago's black wards, ran a sensational headline, "Black Parley Comes Out Against Busing," over a portrait of Coretta King—triumphantly raising her hands at Gary—on page 1.[49] The issue was no longer prayerful black dignity versus trashy white hatred, as King had striven so successfully to make it. The exploitation of busing's unpopularity—especially black and liberal divisions over it—worked wonders for Nixon. Before his affirmative action initiatives bore fruit, the remnants of the civil rights movement were looking for ways to change the terms of the battle. The direction of progress in civil rights—if there was to be any more—was open and in great flux.

The 1974 Convention

Some of the convention organizers decided to try again two years later, in Little Rock, Arkansas. The city was once a symbol of white power, just as Gary had been a symbol of black power. Organizers held the 1974 convention at Central High School, a historic civil rights battlefield. The convention made a great point of lauding Daisy Bates, the leader and inspiration of the Little Rock Nine, the children who had put their bodies on the line in the face of white mobs to desegregate the school in 1957.[50] With the aid of federal troops, they had succeeded. But Little Rock was a complex symbol. By the 1970s, Central High also represented the growing wave of white flight: The school was now 45 percent black, with a black principal, and black teachers.[51] By that process, it had become a symbol not so much of the victory of integration but of growing black power, thriving in the heart of a largely unwilling white southern city. Little Rock was also the one major civil rights battle in which King had played no role. Thus it was an ideal place to dramatize the importance of unmemorable grassroots community activists, on whom, convention organizers believed, past and future successes depended.

The convention capitalized on national trends, which looked much better that year for black political power than for desegregation. Resistance to desegregation culminated in 1974 in the NAACP Legal Defense Fund's first major defeat in its three-decade desegregation campaign. The Supreme Court ruled, in *Milliken v. Bradley*, that white flight to the suburbs was a permissible way to evade desegregation orders: Courts could not desegregate entire metro areas. Desegregation had to stay within the antique political borders that growing millions of commuters—and Congress's massive subsidies to highway construction and unprecedented house-buying—ignored.

Electoral gains for black candidates, by contrast, had never been more dramatic. In the year leading up to the second NBPC, three black firsts marked a new era in urban politics. Coleman Young was elected mayor in black-majority Detroit. Tom Bradley was overwhelmingly elected mayor in the nation's third-largest city, Los Angeles, which was then only 18 percent black. Most significant, Maynard Jackson was elected mayor in Martin Luther King's birth and burial place, Atlanta, a southern city as well as a city in which black voters were a minority. Jackson won about 30 percent of the white vote and almost 60 percent of the total vote.[52]

The organizers of the second National Black Political Convention did not want Jesse Jackson to play a role there, after his triumphal, crowd-pleasing speech in Gary. Still shunning charismatic leadership, they did not invite him. The convention's planning chairman, Leon Modeste of New York, supplied the reasoning behind the snub: The Little Rock gathering was not for "big names or superstars" but rather for "people willing to work at finding ways of controlling the goods and services we receive in the community."[53] The decision to exclude Jackson was a reaction to his growing dependence on the cotton candy of media attention. But could a new "agenda"—or any other result—bring more alchemical substance out of incantations of racial unity than Jackson's scenery-chewing antics? The second convention began inexorably to settle that question.

The only elected officials of "national reputation" involved in planning the 1974 convention, according to *The New York Times,* were Amiri Baraka's previous cochairs, Mayor Richard Hatcher of Gary and Congressman Charles Diggs of Detroit.[54] Then Diggs dropped out right at the start of the convention.[55] Although Black Caucus chairman Charles Rangel, Harlem's congressman since 1971, had vowed in February 1974 to get more elected officials involved in the NBPC, the CBC refused to participate as a body, and some of its members declined to endorse the convention. Rangel himself never showed up. Los Angeles mayor Tom Bradley told the press that he would not go to Little Rock because nationalists had apparently taken control of the convention.[56] Hatcher soon threatened to drop out, unless the convention returned to its original, moderate theme of "unity without uniformity" and took "a more middle-of-the road" stance, an obvious reference to widespread reports that nationalists had taken over the convention.[57] Coleman Young unsurprisingly announced that he would not attend. His press secretary explained, "He finds this year's convention is no better organized than the last one."[58] Nationalists in the NBPC threatened to disinvite Atlanta mayor Maynard Jackson, and almost succeeded. Jackson was perceived as a moderate, pro-business politician with little interest in black unity and little faith in separate development. "The nationalists contended that persons such as Mr. Jackson who had not participated" in the convention two years previously "should not be allowed to do so now," according to *The New York Times*'s Paul Delaney.[59] Coretta King, Louis Farrakhan, a spokesman for Elijah Muhammad's Nation of Islam, and Beulah Sanders, president of the National Welfare Rights Organization, all "indicated" to local reporters that they would attend the convention. But there was no mention of their presence in subsequent local or national press coverage.[60] The second convention nonetheless raised tremendous hopes and attracted some of the most promising new voices in African-American leadership, including Maynard Jackson. Hatcher and other voices prevailed in pushing a moderate line, and made the moderate, interracially appealing Maynard Jackson the keynote speaker.[61]

From the point of view of the grassroots power strategy, the withdrawal of so many limelight-stealing figures of "national reputation" was a blessing. Leon Modeste was confident that the absence of famous figures would make the second convention more productive than the first: "After the Gary convention, people thought we would just dry up and blow away." But Little Rock was going to be "a serious, working convention," not one for "finger popping and partying."[62] Chicago columnist Vernon Jarrett, one of the most influential black voices in the national press, observed on the eve of the convention that the "celebrity roll call" of the Little Rock convention was scant, compared to that of Gary. "And therein lies the significance of this convention. It is probably the first time in nearly two decades of political struggle that the focus will be on the unknowns." Having survived some infighting himself, Maynard Jackson urged the crowd to "stop fussing and stabbing at each other so that we can begin to channel our frustrations into action," especially local action. He urged the full diverse range of black people to work together.[63]

Hatcher's speech, the most publicized of all convention statements, diverged somewhat from the overall tone and called for united black leadership. Established, high-profile black leaders appeared more united in their absence from the convention than anything else. Though Hatcher was roundly criticized for blaming every black leader but himself, he tried to show magnanimity by inviting absent black leaders to "return to the fold," naming not only Charles Diggs, Coleman Young, and Tom Bradley, but also the NAACP president Roy Wilkins, Urban League president Vernon Jordan, CORE's Floyd McKissick, and Republican senator Edward Brooke of Massachusetts (who was not a CBC member).[64]

The most conspicuous of these missing leaders was Wilkins, about whom Hatcher said, "It is time he stopped defending our grandfathers and started defending our children." Hatcher shrugged off critics of his speech, saying he meant it to be "conciliatory in its call for black leaders to get together." It was important to give the widest possible platform to "leaders in different camps who have the genius and moral stature to reawaken this country to the continued desperation of black Americans." Acknowledging that the NBPC had not yet done that, he was inviting all black leaders to step up and pitch in. "Since the death of Martin Luther King, Jr., black America has not had a spokesman to interpret its dreams and articulate its dreams."[65]

Hatcher might have been able to save the convention from the charge of divisiveness had it not been for Baraka's insistence on gestures of opposition to Israel. Baraka "attacked the black members of Congress for embracing Israel in its struggle against the Arabs and said the United States had stood by and watched thousands of Africans die of famine and drought," according to the most thorough local reporter, James Merriweather, one of the first black reporters at the *Arkansas Gazette*.[66] Tacking away from Baraka, California congressman Ron Dellums vented his irritation with nationalists when he called for a broader unified front: Black folk were "not the only niggerized people." He came to Little Rock because he was "concerned with something besides myself."[67] Dellums echoed Baraka's and Hatcher's frustration with the absence of most black leaders, however: "Any black elected official who understands why he or she is in political office has got to come here."[68]

Jesse Jackson's absence moved no speaker to complain, however. Until he just showed up, that is, at the last minute.

On the second day of the convention, Jesse Jackson first appeared on the religion page of the *Arkansas Gazette* in a small ad announcing that he was slated to speak at Mount Pleasant Baptist Church, on the closing day of the convention.[69] Merriweather of the *Gazette* extracted only one comment from convention leaders about Jackson's surprise appearance. At a press conference at Central High School, Congressman John Conyers of Michigan said Jackson's appearance at a local church may not have been "purely accidental." Merriweather noted that Jackson arrived later that morning, a Saturday, at Central High, after the press conference. Jackson dodged the reporter's question about not being among the initial invitees: He said he would attend the convention as a delegate that day and that Hatcher and Baraka had invited him.[70] Jackson, meanwhile, did what he did best. He contentedly drew more attention than anybody in town—certainly than any invited guest to the convention. According to one witness, when Jackson made his "impromptu appearance" at Central High, "the press who were inside covering the workshops, etc., left en masse to check out the Country Preacher who 'just happened to be in the neighborhood.'"[71] The suspicions that were directed at Jackson, bordering on paranoia, only made his critics look weak, if not indeed jealous. Jackson sounded sporting, by contrast.

An "overflow crowd" of one thousand came to hear Jackson's sermon on Sunday at Mount Pleasant Baptist: "The Struggle for Justice: A Challenge for Christian Men." He won rounds of applause with lines like "Hands that picked cotton 10 years ago can pick presidents this morning," and alluding to black slugger Hank Aaron, who was on the brink of breaking Babe Ruth's home run record, "In 1947 we were outside the ballpark. . . . Now we are about to break all the records."[72]

Across town, the prominent comedian and bestselling author Dick Gregory closed the convention later that day, drawing only three hundred. Few heard what was in some senses the great lesson of the convention movement. Gregory spoke about "the Convention's near-obsession with unity or the lack of it." To Gregory, disunity just meant both sides were serious.[73] Chicago's Vernon Jarrett devoted a column to the same idea, "The Disruptive Concept of 'Unity.'" Jarrett was "ready to write off 'unity' as one of the most misused, disruptive and disunifying words ever coined." Only when it was "confined to the realm of inspirational oratory" was it safe. "Frequently at Little Rock," Jarrett wrote, he had wished that "some courageous delegate . . . had said loud and clear: 'We have an urgent job to do. We black people have 14 million citizens of voting age. We can have an impact on this nation's political life. We cannot afford to wait for unity among us.'" Jarrett compared the quest for unity to other excuses for delay of black liberation, for example, the "hoax" that Booker T. Washington believed in, that black people had to wait till they were "sufficiently educated." Generations had been told—and often told themselves—"when you blacks develop enough skills" or "establish your own economy," then you can expect freedom. The new version was simply "When you Negroes get yourself *unified,* the white world will be ready to bargain with you."[74]

After Little Rock

After the Little Rock convention, the press reported a general air of disillusionment among delegates, similar to that reported after Gary.[75] Reports on attendance were disappointing.[76] The black press filled its postmortems with criticism.[77] The main black weekly of Memphis editorialized that "a dismaying exhibition of disorganization, disunity and immaturity" at Little Rock, punctuated by "too much vacuous rhetoric and pointless ideology," had driven away "an important segment of the black leadership such as the NAACP and the National Urban League. Without the support and active participation of these two centers of power, the Black Convention cannot attain national importance or influence the course of political thought and action in the black community."[78] *The New York Times* strove for balance: "Low Key Black Meeting/Many at Little Rock Conference Hail Absence of Division and Controversy."[79] Some came to the convention's defense, mostly by saying, as after Gary, that the mere fact that it happened—that black people could hold their own political convention and keep it going from beginning to end—marked tremendous progress from where black Americans had been before the civil rights movement.[80]

The most stinging criticism of the Little Rock convention—and the whole project of black political unity in the 1970s—came from Harold Cruse, the uncompromising black nationalist historian and strategist.[81] Though Cruse had long taken a separatist stance, he worried that post-1960s nationalists failed to comprehend their debt to previous militants, who were integrationists. Cruse respected the turn that "militant" pragmatists took from protest in the 1960s to electoral politics in the 1970s—where the results and reasonable hopes were now being generated. He did not name Bayard Rustin, but this was the shift that Rustin had foretold and endorsed in his famous 1965 essay, "From Protest to Politics." Unlike Rustin, however, Cruse wanted a black nationalist vanguard to lead, or at least to form a launching pad and pit stop. Cruse had been drawn to the first NBPC in 1972, when its purpose was a "loudly proclaimed threat to form an 'Independent Black Political Party.'" But the 1972 conventioneers ultimately lacked the nerve to commit themselves to a third party. Then the 1974 NBPC "repudiated" even the verbal commitment of 1972 to "vanguard politics."[82] It was the worst kind of anticlimax.

Cruse's 1967 *Crisis of the Negro Intellectual* had been a manifesto for a new, improved nationalist movement—the only discernible alternative to the left- and labor-based alliances of the Popular Front, New Deal, New Left, and Great Society. Any movement that answered Cruse's call to arms would have to be strategically nimble and historically informed. A true vanguard "knows what *it* wants," he wrote in 1974. And a true vanguard has nothing to fear from coalitions, since it has a clearheaded basis to form them and to dissolve them at will. To Cruse, that meant that "in the seventies and eighties to come," a black vanguard "should consider 'coalitions' (with either whites, browns, *or even other blacks*)."[83] Such coalitions will be "purely tentative, tactical and conditional"—in other words, realistic politics, as practiced everywhere by experienced grown-ups.

It was probably as galling to Cruse as it had been to Baraka and other militants that a very different black vanguard *was* emerging, or rather reemerging. Though the NAACP was not the only black forum of the decade, it appeared to be by far the most respected and durable one. The CBC, for example, survived, though it never developed the clear-cut identity and program for which people envied the NAACP. The CBC was just that, a caucus, as provisional and nonbinding as any of its shifting membership needed it to be. The Urban League abided quietly on the sidelines, doing effective work. Jesse Jackson's Operation PUSH was integrationist and pragmatic like the NAACP, corporate-oriented like the Urban League, and it had absolutely no identity in the press beyond its charismatic leader, like the SCLC. The NAACP remained prominent and would soon weather a withering decline in membership, potentially crippling legal challenges, and a succession crisis. It had not only survived the energetic and resourceful challenges of the post–World War II movement, whose spellbinding leaders—James Farmer, King, Malcolm X, Huey Newton, Stokely Carmichael—had all been sidelined and left without significant institutions to survive their fleeting fame. The NAACP had learned from them. Most notably, it would soon resolve its succession crisis by choosing a southern preacher as its new figurehead: Benjamin Hooks, who rose from the city where King had fallen. Indeed, King was reputed to have spent the evening with Hooks at Hooks's home the night before he died. So the organization kept in step with its main rival now, the unorganizable Jesse Jackson.

Jackson's dramatic events had an undeniable power. More tangible kinds of power were available to charismatic black leaders—such as supervising big-city governments when investment capital and taxpayers were fleeing to the suburbs—but that kind of power was not necessarily of greater long-term practical benefit to poor people in the inner cities. Jackson's descent upon Little Rock was an example of his limelight-stealing manipulation of the media and, through it, of a degree of public opinion. He was criticized for opportunism. Yet no one could deny his genius for seizing opportunities. He was a force who could be harnessed for good—and perhaps it is not his fault that there was no mass movement to harness him, to discipline him, to bend his strengths toward achievement of tangible goals that would benefit the masses.

Jackson himself told a crowd in Norfolk, Virginia, that the civil rights movement was "dead."[84] Jackson did keep a part of King's legacy alive: the part that drew media attention. In hindsight, Americans still exaggerate King's effect on the national media: Reporters and editors did sympathize with him greatly at times, but especially in his last years the coverage was often negative and occasionally very damaging. Jackson never was to enjoy the national press support that King enjoyed during his halcyon years, but he was to become an expert surfer of waves of attention, and occasionally to become the wave machine himself.

In retrospect, the movement was at a standstill and a crossroads in 1972–74. The black political conventions had demonstrated that although black unity might be an electoral force, it was primarily a defensive and reactive one. Black unity was not a force that anybody could use, as King had, to take aggressive, offensive initiatives. When some politician or police department appeared to attack black people's interests or self-respect in a general manner, that is, black voters would rally at the polls to rebuff the assault. But beyond that, black America was a population, full of all the diversity, individuality, and contention of the rest of America. It was not an interest group. In the 1950s and early 1960s, it had been plausible to conceive black America as an emerging nation, struggling to break free from severe oppression in the South and some northern inner cities. But through a combination of victories and defeats, black Americans no longer had the severe incentives of systematic humiliation and deprivation to make unified claims on new legal and political territory. And because they were no longer systematically silenced by segregation and other forms of legal repression, no group could plausibly claim fully to represent them in the contention for political spoils. The quest that animated the conventions yielded no tangible new achievements, no new map or plan. Institutions and programs turned out to be just as evanescent and vulnerable as charismatic leaders.

A large portion of the black population—by many measures, a growing one—remained humiliated and deprived by poverty, however, and Jesse Jackson would continue to try to give them a voice, as King had died trying to do. But the black conventions could neither organize that population as an independent force nor unify it with black elected officials, who were behaving more and more like middle-class leaders, maintaining whatever slice of the pie they could hold on to.

The black middle class was the great beneficiary of the civil

Rivals and critics accused Jesse Jackson of hogging the limelight and chewing up the scenery. He kept the cause of civil rights— and the plight of the poor whom King had died trying to save— in the public eye, however, more than any other leader.

AP Images

rights era: It had been liberated and enlarged by the movement's great political victories, as well as by the unprecedented economic growth of the 1940s through 1960s. The NAACP, representing that black middle class, was moving toward a coalition with other populations, composed of white women, recent Spanish-surnamed immigrants, and other upwardly mobile groups that together formed a majority coalition, rather than the outcast minority group that the NAACP had spoken for in the past. That new coalition would emerge from the 1970s, though it was barely discernible in 1974. The quest for black political solidarity having run aground in Gary and Little Rock, the time had come to reconstitute the social democratic coalition that the civil rights movement had so often been attached to.

CHAPTER THREE

A Coalition for Full Employment

As the second National Black Political Convention faded, a different group staked its claim to King's legacy, mustering sufficient force to get the old engine of progress moving again in Congress. In 1974 Coretta Scott King, representing the civil rights movement, along with Murray Finley, president of the Amalgamated Clothing Workers of America, representing the labor movement, formed the Full Employment Action Council. Rather than try to unify black voters, the new force created by the civil rights movement, the council sought to uplift those left behind by the movement. It spoke on behalf of a vast, mostly white population who shared something with the black poor: the growing menace of unemployment, which reached a postwar high in 1975. The council's immediate goal was passage of ambitious legislation that had just been introduced in Congress—legislation more radical than any that had passed in the 1960s. The Humphrey-Hawkins full-employment bill would require a complete transformation of economic policy, spreading the direct benefits of federal intervention to working and poor people.

Rather than create a new institution, the council was reviving an old coalition with an old ambition: educated black and white liberals working together with union leaders to improve the lives of the underprivileged. The council represented, as the *Pittsburgh Courier* put it, "the same coalition of minority, labor, religious and women's groups that pushed 1960s civil rights legislation."[1] More than consolidate the gains of the civil rights movement, the council attempted to reconstitute modern liberalism, the political base that had buoyed the civil rights movement up with experienced allies and winsome self-assurance. The old band from the heyday of the civil rights era was getting back together. The great social-democratic moment in Western history, known in the United States as progressivism, would either come back to life or go out with a bang.

Full Employment Gets Traction in Congress

Inside Congress, leadership came from Senator Hubert Humphrey, the aging liberal hero and former vice president, who had strong ties to labor leaders and mainstream civil rights leaders. As a powerful northern senator and party leader, Humphrey had led the Democrats in their historic shift, beginning in the late 1940s, away from their heritage of white supremacy and states' rights. Humphrey—who like most of his generation defined liberal as centrist, and who was proud of the deals he had made with conservatives and southerners—broadened the appeal of full employment. No doubt recalling the ways Republicans and independent business executives had leapt to fund ghetto programs in response to the rioting of the mid-1960s, Humphrey offered a path to "an American future in which the work ethic is to be conserved" by employment opportunities, "rather than undermined by the lack" of them.[2] He argued that his full-employment initiative would do more to restore safety on city streets than the Nixon administration's "much-touted war on crime," which had not reduced crime. Unemployment was much higher among crime-prone populations in high-crime areas than in the population at large: "Between one-third and one-half of the cities' post-adolescent black youths are out of school and out of work." He tied his initiative to America's bicentennial, soon to be celebrated: Enactment of full employment "would be the best way of celebrating the commitment of the Founding Fathers to the 'inalienable rights' of human beings."[3]

House leadership came from Congressman Augustus Hawkins, who represented the Watts section of Los Angeles and was one of the oldest members of the Congressional Black Caucus. Hawkins had been a New Dealer in the California Assembly since the 1934 election, where he had worked for fair-employment legislation and other social-democratic causes. First elected to Congress in 1962, Hawkins hewed to Great Society integrationism, much influenced by A. Philip Randolph and his remarkably successful union of rail-road employees.[4] Like King, Hawkins favored coalition politics, eschewing nationalist proposals for a separate black party. According to political scientist Robert C. Smith, Hawkins was "the most outspoken Caucus member in opposing the 1972 National Black Political Convention." Hawkins had even expressed some discomfort with the formation of the racially exclusive Black Caucus.[5]

Hawkins began drafting the full-employment bill in 1973.[6] The Humphrey-Hawkins bill, introduced in June 1974 as the Equal Opportunity and Full Employment Act of 1976, sought to establish a "judicially enforceable right" to a job—meaning unemployed people could sue if the government failed to provide them a job. The quaintest statement Hawkins made, from the perspective of later, more conservative times, dismissed "that economic mentality which rejects any Federal obligation to deal with the problem of widespread unemployment." That mentality, "widely prevalent prior to the New Deal," had obviously been overturned by the political successes of the New Deal and by the massive federal spending that finally ended the Depression in World War II. Before those lessons were learned, many Americans had understandably "held to the belief" that widespread unemployment should be left alone, to be "solved in a 'self-regulating' economy." To Hawkins, it was a self-evident truth that modern realities had repealed such outmoded thinking. "Saving human beings from economic disaster through commonsense planning demands no less attention than protecting the banks, saving the railroads, and helping industrial giants survive."[7] He could not foresee the day when faith in self-regulation would become politically plausible again.

The recession of 1973–75, on the heels of the 1960s riots, Vietnam, Watergate, and the first energy crisis, shook the confidence that had characterized America in the unprecedented economic boom that began in World War II. In May 1975, unemployment peaked at 9.0 percent. High inflation—over 12 percent in 1974—crippled the economy simultaneously, in a twist that was considered theoretically impossible till then. By 1976, panic over the economy had made a majority of Americans more concerned with domestic than foreign policy for the first time in forty years.[8] Many liberals thought the time was finally ripe to revive and redeem the New Deal's promise, to save the capitalist system from self-destruction. Fundamental reforms began to seem urgent again, as they had in the 1930s. The question was whether they could become politically feasible again, too.

Coretta Scott King's Role

Martin Luther King's widow was the most visible leader of the full-employment cause outside Congress. She remained a mysterious, elusive force, since she generally kept quiet around reporters. "I'm not a ceremonial symbol—I'm an activist," she told Barbara

Reynolds of the *Chicago Tribune,* who had just published a scath-
ing exposé on Jesse Jackson. Mrs. King generally refused to talk to
the press, she explained, because her name would create headlines
about things other than the cause she was fighting for. Building the
King Center to carry on her husband's work of nonviolent social
change was phase one of that cause. "In Phase 2, Mrs. King is re-
building the New Deal–Civil Rights coalitions into a movement
for full employment," Reynolds reported. Mrs. King explained
that this focus was not really new: "That's where my husband was
going. People couldn't see the economics of the movement because
of the drama." A job and an income must become as constitu-
tional as the right to vote. That was why Mrs. King and Murray
Finley had "pulled together a team of economists and a cadre of
labor, Jewish, and political groups to make full employment a national priority." Mrs. King, chafing under the growing emphasis
on affirmative action at the expense of all other civil rights programs, said, "I am not talking about a system that pits women
against men or one ethnic group against another, but rather a new
system that includes everybody."

Reynolds echoed a widely held view that Mrs. King "has the
respect to lead the movement and correct its drift since the death
of her husband." But Mrs. King said that she did not believe in
doing that: "No one man speaks for whites, no one man speaks for
blacks. Martin articulated the concerns of a coalition, SNCC,
CORE, SCLC, and others. . . . It is more crucial to develop leadership than to project a singular individual." Reynolds added, "Mrs.
King emphatically refuses to comment on the role of the Rev. Jesse
Jackson as a civil rights leader."[9]

On the anniversary of King's death in 1975, Mrs. King testified
before Hawkins's House Subcommittee on Equal Opportunities
that the full employment law would be "a real tribute to him." A
new tribute was due, these seven years later, given the increasing
importance of the work that King's death had cut short, and the

lack of progress since then. Mrs. King told the committee that it was "so appropriate that this hearing was scheduled on April 4th, which is a tribute to my husband and his work."[10]

The Bill

Full employment was actually a milder proposal than the comprehensive economic planning act that Humphrey and Senator Jacob Javits, the New York Republican, had cosponsored. For a time, the Humphrey-Javits bill eclipsed Humphrey-Hawkins in its efforts to apply the lessons of World War II and the Cold War to the 1970s: that planned government spending on the most advanced industries can reverse economic downturns. But Humphrey-Javits never came to the floor for consideration, and Humphrey-Hawkins—partly because it was less radical and partly because the Congressional Black Caucus pushed so hard to get it on the docket—became the compromise proposal for congressional liberals to end the recession of the early 1970s.[11]

In its original form, the Humphrey-Hawkins bill was based on the 1945 employment bill, which aimed to resurrect the ad hoc employment and public-works programs of the New Deal. New Deal programs had always been understood to be temporary, but the 1945 bill attempted to convert them into a frank, Keynesian acknowledgment of government's role in rescuing and sustaining capitalism. More directly, the 1945 bill aimed to perpetuate the economic salvation of wartime subsidies. The original 1945 bill, written by Representative Wright Patman of Texas, would have required the federal government to provide jobs to all who sought them. At the start of each year, the government would forecast the economy's employment level and then spend enough to bring it up to full employment. Conservatives quickly amended away the job-creation mandate and the spending. Truman signed the revised, largely symbolic bill in February 1946.[12] The main legacy of the Employment Act of 1946 consisted of the yearly President's Economic Report, which the act ordered, and two institutions that helped to politicize the economics profession, as it simultaneously struggled for academic legitimacy as a "science": the President's Council of Economic Advisers, and Congress's Joint Economic Committee. Full employment remained on American liberals' ideal agenda over the postwar era, though rarely near the top of it. Growth-stimulating policies, and generally flush times, kept the idea in the background—except in discussions of minority groups, where unemployment was almost always high. The Humphrey-Hawkins bill was an effort to bring black voters' concerns into mainstream economic policy brokering during the most serious recession since the 1930s—a time when the menace of unemployment spread to the general population.

Early in the process of pushing the new full-employment bill, however, Humphrey expressed some faintness of heart. Would voters resurrect countercyclical spending when so many were drawn the other way, to the tax revolt?[13] Inflation (in double digits from February 1974 through April 1975) already plagued not only big banks but also millions of middle-class consumers, especially those living on fixed incomes or looking forward to them in retirement. On King's birthday in January 1975, according to *The Washington Post,* "Humphrey said people had told him the bill has little if any chance of passage. 'People say that this is dreaming, but let us dream a little.'"[14]

Despite congressional hearings on the bill and Mrs. King's testimony in 1974 and 1975, no real action on Humphrey-Hawkins occurred until 1976, when unemployment remained stubbornly high, despite the official end of the recession in March 1975.[15] In an editorial in March 1976, *The New Republic* said that Humphrey-Hawkins was "the only comprehensive economic plan the Democrats have produced in this recession, and probably the only alternative they have to offer to *laissez faire* policies that have created such high levels of unemployment and industrial stagnation."[16]

Revising the Dream

Since King's death, speakers and placard-carriers in his birthday demonstrations had often emphasized King's commitment to jobs and economic justice as the essence of his dream. But jobs for all, at decent wages, through legislation, became the main—often the exclusive—emphasis of those demonstrations from January 1975 on.

The Humphrey-Hawkins bill became decidedly less dreamy after revisions in March 1975 and in late 1976. The right to sue the government for a job was cut. The public service jobs were to be "temporary" and "residual" jobs only (meaning the jobs would go to someone who had applied for benefits under the act only if the jobs could not be filled by normal means). Full employment was officially defined as a 3 percent unemployment rate for people over sixteen. The timetable to reach that was set at eighteen months. The Joint Economic Committee, chaired by Humphrey, held hearings in March 1976 and the House Committee on Education and Labor approved Hawkins's substitute bill. Hawkins's revised bill also changed the definition of an adult from sixteen to twenty. He added a provision that prohibited government intervention in the "private sector" except where authorized by other legislation. Perhaps most fatefully, Hawkins also put a ceiling on the inflation rate. The government's employment efforts would effectively halt if inflation passed a point that the president deemed inconsistent with "reasonable price stability"; the president's "goal" would be to prevent a rise in the consumer and other price indexes above their levels on the day of the law's enactment. This was intended to appease critics who argued that employment increases meant price increases.[17]

That point was hotly disputed, by Mrs. King among others, in the hearings. She took the simultaneous increases in the current data in both unemployment and inflation to imply that the old rules no longer applied. According to standard economic theory, embodied in the "Phillips Curve," when unemployment rose, inflation fell, and vice versa. But the startling new reality of simultaneous increases in inflation and unemployment, Mrs. King and others argued, clearly broke the connection. Therefore fears of inflation should no longer stifle employment-boosting policies, as had happened in the past. Employment-boosting policies were the logical extension of the civil rights victories that everybody had recently been so proud of, victories her husband had died for. Now that reality no longer supported the theory of an employment-inflation connection, Americans were free to pursue full employment without fear.

The Ford administration, however, was blind to the new reality. In one of her most dramatic statements, Mrs. King told a Senate committee in May 1976 that the administration's "current policies amount to nothing less than the repeal of the civil rights acts of the 60s, and the gutting of the promise of justice." She was trying to re-create the moral clarity that her movement had enjoyed in facing off against Bull Connor and Sheriff Jim Clark. "What good is the legal right to sit in a restaurant if one cannot afford the price of its food? And what good is the promise of fair employment when there is no employment for black Americans?" "Nothing would facilitate the improvement of black-white relations [more] than the elimination of competition for jobs which would result from this bill."[18] Anticipating that the persistent economic crisis would weaken the GOP, sponsors began a stronger push for the bill.[19] But sponsors conceded that they expected President Ford to veto it.[20]

The compromises that Hawkins and other sponsors worked into the bill were still not enough to persuade Democratic presidential nominee Jimmy Carter to embrace it. Carter, then governor of Georgia, had a complicated relationship to black voters. During the primaries that year, Carter got significant black support as a new kind of southern Democrat who openly courted black voters yet could also win statewide office in the South. Early endorsements came in from Detroit mayor Coleman Young, from the unrelated Georgia congressman Andrew Young, King's former aide, and Martin Luther King, Sr., who, after making sure that Nelson Rockefeller would not run for the GOP nomination (Daddy King, like much of Atlanta's older generation of black leaders, remained a Republican), vigorously supported Carter's bid for the Democratic nomination. Coretta King also endorsed Carter. While much of black Atlanta did not support Carter (who had always done better among black voters outside Atlanta than in), the King family and others saw his repudiation of his racist predecessors as a helpful step.

In the 1976 election, black voters generally had not followed the independent course that the NBPC, and then Jesse Jackson, had urged upon them.[21] They did, however, mobilize effectively enough in support of Carter so that, in a close election, their votes proved decisive. *Congressional Quarterly* reported that Carter's margin of victory consisted entirely of black votes in thirteen states (worth 216 electoral votes), including Mississippi.[22] As one Urban League officer put it, "If Ford had gone to black churches in Ohio, he might still be president."[23]

It was the first time since reestablishment of voting rights in 1964–65 that black voters could claim to have made a critical difference in a presidential election. According to journalists, civil rights leaders, and black politicians, black voters believed the new president owed them a great debt in return.

President Carter Comes on Board

Urban League president Vernon Jordan grabbed attention by attacking Carter for defaulting on his debt only six months after his presidency began. Jordan said, "We expected Mr. Carter to be working as hard to meet the needs of minorities and the poor as he did to get our votes. But so far, we have been disappointed." The administration had "fallen short on policies, programs, and people." Since Jordan was seen as the most moderate and least contentious of civil rights leaders, and the one closest to the president, this was front-page news. Jordan escalated the criticism at the Urban League's annual convention a few days later, leading a litany of complaints with "We have no full employment policy." Other black leaders and journalists suggested that Jordan would only speak that way if the tide of black feeling pushed him that way. As the headline of a Faith Christmas column in the *Los Angeles Sentinel* put it, "We Provided the Votes, Now We Want the Oats."[24]

Jordan's private correspondence with Carter aides reveals that the denunciation was mostly theatrics: He maintained close working ties with the administration.[25] But Carter had to make a public show of respect to black voters. If sufficiently outraged or insulted by Democrats, black voters would stay home; if by Republicans, they would turn out in high numbers. In a sense, black leaders in this case were making it easy for Carter by offering him an already compromised full-employment bill. Representative Hawkins, in a column in the *Los Angeles Sentinel,* tried to find "a middle ground" between Jordan and Carter.[26]

By 1977, a black leadership summit—the first major strategy session among leaders of the major civil rights organizations since 1963—took up the full-employment cause. "There was universal agreement on jobs," said Vernon Jordan, who hosted the meeting.

Carl Holman, head of the National Urban Coalition, compared the meeting and its purpose to the March on Washington that King had led fourteen years earlier that month. Many at the meeting said things had gotten worse for the black poor since then: black unemployment had been 10.2 percent in 1962 (when white unemployment was 4.9 percent); in 1975, black unemployment was 13.8 percent (white unemployment was 7.9 percent). The 1963 march was "a march for jobs and freedom," Holman said. "And to the extent that legislation resulted in an opening up of public accommodations, you could say that represented a certain amount of freedom. But the failure was jobs—not in terms of those who marched, but in terms of those who weren't listening. We want to change that this time."[27]

Huge rallies made the front pages at the end of the summer of 1977, stretching from the anniversary of King's March on Washington and "dream" speech on August 28, through Labor Day. Governors and mayors joined the American Federation of Labor–Congress of Industrial Organizations in proclaiming "full employment week," the aim of which was passage of Humphrey-Hawkins. Demonstrations were planned in New York, Washington, and a hundred other cities "under auspices of a coalition made up of unions, civil rights groups, churches and other organizations." Meanwhile, "quiet talks" were in progress, according to A. H. Raskin of *The New York Times*, aimed at "modifying" the bill to "make it more acceptable to the White House."[28]

White House negotiators met with congressional sponsors to make further changes, announced in November 1977, that set a 3 percent unemployment goal for adults but a separate 4 percent goal for sixteen- to nineteen-year-olds, over five years. While the 3 and 4 percent figures and the assertion of a "right" sounded like mandates, the other new language was all hedges and escape hatches: The bill established the right not to an actual job but rather "to full opportunities for . . . employment," from no specified source, and only "as a national goal."[29] Along with inflation targets that could easily provide a pretext for ignoring the employment targets altogether, this all felt a far cry from the right to sue the government for a job, as Hawkins had originally proposed.

The cause was far from lost, however. Unemployment hawks—namely unions and Great Society liberals—still had great power, intellectual legitimacy, and, perhaps most important, confidence, through much of the 1970s. The monetarist faith of inflation control at all costs had not yet become the national religion. Jimmy Carter's appointment of an inflation hawk, Paul Volcker, as chairman of the Federal Reserve Board, was still in the future (August 1979).[30]

The final push began in the tenth year after King's assassination: 1978 began with King's birthday celebration at Ebenezer Baptist Church in Atlanta—extended to a five-day extravaganza, chaired by Andrew Young (newly appointed by Carter as the ambassador to the United Nations) and the president of the Coca-Cola Company.[31] The idea was to take advantage of Democratic control of the White House, with a president who owed his small majority to high black turnout, in time for what would have been King's jubilee fiftieth birthday, the following January.

Corporate sponsorship of the event was significant for its reflection on the weakening of the civil rights movement. It highlighted the civil rights groups' inability to raise sufficient funds from their own rank and file. Jesse Jackson had shown major corporations, who worried about their public image, how easy it could be to buy a pass from civil rights leaders, and to ingratiate themselves with black consumers, by sponsoring their events.[32] It also signified civil rights leaders' shrinking confidence in the common ground they had with white rank-and-file union members, or at least in the power of union leaders to defend that ground.

Mrs. King and other full-employment crusaders held on, however, to the labor–civil rights alliance. Full employment would prove to be the alliance's last significant common cause as well as the last serious effort to revive a social-democratic policy for the American majority.

For the Carter administration, the bill was enough of a public relations problem that the president sent one of the senior administration officials who favored Humphrey-Hawkins, Secretary of Labor F. Ray Marshall, to speak that January at King's five-day birthday celebration.[33]

The forces assembled there found themselves fighting to establish not only King's goal of economic opportunity for all, but its receding context: the institutional order that King had taken for granted. In King's day, bankers and industrialists jockeyed with government officials and union leaders to set the tone and pace of public life. Liberal thinkers had celebrated and justified that "pluralist" order as one in which no single "interest" would dominate; rather, the self-interested contention would stimulate economic growth.[34] But since the 1960s, partly because of the civil rights struggle, certain liberals were coming to see unions and government as part of the problem.[35] A tone of nostalgia sat awkwardly on the "progressive" forces who fought to carry on King's work, but they found themselves essentially in a conservative position of seeking to defend a once-established order that was eroding. Gary mayor Richard Hatcher told the crowd that the private sector must involve itself in decision-making processes to ensure that everybody who seeks a job can find one. "That kind of commitment will ensure that Martin Luther King's dream will become a reality," he said.[36]

Final Hurdles

Just when the full-employment bill raised its highest hopes, another signal death shocked what was once called the civil rights community: Hubert Humphrey died, two days before King's birthday, on January 13, 1978. Coming on the heels of Harry Truman's death in late December 1972, and Lyndon Johnson's in January 1973, Humphrey's death confirmed the New Deal–labor coalition's slippage from the field of power. In many ways black voters held Humphrey in even higher regard than Truman or Johnson, and his death inspired the black press to go all out with oversized headlines and front-page photo spreads on all the patriotic pomp devoted to an old friend and champion of the people. The major black weekly of Congressman Hawkins's hometown, the *Los Angeles Sentinel*, compared Humphrey to the great black leader whose birthday shared the headlines with his death: "Like the late Dr. Martin Luther King Jr., Hubert Humphrey had a dream. His dream was simply to make sure that every man, who is able, has a job and is able to stand on his two feet as a man. We cannot afford to let that dream die, just as we cannot afford to let Dr. King's dream die." There was one way to make sure that Humphrey did not die in vain, the paper added: "The Humphrey-Hawkins bill is one of the last hopes we have for the future. But it can only be meaningful if we push . . . Congress to make sure the bill . . . is not too watered down to be effective."[37]

Humphrey's deathbed wish was passage of his eponymous bill. In hearings shortly after Humphrey died, Senator Don Riegle of Michigan referred to the new Senate office building then being built in memory of his predecessor Phil Hart, emphasizing that "another kind of construction needs to be built in the memory of Hubert Humphrey and Martin Luther King": full-employment law.[38] Republican Edward Brooke, the lone African-American in the Senate, said that "just as Dr. King was the father of the civil rights revolution, Hubert Humphrey was its legislative father."[39] As with the 1968 housing act, the bill's advocates unabashedly invoked the name of their fallen hero to push for passage.

In the event, the bill was watered down by several eleventh-hour amendments—though some poison pill amendments were defeated, including one from Ohio Republican John Ashbrook, which would have required a balanced budget. The revised bill passed the House 257 to 152 on March 16, just twenty days before the tenth anniversary of King's murder.[40]

Mrs. King defended the revised bill, hoping it would pass by June that year. "We feel real good," she affirmed. "Perhaps we can make some progress while opponents don't realize it's being done." She said more supporters of civil and human rights had come together than since, as the *Atlanta Daily World* paraphrased her, "the times poor people ban[d]ed together for the passage of the 1964 Civil Rights Act and the Voting Rights Act of 1965." "It has taken 10 years for the legislation Martin was talking about to get to this point. The Humphrey-Hawkins bill will be the next big step in human rights to be implemented so that the poor can be involved in the greatness of this country."[41] Part of her confidence came from Jimmy Carter's new willingness to support the bill.

That was indeed a turn in the tide. Just before the tenth anniversary of King's death, in April 1978, Chicago's black columnist Vernon Jarrett touted Jimmy Carter's now unhesitating, "enthusiastic" support of the (admittedly "softened") Humphrey-Hawkins bill.[42] That same day, Ossie Davis—who had recently portrayed King in an NBC documentary—addressed a rally in New York. King's widow joined Hubert Humphrey's widow, who had assumed her husband's seat in the Senate, on stage. The rally focused on employment, making demands on Mayor Ed Koch and Governor Hugh Carey to create jobs, and demanding congressional passage of Humphrey-Hawkins.[43]

A few weeks later, Jarrett turned up the heat on northern white liberals. A number of southern Democrats were supporting the bill. Jarrett quoted Mrs. King saying she was "feeling more and more optimistic"—after talking with Senators Sam Nunn and Herman Talmadge of Georgia, and "several other Southerners," including Arkansas's Senator Dale Bumpers. It was "a real pleasure" to talk to Democratic senator James Sasser of Tennessee, she said, "And we're not writing off Sen. [Ernest F.] Hollings [D–South Carolina]." By contrast, prominent liberal senators in the North, notably Democrats William Proxmire of Wisconsin and the former vice presidential nominee Edmund Muskie of Maine, were failing to support the bill. Lobbyists for the bill were mounting a public crusade for final passage. Jarrett urged his readers to turn out for the rally the following Sunday to kick off the effort, led by Congressman John Conyers and other Black Caucus members, midwestern labor leaders, and representatives of the Full Employment Action Council, at the Radisson Hotel downtown. "It will be interesting to see how many Chicagoans that afternoon value football over full employment."[44]

One Chicagoan, Jesse Jackson, got credit for bringing some Republicans over to vote for the bill. Jackson called on Bill Brock, the chairman of the Republican National Committee (RNC). The GOP had gotten a reputation for countenancing bigotry in order to recruit the white southern voters who felt betrayed by Democratic support of civil rights. Jackson was helping Brock shed that reputation. Jackson spoke, for example, at the Republican off-year convention in 1976, telling the delegates that black voters were not welded to the Democrats: It would not take much to win them back to the party of Lincoln, which could help the GOP in close states. The GOP—still led by moderates like Brock; his fellow Tennessean Howard Baker, the Senate minority leader; and former vice presidential nominee Senator Bob Dole of Kansas—was waging a now-forgotten campaign to capitalize on the growing view that Democrats took black voters for granted. The RNC increased its spending on recruitment of black voters from $50,000 in 1976 to $250,000 in 1977.[45] In return for promoting the GOP among black voters, and perhaps making moderate Republicans feel good about their party, Jackson would push for amendments to the full-employment bill that would keep the GOP from supporting a filibuster. Where the CBC had openly opposed such amendments on principle—taking, Jackson said, "a stance of all or nothing"— Jackson said, "I'll take something over nothing any day." Brock set up a meeting between Jackson and Howard Baker. Baker agreed to prevent a filibuster in exchange for some weakening amendments.[46]

Carter once again became the biggest obstacle. He would not use the necessary force to make his Senate supporters bring the bill to a vote. His support for the bill was no longer so "enthusiastic." The CBC called a meeting with him at the White House in September that blew up all over the headlines: "After [the incoming CBC chairman John] Conyers reportedly pointed out that if the bill did not pass the President would be blamed, a shouting match erupted between Conyers and the Vice President [Walter Mondale], as well as the outgoing caucus chairman, Parren Mitchell [D-Maryland]." Conyers stormed out.[47]

Two days after the White House breakdown, Coretta King led a thousand protesters in support of the bill at the Capitol.[48] Carter capitulated and agreed to push congressional leaders to bring the bill to a vote in the Senate. The next evening, at the CBC's annual Washington banquet, Carter called caucus members his "brothers and sisters." The dinner drew its largest crowd ever: estimates of eight to ten thousand rivaled the Gary convention six years earlier.[49]

The Senate approved some weakening amendments over the following week, and the bill passed the Senate, without a filibuster, "decisively" on Friday, October 13, 1978.[50] Ashbrook's idea—to add a balanced budget to the act's goals—had come back to qualify, perhaps to mock, the main goal of ending unemployment.[51] The most irksome amendment hardened the bill's previously vague goal of reducing inflation. The goal was now 3 percent inflation in five years and zero inflation in ten, a provision for which Senator Richard Lugar of Indiana led the fight.[52] President Carter signed it

Coretta Scott King helped to reconstitute the labor–civil rights
coalition that her late husband's movement had often relied on,
especially in lobbying Congress. The last major effort of that
coalition was the campaign in the mid-1970s to enact a
full-employment law. Despite amendments that diverted
the legislation from many of its original goals, she supported
the resulting Humphrey-Hawkins Act. President Jimmy Carter,
after considerable evasion of and resistance to stronger versions
of the bill, supported the final version as well. He signed it
into law in October 1978.

Courtesy of the Jimmy Carter Presidential Library

into law on October 27, 1978. Mrs. King got much of the credit. "I believe we are now on the way toward dealing with one of the most basic human rights," she announced.[53] Her hope, tempered by decades of frustration and setbacks, which had often led to devastating loss, was almost lost in the clamor of shorter tempers.

A Toothless Bill?

The Washington Post, which had previously supported the principle of full employment, went so far as to pronounce the final form of Humphrey-Hawkins "a bad bill," because it sought to legislate goals "that are obviously unattainable in reality."[54] Certainly the political reality of the mid-1970s made it look like a gesture of nostalgia.

On the other hand, it had been objectively unrealistic to hope for massive social change twenty-four years earlier, when Coretta King and her husband moved to segregated Montgomery. That city had since become a symbol of dedicated struggle triumphing against the odds, however, and a historic step forward that inspired oppressed peoples around the globe for years to come.

Mrs. King told reporters at the King Center that the new full-employment law was similar in effect to the history-making Civil Rights Act of 1964 and the Voting Rights Act of 1965. (She did not mention the 1968 housing act.) Time would tell just how seriously the courts would enforce, and the white masses would respect, the new law. She added, a bit defensively, that the Humphrey-Hawkins Act was more than a "symbolic gesture." "Certainly we would have wanted 10 million jobs by next week if that were possible," she said. "We got the first step, but if you don't get the first step, you don't ever move."[55]

Gus Hawkins felt the same way, judging the new law—"a modern-day Magna Carta"—to be a great achievement after so much effort against such great opposition.[56] It laid a basis, John

Conyers added, paving many pathways for subsequent advances. The new law required the president to outline a specific plan of action every January—around the time of King's birthday—till 1983, when unemployment would have to reach 3 percent. That would keep the issue in the news and give activists a fire to hold the president's feet to. It ended the "piecemeal" approach to employment policy and brought all federal efforts under a single umbrella, Conyers said, for which the president is held publicly responsible in yearly reports. Charles Rangel noted that the regular public exposure of the executive branch to scrutiny of its legal requirement to make steady, irreversible progress toward full employment was a great achievement. Despite the deletion of many "substantive" provisions, which was politically necessary, the new law was a "tremendous political victory for the poor and the unemployed of our country."[57] It was a foundation to build on.

In historical perspective, this is compelling. Compared to Hawkins's original draft of 1974, the surviving law does look pretty toothless—just as the 1957 and 1960 civil rights acts, in their final form, looked toothless. Still, as civil rights leaders had said at the time those two incremental acts were passed, if you are digging a ditch with a spoon, and somebody comes along and offers you a shovel, you do not turn him down because he didn't offer you a bulldozer.[58] The historical standard that had cropped up since 1957 and 1960 was the millennial standard of the civil rights acts of 1964 and 1965: That was the standard that made the Humphrey-Hawkins Act look small. But that standard was the rare, historically unusual, and thus unrealistic and rather unfair one.

The CBC leaders' optimistic glosses on the bill's final passage reflect a certain pride of ownership. They had had the bill at the top of their agenda for four years.[59] Outright failure to get action on it would clearly have been more embarrassing than a watered-down bill, and nearly every bill is watered down to some degree.

The bill did establish the power of the Congressional Black Caucus to lead a successful legislative campaign in the face of nearly overwhelming opposition. Several black supporters of the bill emphasized that when they tried to put the victory in the perspective of history.[60]

The Urban League's Vernon Jordan emphasized that the new law, despite its copious disappointments, was "vitally important to working people. It mandates measures by the President to comply" with the goal of reducing unemployment to 4 percent, or "to face the politically difficult task of explaining why the goal would not be fulfilled." That was "an important step on the road to full employment." Maybe it was as much as legislation could do. At any event, the achievement was bigger than the disappointments in context: The bill's supporters "managed the impossible[:] to get an historic full employment Bill through one of the worst Congresses in modern times."[61]

Perhaps the shrewdest judgment came from Annette Samuels of the *Amsterdam News,* just before final passage. The congressional attention given to the bill showed that its backers had a serious measure of power. The caucus's compelling Carter to put his resources and leadership on the line for a final Senate vote, in particular, clearly showed "the potential power of the Congressional Black Caucus. . . . But it also highlighted the weaknesses of the Black community." Thousands had attended the Black Caucus's legislative weekend—designed among other things to bring the black "community" into "the legislative process." But that community did not get what it wanted—in part, perhaps, because it was not brought into the process till near the end. This was nothing like the mass surges of protest in the streets, and organized economic leverage in the boycotts and marches of King's era. Not only did congressional politics weaken and delay the Humphrey-Hawkins bill, but it outright cut several other vital programs, in the "spirit of Proposition 13," the 1978 California ballot initiative that put a 1 percent ceiling on property taxes, launching the "tax revolt" that defined a new era of opposition to paying for education, welfare, and government services in general. "Yet no groundswell of indignation, such as that made by women over the past two weeks when defeat of the Equal Rights Amendment extension bill seemed imminent, has come from Black and poor communities."[62]

One of Gus Hawkins's legislative assistants, frustrated with key liberal senators' failure to support full employment, emphasized the contrast to the 1960s. This less-than-millennial result was just what life was like when no mass movement bore down upon the standard operating procedures of jawboning, lobbying, and logrolling. Liberal senators weren't supporting the bill "because they haven't felt the pressure from enough of us. It's that simple."[63]

Annette Samuels elaborated: More than 9 million black Americans were registered to vote. Yet in the 1976 presidential election, fewer than 6 million of them voted. More than 7 million black Americans were eligible to vote "who remain unregistered and outside the political system." Black Caucus members continually complained, Samuels said, that "the Black community still has difficulty understanding the impact that letters, calls and telegrams have on their Senators and Congresspersons." The caucus needed to remind voters "that poverty did not stop the cotton pickers, tenant farmers, seamstresses, domestic workers, laborers, students and thousands of poor people of the sixties from fighting and giving up their lives for a yet to be realized freedom." The sixteen Congressional Black Caucus members, "stacked up against the 419 other members of the House" and one hundred senators, were "playing a tough game of poker." They called for a massive voter-registration drive and a massive get-out-the-vote campaign. "The next play, it seems, in this game of life and death poker is in the hands of the Black and poor community."[64]

Conclusion

Without a mass movement threatening order in any organized or sustained way in the streets, or some other kind of national emergency, it was extremely unlikely that any social legislation would live up to the highest expectations of its supporters. In politics, an inch or two of territory required extraordinary effort. Even the inches could only be contemplated on rare occasions.

The victory of compromise legislation like Humphrey-Hawkins always tends to wither under attack from those who imagined that stronger legislation was possible. The critics who cried empty symbolism in this case had a point, but only to a certain extent. For Humphrey-Hawkins had laid down a significant principle.

The right to an economic livelihood, adumbrated by agrarian and labor organizations in the nineteenth century[65] and again in the New Deal, was specified in the Four Freedoms as "freedom from want" and in the Atlantic Charter as "improved labor standards, economic advancement and social security" for all. Its worldwide appeal was enshrined in Article 23 of the Universal Declaration of Human Rights in 1948 as "the right to work." Martin Luther King had reasserted the right to work in the civil rights movement. The Humphrey-Hawkins Act revived it once again. But the form it took, in the surviving husk of the original bill, was also a creature of the 1970s, when a depressed economy and "stagflation" raised serious doubts about the continued power of modern governments to moderate the business cycle. At any rate, the enactment had enshrined in law the political principle of full employment as a major national goal—on a par with curbing inflation.

Hubert Humphrey told an interviewer in 1976 that sometimes all you can do is articulate a goal, a founding principle. Reality simply does not offer a choice of doing something better.[66] But founding principles boldly stated, or memorably enshrined in law, have a better chance of getting embodied in substantive social and political changes later on, when reality may be less stingy with its opportunities. For Murray Finley and Coretta King, speaking for the "labor, religious, civil rights, and other organizations" in the Full Employment Action Council, the full-employment law was no empty gesture. Rather it had made "full employment the central priority of economic life"—at least it would do that if people demanded that their representatives live up to the terms of their contract. By providing a "framework for a concentrated and flexible attack" on unemployment, the law was "an essential first step" and "an enormous improvement."[67]

If the result was only a framework, whose content and significance would await future action, the Humphrey-Hawkins battle had also tested the shift back to a coalition strategy, after the nationalist experiments of the National Black Political Conventions. The campaign for the law was an effort to vindicate the cooperative alliance approach to freedom and equality, to which King was as devoted as he was to nonviolence. In the thick of the battle over full employment, a columnist in San Francisco's black weekly cut to the quick of the coalition strategy: "The Black Caucus realizes that American Blacks live outside the mainstream of American life." The caucus's investment of so much of its resources and attention over four long years in the Humphrey-Hawkins bill was the great illustration of that: The bill would "provide jobs for unemployed Blacks and for others who are not Black in need of some form of employment."[68] But the record of job creation over the next several years was dismal, particularly for black workers: In 1981, when white unemployment was 6.3 percent, black unemployment was more than double that, 14.3 percent. In 1984, white unemployment was 6.5 percent and black unemployment was 15.9 percent.[69] From that perspective, the fight for the Humphrey-Hawkins bill had shown that even in broad, 1960s-style coalition with labor, black Americans had little political power to effect major social changes on a par with those achieved during the 1960s, when a mass movement was active in the streets. The reconstituted coalition—leaving aside the question of whether it could be sustained—had not achieved more tangible near-term gains than the independent, coalition-free strategy. The National Black Political Convention organizers had tried to make black voters a potent force in electoral politics, the way labor had become a potent force during the 1930s. It was now clear that, when they were not organized in a disciplined mass movement, black Americans were not that potent force—at least not when playing offense. But when they were attacked, or when they perceived they were being attacked, a negative, reactive unity and power could yield another kind of meaningful victory.

CHAPTER FOUR

Legalizing the Legacy

THE BATTLE FOR A MARTIN LUTHER KING HOLIDAY

Coretta Scott King and many others metabolized the hard lesson of the Humphrey-Hawkins battle, which turned out to be the lesson of the entire post-1960s period. The American political system could be compelled to make gestures in black America's direction. But it was not going to yield the millennial sorts of changes it had yielded in 1964, 1965, and 1968. In that respect, the post-1960s period resembled most periods in the struggle for black freedom: The streak of major victories that King represented was history's great exception. Nor were protesters about to come out again in disciplined, steady solidarity for a long siege like the Montgomery boycott of 1955–56. Perhaps the time had come to revisit the aging victories of King's era directly: to test America's commitment to the principles it had claimed to embrace, when, in response to the protesters of the mid-1960s, America granted the rights it had so long denied. King had become a symbol. He had died for those historic victories in the struggle for freedom and equality. If his survivors could not keep moving forward with his work, would they slip backward? Would the victories evanesce like a dream after all?

Battening on to that quandary, King's legatees achieved their most decisive political victory in the entire period since King's death—while setting no expectation whatsoever of substantive change. The campaign for a Martin Luther King national holiday began in earnest in 1979 and very nearly achieved its goal that year. The campaign was an implicit acknowledgment that if substantive gains were no longer feasible, symbols were still important. Perhaps the symbolic concession of a holiday devoted to a martyr for civil rights would provide recurring leverage, or at least publicity, to advance his unfinished cause.

Mrs. King and her congressional allies saw that many Americans believed they had reached their limit in the granting of rights. Over the previous twenty-five years, the country had given a tremendous advance to black Americans. How could they ask for more? King's survivors insisted that the important business was actually just beginning, that America had only partially granted equal opportunity and basic human rights. Certainly King died believing that. But in hearing so often that America had given them so much already, Mrs. King and others grasped that they could lose what they had gained. To set a King holiday as their new goal was to force America to keep the gains of the past in view, to reaffirm those gains in some way—to protect them, with ritual regularity, from misdeeds that could be done in the dark. The nation would have to pay tribute in broad daylight to the one man who represented those gains, on the level they paid yearly tribute to George Washington, Christopher Columbus, and Jesus of Nazareth. Martin Luther King's meaning might continue to get marginalized and mangled, but it could not get swept away altogether. His words and work would always be in the national spotlight once a year.

The battle for a King holiday gave its supporters an added tactical advantage, though Mrs. King and her allies may not have initially realized it. It would force those who sought to disparage, to minify, or to co-opt King's legacy to fight in the open arena. As the guardians of King's legacy kept up the battle over another four years—the holiday did not become law till 1983—they found that they were providing a platform to those who thought America had given way too much to black protesters in the 1960s. By letting all sides with a stake get on the record, the holiday debate aired and immortalized the obsessive rants of right-wing King-haters, who rose up to expose King as a national villain, unworthy of the nation's honor. The haters appeared to attack not only Martin Luther King but the entire African-American population whose cause King symbolized. Their tactics were guilt by association, and character assassination, evoking memories of the McCarthy era. Would these ruthless, paranoid-sounding King-haters—who gave expert testimony against the holiday legislation—be allowed to carry the day?

President Carter Backs the Holiday

The idea of a national holiday honoring King had been kicking around nearly since King's death. Several members of Congress had introduced King holiday bills on April 8, 1968, the day before King's funeral. In every year since then except 1972, a holiday bill was introduced.[1] The R&B singer James Brown had an audience with President Richard Nixon and his aides in the spring of 1972. A King holiday was Brown's only request. Nixon refused, saying that Dr. King would not want Nixon to exploit his memory for electoral gain in the coming election. The president vaguely left open the idea that he might support a holiday after the election.[2] Holiday proposals popped up on various other occasions, and a House committee even held exploratory hearings on the idea in 1975.[3]

King holiday bills failed to pass for fifteen years after his death for the same reason that nearly all legislation fails to pass: Nobody made those bills the most important thing in their lives.

Even members of the Congressional Black Caucus—and their occasional allies—looked at the holiday as a substitute for truly substantive action, especially in light of the recent disappointment of
Humphrey-Hawkins. Even so, the substitute was going to require
tremendous work and coordination of forces.

The year 1979 began with good omens. Though several black
leaders had recently been calling President Carter a traitor, Mrs.
King maintained strong and friendly relations with him. Her center awarded Carter its eighth annual Martin Luther King Nonviolent Peace Prize on King's fiftieth birthday, in January 1979.[4] The
president accepted the award at Ebenezer Baptist Church, announcing, as Birmingham's black newspaper put it, a big "Push to
Make King Birthday Nat'l Holiday."[5]

The principal holiday sponsor, Michigan's John Conyers, who
had introduced a King holiday bill in every Congress since King's
death, amplified the irony that he had been touting for years. "The
passing of time ordinarily has a way of tarnishing or weakening
the memory of even the greatest leaders." Not so with King, "for
whom affection, respect, and devotion have grown" with time.[6]
This optimism contrasted with the gloomy picture that Conyers
and other holiday supporters drew of the recent history of race
and poverty.

In the Senate, Charles Percy was a sponsor of the holiday bill,
along with his fellow midwestern Republican Bob Dole and midwestern Democrats Birch Bayh and John Glenn.

The only easterner among Senate sponsors then was Ted Kennedy, who had been building a campaign to take the Democratic
nomination away from Carter. Kennedy took the occasion to up-
stage the president by inserting a speech into the Senate record that
he had given at Ebenezer, three days before Carter. Kennedy had
been a "show-stopper," *The Washington Post* reported, punctuat-
ing his speech with King's line "Now is the time," which the crowd
of seven hundred turned into a "raucous" chant. When Kennedy

announced that he would introduce a King holiday bill, "[the] Rev. Martin Luther King Sr. whooped like he had never heard it before."[7]

In his State of the Union address on January 20, Carter called formally for King holiday legislation and pledged his support. The conservative *U.S. News & World Report* did not view the King holiday bill as the initiative of Coretta King, John Conyers, or the Black Caucus: It was a political move, and it was Carter's.[8] The holiday was a symbolic prize in the struggle between Ted Kennedy and Jimmy Carter for control of the Democratic Party, and thus a bellwether of the party's electoral prospects.

Holiday supporters were confident. With the support of the president, and with black voters emerging as a bone of contention between the president and his fearsome Democratic challenger, and with the support of key Republican leaders, the time had come to show some respect for King's legatees. If the economy could not bear wholesale redistributive legislation, or strike a healthy Keynesian balance of supply and demand, surely it could afford a ceremonial tribute. The bill had more than ninety sponsors, and its floor managers had counted roughly 268 votes (a comfortable majority in the 435-member House).[9]

In late March and June 1979, the Senate Judiciary Committee began holding joint hearings on the King holiday with the House Committee on Post Office and Civil Service, which had jurisdiction over holidays.[10] The only previous hearing on the holiday had been marooned as a dry run, back in 1975.[11] The 1979 hearing was longer, higher profile, better attended, and had testimony from more famous witnesses.

Opposition to the Holiday Bill

The opposition witnesses in 1979 included the holiday's only two ideological opponents in the House: Larry McDonald of suburban

Atlanta, a Democrat but a member of the John Birch Society; and John Ashbrook of rural Ohio, the Republican who had fought so hard against the housing act in 1968. According to Michael Barone's *Almanac of American Politics,* McDonald faced frequent charges that he was "more interested in advancing his right wing views than in serving his constituents." McDonald accomplished little but had "put together some very creative amendments to help his fellow members express their disapproval of abortions and homosexuals." Ashbrook was "by any measure one of the most conservative members of the House" yet served on its most liberal committees; his career was "almost a catalogue of lost causes."[12] The pair emphasized King's alleged associations with communists and subversives and his violence-inciting tactics, echoing the attack politics that Ashbrook had mastered during King's lifetime. The difference was that Ashbrook's rhetoric appeared far less popular and respectable now in Congress.

Nearly everyone else who opposed the holiday in Congress over the next few years eschewed the anticommunism of McDonald and Ashbrook. (Senator Jesse Helms of North Carolina would echo them as the bill neared passage in 1983.) And nearly all granted King's moral stature. Except for these two right-wingers, holiday opponents confined themselves almost wholly to three nonideological objections: the expense of paying federal employees to take another day off; the potential unfairness of singling out one great black leader, when many others, like Booker T. Washington or George Washington Carver, or white leaders like Theodore or Franklin Roosevelt, might equally deserve that level of recognition; and the related rashness of leveraging King up to the level of Columbus, Washington, and Jesus before sufficient time had passed to gauge his relative historical significance. Holiday supporters often charged opponents with insincerity on these points, imputing secret, immoral motives to them. McDonald and Ashbrook frequently supplied explicit content to fit the imputations.

At the start of the hearings in 1979, it appeared that the most prominent opponent of the King holiday would be someone else. Strom Thurmond had no rival among segregationist senators. He had led the unsuccessful and short-lived southern effort to secede from the Democratic Party after Harry Truman broke the party's tradition of white supremacy in 1948. Thurmond more impressively organized the amazing show of regional unity known as the "Southern Manifesto" of opposition to the Supreme Court in 1955. In disgust over Lyndon Johnson's final repudiation of the party's historic (and until recently transregional) commitment to states' rights and white supremacy, Thurmond became a Republican in 1964. Though Thurmond introduced extreme anti-holiday testimony, his own public opposition appeared halfhearted and would ultimately evaporate—as the old white South's united front against King would.

From the start, Thurmond shared a surprising basic premise with holiday supporters: He did not want anyone to think the civil rights movement was "completed" and "part of history." Thurmond was sure that "Dr. King, if he were here today, would find that his drive for social change, although highly effective, still has other avenues to travel. Indeed, the very existence of the Martin Luther King, Jr. Center for Social Change indicates that his work goes on, as well it might." Why stop to commemorate that work now—as though all that history were settled and behind us? Americans reserved calendar-changing stature to Christopher Columbus and George Washington. America still denied holidays, Thurmond noted plaintively, to Booker T. Washington, George Washington Carver, Thomas Jefferson, Benjamin Franklin, Abraham Lincoln, Dwight Eisenhower, and John Kennedy. Following Lincoln's example at Gettysburg in 1863, Thurmond disqualified himself—along with everyone living—from hallowing freshly dead heroes. A historical commemoration was premature. Holidays were intermissions from the present. They were backward-looking, one might say conservative, affairs. They were also costly: The Civil Service Commission estimated a holiday would cost $195 million in direct federal expenditures, and millions more in lost private production.[13]

Still, chances looked good for the holiday in 1979, above all because the Carter administration decisively countered Thurmond's objection to the cost. The White House's Office of Management and Budget submitted what could be called a plausible denial of the Civil Service Commission's calculation that a new holiday would cost taxpayers $195 million each year in direct federal revenues. Rather than dispute the CSC's figures, the OMB claimed that "work not performed on a holiday . . . is normally made up to some extent during the remainder of the year."[14] It was the sort of argument that could be used against any cutback of resources: It was a statement of political will rather than financial calculation.

That boded well for the pro-holiday side. Carter's support came more quickly and more decisively than it ever had for the full employment bill. He could afford to support this bill. Ted Kennedy managed to claim credit for introducing the administration's fiscal counterthrust into the debate.[15] The competition could only increase optimism about passage.

Coretta Scott King's Role

The testimony of Coretta King gave the pro-holiday side its emotional power. Her pietà-like irreproachability seemed to grow even as her husband's flaws were exposed over the years. Nobody, after all, had borne those flaws—and the vulnerability they translated into—more directly or more intimately than she. It was perhaps scant consolation that King's enemies had to treat his widow with circumspection and, if pressed, a show of respect: To attack her, as they had done her husband, would be bad public relations for their side. There were a few other silver linings in her bereavement. Her own steady character was one. Her regal reserve was often compared to Jackie Kennedy's, though she never tested her followers' loyalty with remarriage, luxury, or fading glamour. Like Mrs. Kennedy, however, Mrs. King lived with the knowledge that her children were so many bull's-eyes for every demented publicity seeker on the planet. Unlike Mrs. Kennedy, Mrs. King kept at her husband's work.

In that work, Mrs. King had one advantage that her husband had never had, namely the nation's memory of him. It would have shocked her husband to learn that his memory had become a political asset. But it was becoming a great one, and so quickly that she had little choice but to make his memory the center of her public career.

Committee members appeared to sense that her career was climaxing in the holiday campaign, in which she was now a far more authoritative presence than she had been in the full-employment campaign. No titles of nobility were permitted by the Constitution they all kept citing. But Mrs. King was certainly "the most noble" of the noble witnesses that Senator Birch Bayh welcomed to the hearings. When Senator Ted Kennedy told her she was "a long-time friend," he meant to compliment her and perhaps to reassure her—or perhaps to seek her complicity, as he turned against her other friend Jimmy Carter. Kennedy compared her to her husband in every way but one: "She does not shake the rafters, but her eloquence shakes the conscience of the American people."[16]

Mrs. King proceeded to describe her husband's uniqueness more factually and dispassionately than any other witness. She spun Senator Thurmond's nod to Booker T. Washington to a different purpose: Previous black leaders "necessarily addressed" issues that "concern blacks exclusively," she said. But King "spoke to us all." This countered both Thurmond's explicit point that other

black leaders might emerge as more important to more black people than King, and what holiday opponents often seemed to imply,
that the holiday would be a concession to the black population
as an interest group, the way Columbus Day had been to Italian
Americans.

But to confine King's leadership to black Americans would,
Mrs. King insisted, diminish his true significance. King was "the
first to lead a mass-based movement which nonviolently struggled
for justice and achieved significant social and legal reforms that
improved the lives of millions." More than any other black American name, King's "is widely known throughout the world." Even
in countries with no black citizens, "buildings, streets, and organizations" bore his name. Fourteen states and hundreds of cities celebrated his birthday. Hundreds of businesses closed and several
major unions observed his birthday by a contractual right they had
negotiated.

Given her and her husband's associations with the American
left during the Vietnam War, it was of some interest that she put
King's legacy on the home side in the Cold War: "in Hungary
alone, there were no less than five churches named after Martin."
Such tributes made it clear that "people who are yearning for freedom everywhere regard Martin as an outstanding example of what
is right about America." She was confident that time was on her
side: "millions of Americans already have a day off on January 15
and the prospects that the number will increase, with or without
Federal legislation, are bright indeed because the holiday drive has
steadily gathered momentum."

Mrs. King rightly predicted that the "principal objection" to
the holiday would be its cost. That generated all the emotional
heat in her testimony. "For those who are sincere in their concern,
this is a legitimate question," she allowed. "But to those who
would use this issue as a smoke-screen to avoid dealing with the

real importance of this bill, I can only say that this is the most reprehensible evasion of all."

She had no qualm about her own fiscal priorities. Workers deserved another day off. King Day would be the first holiday to honor "an American who gave his life in a labor struggle." She thought a prosperous America owed itself a holiday to requite all the labor that had gone unpaid before the Civil War. One day was a lot less to ask—and it had firmer logic to recommend it—than the pounds of flesh that some die-hard veterans of the 1960s had demanded for themselves as the probable distant relatives of slaves. "I am not asking for reparations to the black community. No amount of money can compensate for the brutal injustice of slavery in the United States. But, given the hundreds of years of economic sacrifice and involuntary servitude of America's blacks, is it too much to ask that one paid holiday per year be set aside to honor the contributions of a black man who gave his life in an historic struggle for social decency?" Who else had the authority—or the nerve—to answer such a question on behalf of the nation? "I think that deep in our hearts," Mrs. King said, "we all know the answers to the questions I have just raised."[17]

Conservatives

Over the next few months, as support for the King holiday grew, one new sponsor marked the tectonic shifts of symbolic alignments in the era. John Danforth was a new Republican senator from Missouri, a millionaire who had unseated the old liberal Democrat Stuart Symington in 1976. Danforth urged his fellow Republicans to join him in honoring King.[18] Armed with a divinity degree, Danforth was helping to refashion the GOP as a crucible for the mixing of church and state—just as Jimmy Carter and Jesse Jackson were using public displays of religion to challenge the Democratic establishment. Danforth believed he was following Martin Luther King's example.

Danforth later revealed that he had gotten to know King and King's father when he served as a board member of King's alma mater, Morehouse College. He did not want champions of the welfare state to have a monopoly on public claims of morality and decency. To Danforth, King's determination in the fight for equality symbolized "the spirit of American freedom and self-determination." Was Danforth's view of King's legacy in step with the growing body of social conservatives, who were campaigning vigorously to take over the GOP and the country? That question still appeared to be open, what with much of the pro-life movement claiming King as an inspiration and model, and with at least two Republican presidential candidates (John Connally and John Anderson) making a great show of repudiating their former opposition to King and civil rights.[19] Danforth signaled a new possibility for conservative Republicans: They could claim some affinity, even allegiance, to King's mantle. They may not have wanted to convince many black voters, and they did not need to. White conservatives in particular recognized in King a model to emulate—notably his use of religious enthusiasm and will-to-sacrifice. Nobody better illustrated Mrs. King's point that King had spoken "to us all."

Other conservatives got in Danforth's way, however, with tough ideological attacks on King's legacy. When Senator Thurmond reconvened the joint hearing, opponents of the King holiday were given the most room they ever had in the record. First was Alan Stang, author of an anticommunist tract, *It's Very Simple: The True Story of Civil Rights* (1965).[20] Stang enumerated King's alleged communist associations more clearly than any holiday opponent had done on the record before. He also did a better job than anyone had in spelling out the claim that King provoked violence. To people who wondered why "violence was so often a hallmark of King's so-called nonviolent movement," Stang answered that "violence was exactly what he wanted," citing King's own article in the April 3, 1964, *Saturday Review.* There King laid out his strategy: Nonviolent demonstrators went into the streets to exercise their rights, and racists resisted by unleashing violence against them, which led "Americans of conscience" to demand federal intervention and legislation. "So," Stang concluded, "the violence he [King] got was not a surprise" and King "did not dislike it. He wanted it in order to pressure the Congress to enact still more totalitarian legislation."[21]

Thurmond called a real live communist next: Julia Brown, a self-identified "loyal American Negro," who worked as a communist organizer beginning in 1947. At first, Brown had thought she was "joining a legitimate civil rights organization[.] Finding that I was a true member of the Communist Party[,] which advocated the overthrow of the United States Government, I decided to leave the organization, but I had to bide my time to avoid suspicion." Soon she went to the FBI to report what she had witnessed. "In 1951, I was asked by the FBI to go back into the Communist Party as an undercover agent to report on their subversive activities." She claimed that only party members attended the meetings she attended. She "frequently heard Martin Luther King discussed." The communist cells she was in were "continually being asked to raise money for Martin Luther King's activities and to support his civil rights movement by writing letters to the press and influencing local clergymen, and especially Negro clergymen that he was a good person, unselfishly working for the American Negro, and in no way connected with the Communist Party."

Brown proposed an ingenious way to counter all that communist influence: "[A] great many Negroes, such as George Washington Carver and Booker T. Washington," provide American youth with a positive example. King, by contrast, provided an example of "agitation and manipulation for goals dictated by hatred and envy." If the committee recommended a King holiday, "The memory of Carver and Washington would be dishonored." If the holiday bill passed, "we may as well take down the Stars and Stripes that fly over this building and replace it with a Red flag." Similar testimony came from Karl Prussion, a former undercover FBI agent.[22]

Larry McDonald then stepped up[23] and brought affirmative action, which had been upheld in the Supreme Court's 1978 *Bakke* decision, into the discussion. He questioned whether King "really found racism repugnant in light of his support of discrimination in jobs and housing so long as the discrimination was in favor of blacks." King's forming a "common front" with the "virulently racist Nation of Islam" in Chicago raised the same question. McDonald qualified his points: "While Rev. King did not advocate race hatred, he did not bar alliances with racists and he did not keep them from his personal staff." McDonald gave a single quotation to back up the second claim: King's staff member James Bevel said in 1966 in Chicago that "we need an army . . . to fight the white man this summer." King's civil disobedience dangerously taught young people "contempt for the law." A King holiday would teach the same lesson.[24]

John Ashbrook did not show up for the hearing, but he joined McDonald in submitting a written statement. "It is not popular and certainly not politically advantageous to speak in opposition to a man who has been canonized by the news media and by many . . . who profess to advocate civil rights," Ashbrook acknowledged. But "Rev. King's motives are misrepresented. He sought not to work through the law but around it, with contempt and violence. How soon we forget. When will politicians learn to accept history as it really happened instead of history as told by the Washington Post?" The issue was whether Congress would "support the fictional assessment of Dr. King" by adopting a holiday that would "take the taxpayers for a ride to the tune of millions and millions of dollars" and whether America's children would "be misled into believing" that King was a great man and learn to speak of him "with the same reverence" they now reserve for Washington and Lincoln.[25]

A Statue in Lieu of a Holiday?

Lack of coordination among conservatives became more evident when King was next discussed on the floor of Congress at the end of July. The provocation was a resolution dating back several years to erect a statue of King somewhere on the Capitol grounds. It actually passed both houses in the 94th Congress (1975–76), but since the Senate version passed only at the very end of term, the House did not have time to consider the Senate amendments. In the 95th Congress (1977–78), the House passed it, but not the Senate. It would cost $25,000, out of contingent funds already appropriated. It would be the first work of art displayed in the Capitol that memorialized a black American. (There were then 681 that did not memorialize black Americans.) Its author, Democrat Jonathan Bingham of New York, said it had passed before with "little or no dissent."

Ashbrook put an end to that. He was "sad" that no black leader was memorialized in the Capitol, but this particular leader would soon be revealed as an "inappropriate choice." Time and history would "show that there could have been much better choices." History had a way of reappraising once-popular leaders—he repeated Thurmond's example of John Kennedy, and added Lyndon Johnson and J. Edgar Hoover. Ashbrook was the difference between little and no dissent in the past. He was the only one to speak against the King statue now.

Rising to speak against Ashbrook was none other than freshman congressman Newt Gingrich. "As a representative of Georgia," Gingrich said that a King statue would be "an important

None of King's old enemies kept up the fight against him after his death more determinedly than Republican congressman John Ashbrook of Ohio. Ashbrook's extreme rhetoric and tactics tainted the entire opposition to the King holiday legislation.

Harris & Ewing, courtesy of the Ashbrook Center for Public Affairs symbol. It is very clear in the black community that this is the overwhelming choice of that community." Gingrich occupied the district adjacent to Larry McDonald's in the booming suburbs of Atlanta. The statue passed overwhelmingly—supported by many who opposed the holiday—408 to 11.[26]

Enactment of the statue statute appeared to be a rehearsal for the holiday vote to come. The vote here easily topped the two-thirds majority necessary to pass on a "suspension of rules," that is to say, quickly, and without the elaborate rigmarole the House insists upon for controversial legislation.

Ashbrook weighed in again on September 27, 1979, before the House committee took final action that year on the holiday bill. Ashbrook attacked the King Center by citing a news story that contained a wealth of damning circumstantial evidence about its finances, particularly suggesting a quid pro quo from the Carter administration, which had greatly increased the center's public funding. The story quoted the artlessly evasive nondenials of a King Center spokesman.[27] Ashbrook seemed to be testing whether any dirt could stick to the great Teflon icon of civil rights, whether his attack on the fundamental basis of the King holiday—as opposed to its price tag—could draw support anywhere but the outer fringes he and Larry McDonald hovered around.

The Holiday Nearly Passes

He had his answer soon. The House Committee on Post Office and Civil Service finally reported the holiday bill to the floor, favorably, on October 23, 1979. Its minority report—signed by only five of the committee's nine Republicans—conspicuously left out any negative statements or insinuations about King or his associations. It included only two objections to the holiday. Most important was a concise—and persuasive—objection to the majority's fuzzy math on its cost. An ancillary concern was whether Congress should single out King—whom the minority praised—for an honor it denied to Jefferson, Lincoln, Theodore Roosevelt, and Franklin Roosevelt. These objections were confirmed as the respectable bases of opposition to the holiday. Fiscal discipline and an unwillingness to put King on a pedestal above long-hallowed national heroes constituted the broadest argument that could plausibly attract a majority.[28]

Opponents of the holiday could have said: Congress already honored King with substantive action, in the Fair Housing Act of 1968. To point to the superfluity of an additional tribute would have bolstered the most effective point that holiday opponents made, though they never emphasized or belabored it: A Martin Luther King holiday would be an odd, cult-of-personality-like gesture, the sort of thing that King had always opposed. To point to Congress's substantive tribute to King from 1968 would also have given holiday opponents the cover of respectability that they clearly sought. It would have backed up their claim that they really respected King; they just did not think a holiday was the most apt way to honor him.

On November 13, 1979, an overwhelming majority of House members—252 to 133—voted to enact a federal holiday in honor of King on his birthday, January 15, every year. But that was not quite the two-thirds majority needed to speed the bill through Congress on the "suspension of rules" that holiday sponsors had somewhat overconfidently attempted. Holiday supporters were able to get the bill on the docket one more time days before the end of the session, on December 5, 1979. This time it could be carried by a simple majority, but congressional rules would allow opponents to delay action on the bill, or to attach weakening amendments to it.

A pro-holiday substitute amendment, offered by Republican Robert McClory of suburban Chicago, appeared to meet the cost argument halfway by changing the date of the King holiday from

January 15 every year to the third Monday every January: a three-day weekend would not be as costly as the midweek interruptions that would occur almost half the time January 15 came up.

Holiday opponents tended to support a different substitute, to divert holiday feeling into a proclamation of commemoration of King's birthday on the third Sunday of every January. The sponsor of the Sunday switch was the conservative Republican Robin Beard, whose district included several white precincts of Memphis and ran east to the outskirts of Nashville.[29] Holiday supporters objected that a Sunday commemoration would eliminate all the honor that the holiday campaign had intended—and that the House had just voted overwhelmingly for on November 13. Cardiss Collins of Chicago's West Side, speaking for the whole Black Caucus, said Beard's version of King Day would be "a holiday in name only. We all know that many commemorative days and weeks have little meaning to the public." She wondered aloud how many present celebrated National Safe Boating Week, National Poison Prevention Week, or Pan-American Aviation Day, Stephen Foster Day, and Leif Ericson Day.[30]

John Conyers and other longtime holiday supporters supported the McClory (Monday) amendment from the start. It passed overwhelmingly, 291–106, on December 5, 1979. That was well over the two-thirds majority that holiday supporters had needed back on November 13, though that was immaterial now. With a simple majority, it appeared that King's supporters had at last gotten their holiday.

But Beard's amendment came up ten minutes later and also carried, though narrowly: 207 in favor of the Sunday substitute, and 191 against. Holiday supporters, led by Conyers and Democratic congressman Robert Garcia of New York City, moved a petition to withdraw the whole bill in response. Thus, after building support for it all year, the Congressional Black Caucus and House liberals killed the proclamation of a national "Martin Luther King

Day" just forty days before King's fifty-first birthday. That was better than yielding to a phony "holiday" on a Sunday—which would have been hard to repeal down the road in favor of a real, weekday holiday. To block the Sunday substitute was the best they could do for now. They kept the possibility open that they could regroup and rally holiday support more effectively in a future Congress.[31]

The Holiday Rises Again

How often does a second chance come? A big event came between the holiday bill's sea-sickening swings and withdrawal in 1979 and the next round of debate and voting, in 1982–83. That event is often described as a revolution: Americans elected their most conservative president since 1928.

How quixotic it appeared—in the face of the man who resurrected the GOP from Watergate and decisively moved the voters away from their familiar ideological center—to revive the holiday bill in 1982. Not only was Ronald Reagan on the record as not supporting the King holiday, but the case against the holiday had certainly grown. The 1981–82 recession strengthened the argument that it was risky to shut the economy down for an additional three-day weekend every winter. Did CBC members actually expect enough Republicans to turn against Reagan and support the holiday? Or did they only wish to dramatize the CBC's own victimization with an operatic auto-da-fé? Was the revival of the holiday bill a desperate existential thrust of American "progressives," who appeared to have nothing now but memories?

At the 1982 hearings, Coretta King once again headed the roster of pro-holiday witnesses, speaking with much less restraint than in 1979. She focused on the "traveling right-wing circus" that specialized in "character assassination and infantile name-calling."

Her ire elevated the significance of the right-wing fringe and seemed to identify it with all opponents of the bill, including the Reagan administration.[32]

Larry McDonald led the opposition's side of the roster. He had one powerful new argument: Government secrecy was keeping America in the dark about King's record. And for once, government secrecy was serving King and his allies. The SCLC and King's assistant, Bernard Lee, had in fact obtained a court order in 1977 sealing the records of FBI surveillance of King till 2027.[33] "If the FBI files had not proved King's involvement with the Communists," McDonald argued, "we can rest assured that they would have been released as part of the attack on the FBI during the 1970's." McDonald insisted the public had a right to see whether the nation's top law enforcement agency had any reason to consider King a security risk.

McDonald piled on. He cited specific black people who had criticized King. He added that Harry Truman had called King a rabble-rouser. He thought it "racist" to reserve a holiday for black Americans: Why not an Indian American holiday? "I happen to be part Cherokee," he said. "Why not a Chinese American? Why not an Hispanic? . . . [W]e are supposed to be e pluribus unum." He returned again to his hope that, "in the spirit of openhandedness," Congress would "open up the surveillance records . . . so that we would . . . have an opportunity to see if there is something there that a future time would prove to be greatly embarrassing."[34]

In giving full hearing to the opposition, the committee had, perhaps unwittingly, done much to expose the ugliness of anti-King sentiment. This was a strange echo of King's own maneuvers to bring the violence and hatred that he believed inhered in the segregation system to the surface—which McDonald and the other professional anticommunists said was the same as provoking violence.

Stevie Wonder—who had joined the holiday campaign and tried to promote it with one of the weakest songs he ever wrote,

Joining Ashbrook in a lonely ideological campaign against the
King holiday in Congress was fellow John Birch Society member
Larry McDonald, a Democrat who represented the suburbs of
King's hometown, Atlanta. Most holiday opponents in Congress
eschewed ideological attacks on King, sticking to bland
arguments that holidays cost too much, and that America needed
more time to gauge King's historical significance relative to
Washington, Columbus, and Jesus. But McDonald's and
Ashbrook's resort to guilt by association and character assassina-
tion gave color to the suspicion that unreconstructed hatred of
King and his cause was the real basis of opposition to the holiday.

AP Images

"Happy Birthday"—isolated the anticommunist attackers further. "Allow me to quote one American leader who seems to understand the value of remembering Dr. King," Wonder said. "I quote":

> There are moments in history when the voice of one inspired man can echo the aspirations of millions. Dr. Martin Luther King, Jr., was such a man. To America he symbolized courage, sacrifice, and the tireless pursuit of justice. . . . To the world he will be remembered as a great leader and teacher, a man whose words awakened in us all the hope for a more just, more compassionate society. . . . His time among us was cut tragically short, but his message of tolerance, nonviolence, and brotherhood lives on. . . . Let us all rededicate ourselves to making Martin Luther King's inspiring dream come true for all Americans.

Wonder's source? Ronald Reagan.[35] Wonder had taken advantage of one of the president's public statements praising King,[36] which had separated Reagan from the extreme right views of McDonald, Ashbrook, and the like—and from Reagan's own comment shortly after King's murder in 1968 suggesting that King's violent end had originated in the strategies he had promoted: The murder "was a great tragedy that began when we began compromising with law and order and people started choosing which laws they'd break."[37]

The most interesting witness against the holiday was J. A. Parker, the black conservative who had established his reputation by publishing a biography of the black communist leader Angela Davis, in which he attacked Dr. King as a more pernicious influence.[38] In his testimony, Parker summed up the case against the holiday more fully and equitably than anyone inside or outside Congress. It was "unrealistic" to rank King with Jesus and Washington, Parker said. Parker named Jefferson, Lincoln, Patrick Henry, Crispus Attucks, Booker T. Washington, General Daniel

"Chappie" James, and Franklin Roosevelt as examples Congress would have to pass over to do that. He complained that holiday supporters were "unwilling to let history make its final judgment on the merits or demerits of Dr. King." Parker could never forget King's calling America "the greatest purveyor of violence in the world" during Vietnam, or his likening the United States to Hitler's Germany. Parker named five "influential" critics of King, without referring to their race (they were all black): Former U.S. senator from Massachusetts Edward Brooke; former NAACP director Roy Wilkins; former Urban League director Whitney Young; baseball hero Jackie Robinson; and nationally syndicated columnist Carl Rowan. To ignore King's "divisive" role was "to ignore the past and rewrite history." The holiday, widely perceived as a sop to black voters, would "further exacerbate the effects of a color-conscious society at the expense of the color-blind society, which should be our goal."[39]

Congress waited till late in the following year to act. Though President Reagan had not yet come out in support of the holiday, he made a strong public statement at the White House on King's birthday in 1983 about "the man who tumbled the wall of racism in our country. Though Dr. King and I may not have exactly had identical political philosophies, we did share a deep belief in freedom and justice under God. Freedom is not something to be secured in any one moment of time. We must struggle to preserve it every day. And freedom is never more than one generation away from extinction. History shows that Dr. King's approach achieved great results in a comparatively short time, which was exactly what America needed. . . . What he accomplished—not just for black Americans, but for all Americans—he lifted a heavy burden from this country."[40]

———

Republican supporters of the holiday included two of the most effective Republicans on Capitol Hill: Majority Leader Howard Baker and Finance Committee chairman (and former vice presidential candidate) Bob Dole. More surprising were the conservative Republicans who followed John Danforth's example. Senator Richard Lugar (then associated with the rising "New Right" in the party) of Indiana and Congressman Dan Lungren of California soon joined the list of supporters.[41] Lungren's change in particular signaled the shift that Republicans were making across their ideological spectrum to support the holiday.

The House committee reported the bill favorably to the floor on July 26. Although Reagan had expressed some disapproval of the bill, nobody was putting up much of a fight against this old initiative, which had been a Democratic project, indeed a CBC project, since 1968. For some, action on the holiday was futile: Reagan was probably going to veto the bill.[42] It had to clear both houses before anybody would find out.

The House vote came in on August 2, 1983. The King holiday had won an overwhelming majority: 338 members—nearly three fourths—voted for it. Of the 338 yes votes, 249 were Democrats—more than enough to carry the bill in the 435-member House. Among the 89 House Republicans voting for the King holiday were Dick Cheney, Newt Gingrich, Hamilton Fish, Henry Hyde, Dan Coats, Jack Kemp, Bob Michel, and Dan Lungren. Among the 77 Republicans who voted no (about 40 percent of the Republican members) were: both Cranes (Phil and Dan, of Illinois), Jim Jeffords, Delbert Latta, Trent Lott, John McCain, and Ron Paul.[43]

The 1983 Senate debate was far more dramatic than the House one, because there was reason to doubt the holiday's fate in the Senate. It now had a Republican majority, elected on Ronald Reagan's coattails. The holiday's initial Senate sponsors included eight

Republican senators, however, some of them conservative. They had to fight back a series of hostile amendments designed to embarrass holiday supporters, or to turn civil libertarians, black nationalists, and "Hispanic" voters against them.

The chief amender has gone down in history as perhaps the chief offender against the King legacy: Jesse Helms of North Carolina. Helms's anti-holiday speeches drew lavish attention from the media, though Helms had never shown much interest in the legislation before: He did not testify in the hearings held in 1975, 1979, 1982, or 1983.[44] For most of the final Senate debate in 1983, however, Helms's attacks and threats to filibuster were the only big news. Helms succeeded in imprinting the extreme anticommunist message on the national memory far more than those who had made the same attacks on King during his lifetime. Armed with the Senate's unique filibuster-enabling Rule 22, Helms resurrected Ashbrook and McDonald's rhetoric while turning their lost cause into publicity—and significant political leverage—that they could only dream of.

But, like Ashbrook and McDonald, Helms played into the hands of holiday supporters. His statement—and headline-making showdown with Ted Kennedy—came at the start of the Senate debate on October 3. Helms went on for some twenty-one pages in the Senate record. He detailed the alleged communist associations and called for the release of the FBI records on King, and for a full hearing in the Senate Judiciary Committee. Helms pitted liberal martyrs against one another, saying that Ted Kennedy (Helms's principal antagonist in the debate over King's past) was picking on the wrong man. Kennedy's quarrel was not with "the senator from North Carolina." Kennedy's quarrel was with "his dead brother who was president and his dead brother who was Attorney General": Both had warned King about his communist associates, and both ordered the FBI to maintain its investigation of him.[45]

Helms's case, as detailed and energetically argued as it was,

Late in the battle over the King holiday bill, Senator Jesse Helms
of North Carolina took up the ideological attack on King that
had failed in the House. Helms took on Senator Ted Kennedy,
who spoke in favor of the holiday. Helms delighted in pointing
out that Kennedy's own brothers, Robert and John, as attorney
general and president, had ordered FBI surveillance of King
because they suspected he had ties to the communists.
Bettmann/Corbis/AP Images

depended too much on tenuous links. For example, he said, "King associated with identified members of the communist party of the United States (CPUSA), with persons who were former members of or close to the CPUSA, and with CPUSA front organizations. In some important respects King's civil rights activities and later his opposition to the Vietnam war were strongly influenced by and dependent on these associations." Helms admitted, "There is no evidence that King himself was a member of the CPUSA or that he was a rigorous adherent of academic Marxist ideology or of the Communist Party line. Nevertheless, King was repeatedly warned about his associations with known Communists."[46] It was all too easily and voluminously refuted, not only by Ted Kennedy, but by Republican Judiciary Committee members Arlen Specter[47] and Bob Dole. Dole said the FBI's investigation was "tainted": The Senate Intelligence Committee's 1976 investigation found that the FBI categorized King as a communist even before it began its investigation. Dole granted "that various congressional investigations may not have uncovered every piece of information contained in the sealed files. However, there were comprehensive investigations, and I believe that if there was, in fact, anything of significance in the files, it would have been uncovered by now."[48]

The anticommunist rhetoric of J. Edgar Hoover and the Birch Society that Helms was channeling—and which several members of Congress freely applied to King back in 1968—had clearly moved outside the mainstream of respectable language by 1983. Thus Ashbrook, McDonald, and Helms probably helped the pro-holiday forces in 1979 and 1983 more than they hurt them. They made it difficult for Republicans to associate themselves with King opponents. Republicans in the Senate voted two to one in favor of the holiday. Of the six senators who had voted in committee against the holiday back in 1979, five switched to yes votes (all but Orrin Hatch) on the final floor vote in 1983.

Yet more strikingly, southerners—even Strom Thurmond—

could no longer go along with the anti-King voices in any sustained public way, even if they wanted to. Black voters now were strong forces in their states in particular (large black populations had been the principal reason that Democrats in those states had resorted to disfranchisement in the first place, around the turn of the twentieth century). A direct assault on a symbol of black power and respect could be disastrous. With the exception of Democrat John Stennis of Mississippi, senators from the Deep South (Alabama, South Carolina, Georgia, Mississippi, Louisiana) all voted *for* the holiday.[49] The regional base of opposition to the King holiday in the Senate was shifting away from the South and to the West and New Hampshire, where black populations were still among the lowest in the country. The only state Senate delegations to unite against the holiday besides Helms's North Carolina were Idaho, Nebraska, Utah, South Dakota, Iowa, and New Hampshire.

In the last hour of the King holiday battle, Helms had an opportunity to get his name in the papers. Helms said at one point that he knew he had a "losing cause." Yet he fought on, knowing he could not win. That posture of the lost cause is central to the Ashbrook-McDonald line, the extreme ideological anti-King legacy. It occurs almost as frequently as the conviction that King incited violence and consorted with subversives.

President Reagan soon let it be known "through aides" that he was leaning in favor of signing now.[50] Reagan made that position public at a press conference two weeks later. Reagan's motives for switching to support of the holiday remain a source of mystery in the minds of some scholars: Robert C. Smith tried to get all Reagan's papers on the holiday decision released; twenty to twenty-six pages (out of 4,811 pages on the subject known to exist) remain secret. Smith, who believes the number is twenty-six, suggests that Reagan's designated trustees are trying "to whitewash his record on race."[51] The bill was finally signed on November 2, 1983.

President Ronald Reagan overcame his initial opposition to
the King holiday bill. Pulling him in the new direction were
moderate leaders of his party—still very strong in Congress in
those days—and also a few notable conservatives, who supported
the extraordinary national tribute to King. With Coretta Scott
King present, Reagan signed the national holiday into law
on November 2, 1983.
Courtesy of the Ronald Reagan Presidential Library

Conclusion

The King holiday was something of a milestone in America's racial history. The disappointment of the Humphrey-Hawkins crusade was not repeated. On the contrary, the holiday was part of a remarkable—though still unheralded—run of successful civil rights legislation in the 1980s, beginning with the extension and strengthening of the Voting Rights Act in 1982, and, after the holiday, comprehensive sanctions on South Africa, passed over President Reagan's veto in October 1986; the Civil Rights Restoration Act, which reversed a major conservative Supreme Court decision, passed over President Reagan's veto in 1988; and finally the fulfillment of Congress's original tribute to King, the strengthening amendments to the Fair Housing Act, also in 1988. The achievements were all the more striking in light of the Republicans' control of the Senate from January 1981 to January 1987, and the initial opposition of the Reagan administration to many of the initiatives.

The conjunction of those substantive victories with the holiday is the strongest evidence against suspicions that the holiday was just a symbolic sop, a bone of consolation thrown out to pacify black voters and distract them from the lack of real progress. The holiday victory marked a new mood, a new disposition, and a new resolve, which, in its lowered expectations, led to greater achievement and perhaps to greater resiliency in an inconclusive, uphill struggle.

This new democratic realism—in contrast to the bureaucratic and judicial leverage, often funded by corporations who purchased a separate peace from Operation PUSH and/or the NAACP—led the CBC and its allies in Congress to work for what turned out to be much more achievable goals than they had reached for in the 1970s. More important, it impelled much of the GOP (even at the height of "conservative" popularity) to support the maintenance of the strictly *racial* achievements—as opposed to the welfare state or labor achievements—of the liberal era, which the Republicans were then systematically repudiating.

The more technical, tactical lesson—an aggrieved minority can gain tremendous leverage by drawing its most extreme and least popular enemies out onto the public stage—had a more uncertain future. Holiday supporters had practiced what the nonviolent strategist Richard Gregg called "moral jiu-jitsu"[52]—using the power of your opponent against him—by encouraging opponents to indulge in character assassination and guilt-by-association. That was a lesson that King himself had learned and tried to pass on in his major campaigns in the South: Draw the ugliness of the system to the surface, make the system's defenders show their un-seemly side; try to maneuver the most impulsive and PR-insensitive defenders—the Bull Connors and Sheriff Clarks—into the spotlight. The public will see them as representatives of the whole cause. As a result, their cause will lose allies—and, inexorably, heart. The antics of Ashbrook, McDonald, and Helms made the holiday seem like a bigger, more meaningful ideological victory than it was. Their nasty words spurred the pro-holiday forces to their highest rhetorical flights. The campaign for a King holiday became a battle of principle against backward-looking and unsportsmanlike at-tacks on a dead man's character. Holiday advocates may not con-sciously have sought that alignment in the congressional debates, but they did exploit it to fullest advantage, and their victory can-not be explained without it.

But how could holiday supporters phrase the lesson, if they wished to pass it on? If you want something, take care to choose John Ashbrook, Larry McDonald, and Jesse Helms as your ene-my's public standard-bearers? Ashbrook died in 1982, McDonald in 1983. (Supporters founded an Ashbrook Center at Ashland University in Ashland, Ohio, which maintains an active program of internships, classes, and lectures. Ronald Reagan, according to the center's website, "personally dedicated the Center on May 9, 1983." Speakers at the center's annual fund-raising dinner have included Dick Cheney, Margaret Thatcher, Charlton Heston, Henry Kissinger, Clarence Thomas, Bill Kristol, Benjamin Netanyahu, Karl Rove, Glenn Beck, John Boehner, and Mitt Romney.)[53] Helms lived on, but as such an outstanding symbol of racial insensitivity and racist innuendo that it was easy for other conservatives and Republicans to dissociate themselves from him. They dissociated themselves because black voters were strong enough to keep opponents of King's work in check on major, headline-generating legislation. The quieter, incremental game of policy changes arguably hurt the nation's poor, disproportionately black population far more in the 1980s than ever before. As real estate and criminal justice policies concentrated and isolated the poor more than ever before, members of the underclass found ever fewer legitimate opportunities to escape. Desegregation and affirmative action paved the way out of the deteriorating inner cities for the talented and upwardly mobile strivers, which was a great triumph for the civil rights movement and for liberal policies, but the same trends drained the inner cities of leaders and role models. Whether protest or political action could address those largely unforeseen developments was a painful question that shadowed the achievement of the holiday and the substantive changes of the 1980s.

History never answers such questions of strategy decisively. Instead, it moves a different question into focus. The next one up was a vexing and preoccupying question from King's era: the perils of charisma.

CHAPTER FIVE

Jesse Jackson's Rebirth

Jesse Jackson would not let Ronald Reagan take credit for turning Martin Luther King into an official American hero. For two days before President Reagan signed the King holiday bill on November 2, 1983, the papers were crowded with news that Jackson was about to announce his historic candidacy for the presidency.[1] He would be the first African-American to contend seriously for a major party's nomination for the highest office in the land. But the real question—since nobody expected him to win the nomination—was how far his charisma would carry the dream of a restoration of liberalism, based on new black political power, in the Democratic primaries. Could Jackson's mobilization of black voters, and other historically excluded constituencies, push the Democrats to realize King's dream of full equality within their party, if not in the rest of the nation? Would Jackson's crusade gather the discontents of the poor into a focused, effectual force—because he could sustain the national publicity that previous movement-resuscitators could not? He was about as imperfect a candidate as could be. Would his polarizing style reenergize the party—or drive it further than ever from the center of the electorate?

Those questions loomed on October 31, 1983, when Jackson made clear his intentions to run in a speech at King's alma mater, Morehouse College. That same day he announced to 40 million viewers on CBS's *60 Minutes* that he would officially announce his candidacy that week. Jackson attended President Reagan's King-holiday signing ceremony in the Rose Garden three days later, on November 2. He made the papers by refusing to criticize the president, of whom he said: "we've all had high and low moments. This is one of his high moments." The next day, Jackson made his candidacy official, to a roaring, overflow crowd at the Washington Convention Center, eleven blocks from the White House. There he accused Reagan of practicing "showmanship" when the country needed statesmanship.[2]

For someone so erratic, Jackson accomplished remarkable things. The vehicle of his accomplishments was the publicity he always sought for himself. The determination with which he sought it often shook the trust of those who knew him best, but it enabled him to do what others could not do. He easily eclipsed King's own appointed successor, the silent, often saturnine Ralph Abernathy, to whom the media had at first looked for signals as to where the movement would go after King's death. The media got far more satisfaction from the ebullient Jackson, who was always lurching into another ambitious or photogenic scheme. From June 30, 1969, when *Newsweek* put Jackson on the cover of its special "Report from Black America" issue, through April 1970, when *Time* put him on its cover, he was King's heir most apparent.[3]

Dogged by critics who dismissed his fame as media hype, Jackson strove all along for tangible leverage, especially in the form of money and votes. Money came first from famous patrons. His richest donors included Bill Cosby, Motown producer Berry Gordy, Hugh Hefner, Quincy Jones, Norman Lear, Ross Perot, and Donald Trump.[4] The Ford Foundation, CBS, and Merrill Lynch also helped fund Jackson's organization, PUSH, and its affiliate PUSH-Excel. Over twelve years of operation, PUSH garnered a total of more than $17 million in federal grants and private and corporate donations.[5] A large mass membership also paid dues to PUSH.

Jackson realized bigger payoffs by targeting the power of the black purse. He developed a strategy of negotiating deals with businessmen who wanted to avoid bad publicity. They could hire more black workers, create black-owned franchises, buy services and products from black-owned businesses. Boycotts by PUSH got results. The Schlitz Brewing Company, for example, conceded to Chicago's "black community" 286 jobs, $15 million in insurance business, $7 million in construction contracts, $1 million in advertising contracts, and additional professional services to black doctors, lawyers, and public relations firms, after PUSH's five-month boycott in August 1972.[6] A month later, General Foods signed an agreement with PUSH to give "black and minority communities" at least 10 percent of its "employment and economic development activities."[7] By the 1980s, similar deals extended to such major corporations as Burger King, Coca-Cola, Coors, Heublein, 7-Eleven, 7-Up, and the Southland Corporation. After the early shows of muscle, the mere threat of a boycott established that a deal with Jackson was part of the cost of doing business. Cynics referred to these deals as "shakedowns." Jackson and corporate spokesmen called them "covenants."[8]

Votes were harder to be cynical about. Though Jackson hogged perhaps more of the limelight than he earned for Operation Big Vote—sponsored by the unions and the DNC in 1976, with methodical work done by the NAACP, the Voter Education Project, and others—he was an undeniably effective enthusiasm-generator for it. *The New York Times* called it "the biggest voter registration and get-out-the-vote campaign since the civil rights movement."[9] It got much of the credit for Jimmy Carter's close victory in 1976—which carried every southern state except Virginia and

Oklahoma.[10] Jackson made himself a credible political candidate in 1984 and 1988 largely on the basis of subsequent voter registration drives that helped to keep the Democrats competitive in the South and in major industrial states in the 1980s. According to one estimate of Jackson's public campaigns, over four years roughly two million new black voters were registered.[11]

Jackson magnified the power of black voters by flirting with the GOP. Like the Black Muslims and the Nixon administration, he took an active interest in black-owned businesses as an idealistic alternative to government dependency. In 1975, he blamed ghetto habits for black America's failure to realize all the goals of the civil rights movement: "We're free to do a lot of things we couldn't do before, but we don't have the discipline to do them." "We're free to have any job, but we have to be disciplined to produce. We're free to go to any school, but we must take the responsibility to learn." He preached abstinence: Ghetto-dwellers must refrain from "narcotics, alcohol, nicotine, and other vices that have sapped our individual strength to cash in on our institutional victories." It had been easy to "focus blame" on white people during the early movement days, but "we now must be honest with ourselves and take the blame for our own shortcomings."[12] He later said that his great complaint about the Reagan administration was that it stole his idea for a war on drugs.

More startling, from the perspective of later years, was Jackson's position on abortion: "It's murder no matter what you call it," Jackson said in March 1973. "We can't solve the problems of a degenerate society by killing babies. . . . Only He who makes life has a right to take it." He added that Medicaid funding for abortion might keep a new black Moses from being born. A few months later, Jackson, known before and after the 1970s as a voice of the American left, declared, "Abortion is genocide."[13]

There were controversies and embarrassments, beginning with what many thought was his career-killing suspension from SCLC in December 1971 for "administrative impropriety" and "repeated violation of organizational discipline."[14] He left King's organization later that month, converting its economic arm—which King had entrusted to him in 1967—into his own multimillion-dollar operation.

Jackson did not so much fill the leadership vacuum as embody all of its unsettled ambiguity. Nobody else could kindle the thrill of a mass movement—that sense that so many remembered from King's day, that they were part of something larger, something more historic than themselves. If civil rights could move again to the top of the nation's agenda, this now-dashing, now-slapdash daredevil from the original movement was the only recognizable national figure capable of pushing it there. No one denied his charisma. Those immune to his charms acknowledged that Jackson alone could draw crowds nationwide and incite them to ecstasies of rededication. Yet Jackson strained the patience of his comrades and allies. His rhetoric was perpetually half-cocked and off-kilter. He embarrassed and sometimes offended his followers. No living figure better demonstrated the unreliability of charisma, along with its irresistibility.

For better or worse, Jackson made himself the most conspicuous claimant of King's mantle. His performance at the National Black Political Convention in 1972, and at countless rallies for Humphrey-Hawkins and lesser causes, had established that nobody else could compete seriously with him for the role—or perhaps nobody wanted to try. Whether the role itself was uselessly outmoded—except for headline-generating distractions—remained to be seen.

Publicity, for Better or Worse

In the summer of 1983, Jackson's voter registration rallies spread across the South, where the greatest concentrations of black voters still were. He had an audience with former president Carter in Georgia. While there, according to *The Washington Post,* Jackson "granted 10 formal press interviews, called two press conferences and attracted impromptu media gatherings in churches and airports. He played basketball with young men and hugged the old women who came to hear him preach. Constantly, he invoked Martin Luther King's name."[15] Jackson's talent for publicity diverted attention from local black activists who resented Jackson's taking credit for the years of drudgery they had put into voter registration. King had provoked similar resentment.

But who could refuse the publicity Jackson brought? In what the *Post* called "a well-orchestrated splash," Jackson induced Ronald Reagan's civil rights spokesman, Assistant Attorney General William Bradford Reynolds, to visit Mississippi to look into violations of black voting rights in June 1983. Reynolds admitted that the alleged abuses in Mississippi demanded federal attention. He sent two federal observers to monitor local voting practices, and raised that to three hundred in July. Jackson led his audience to believe that a daring outsider could pressure this most conservative administration into substantive concessions. In public meetings, Jackson and Reynolds were filmed singing "We Shall Overcome" together.[16]

Jackson did it again even more sensationally the following month, when disunity among established civil rights leaders was more conspicuous than ever.[17] Bayard Rustin—who had organized the 1963 March on Washington—led the list of those who opposed the reenactment of the march on its twentieth anniversary in August 1983. Yet the reenactment happened, and it turned out to be the largest civil rights demonstration since the 1960s.[18] Jackson "appeared to draw the most fervent response from the crowd" of two hundred thousand, according to *The Washington Post.* His much-rumored plan to run for president played prominently in news coverage of the event. Much of the crowd, according to *The*

Marchers demonstrated their opposition to the rightward drift
of the U.S. government in their 1983 commemoration of the
twentieth anniversary of the March on Washington, where King
had given his "I have a dream" speech. The huge crowds who
showed up to finish King's unfinished business inspired *The New
York Times* to proclaim, "Left Revives." Many in the crowd
found an outlet for their hopes of renewed progress in urging
Jesse Jackson to run for president.

Leonard Freed/Magnum

New York Times, "erupted in spontaneous shouts of 'Run Jesse run, run Jesse run.' "[19]

Black politicians and surviving protest leaders alike saw Jackson maneuvering for a presidential run, and feared he could short-circuit the work they were trying quietly to carry on.[20]

But Jackson could point to the crowds, who kept encouraging him to run for president. If Jackson was a demagogue, he had the advantage of having a larger following than any of his critics—and was arguably more practical as well as more courageous, in that he dared to rally discontented masses of not just black voters but, increasingly, Hispanic, poor white, and other have-not constituencies against the popular rightward trend. *The New York Times,* reporting on the coming together of those masses in coalition with other forces opposed to the Reagan administration, headlined its lavish front-page coverage of the reenactment of the March on Washington with a more startling claim than any Jackson had made: "Left Revives."[21]

If not the left, the new class of black elected officials saw its fortunes soar that year. In November, Wilson Goode was elected mayor of Philadelphia, the nation's fifth-largest city, and Harvey Gantt was elected mayor of Charlotte, the booming commercial center of the New South. Both cities had white majorities—as did Chicago, the third-largest city, where Harold Washington became the first black mayor earlier that same year. Richard Hatcher also won an unprecedented fourth term in black-majority Gary. These historic successes ripened the rumors that Jackson would not be able to resist pushing the trend as far as it could go. If Jackson could ride the surging tide of black power to elective office or even an unofficial position as kingmaker or powerbroker in the Democratic Party, he would diverge strikingly from King's path. Jackson—and his audience—struggled throughout his public career to gauge his relationship to the martyr who, as biographer Marshall Frady put it, gave Jackson his advent.[22] To what extent would he be King's true heir? For many of Jackson's critics, and often for Jackson himself, that question was a handy summary of all the questions that lingered about Jackson's character, his stability, his honesty, his overweening egotism, his opportunism. Memories of King unavoidably shaped Jackson's image, including his self-image. But Jackson's own increasingly familiar flaws—and his sometimes astonishing feats—also shaped the public memory of King.

Miracle on the Road to Damascus

The month after Jackson announced his candidacy, he defined the moment—and upstaged President Reagan—again. On December 5, 1983, Syria captured a black U.S. Air Force lieutenant, Robert Goodman, sole survivor of a crew shot down while bombing Syrian positions in Lebanon. Americans grasped that they might soon have a new black martyr, or a rare chance to save him. President Reagan told a press conference that release of Lieutenant Goodman was a high priority.

Reagan dispatched his special envoy, Donald Rumsfeld—then known as the former secretary of defense to Gerald Ford—to Syria to try to negotiate. Rumsfeld came back empty-handed. Jackson offered to try. The State Department and Jackson's campaign staff objected to his risky proposal. President Reagan did not return Jackson's calls.[23]

Jackson went ahead anyway, meeting the lieutenant's mother at New York's JFK Airport on his way. Goodman's guards were excited to hear that "Jackson" was coming from America—pestering Goodman as to whether it was Michael or Reggie. Syrian president Hafez al-Assad, perhaps the most secular leader in the Middle East, finally agreed to meet Jackson, though he kept Jackson waiting a day past his scheduled return home to the United States. What other presidential candidate would put up with such a show of disrespect? Jackson told Assad that he was "just a simple country preacher."

Two days later, on January 3, 1984, Assad released Goodman into the hands of Jackson and the Secret Service agents who traveled with him. "Jesse Jackson Steals Campaign Spotlight From Fritz Mondale," ran the *Wall Street Journal* headline: "Release of Downed U.S. Flier Dominates the Day's News As Candidate Gets Boost." *Newsweek*'s headline that week had been "Can Anyone Stop Fritz?" Jackson suddenly appeared to be the only answer.

The moment was awkward for the Reagan administration, and for experienced Democrats and pundits who believed in diplomatic protocol. But Jackson brought home an honored young American whose family and country were deeply anxious about his fate. It was not Lieutenant Goodman's fault that his commanders had failed to save him. Who could rain on his savior's parade? The papers and airwaves were full of the phrase "You can't quarrel with success." Only conservative columnist George Will felt obliged to stand out from the crowd, saying with buttoned-down brio, "Well I can quarrel with success." ABC's Sam Donaldson and other pundits admitted they were flummoxed. But they were good sports about it, as indeed President Reagan was.[24]

Uphill Battle with His Inner Demons

Damascus was perhaps Jackson's most astonishing feat ever, but it did not carry him far in the campaign. The worst blunder of his career soon followed. Both peak and plunge were measured not as diplomacy or politics, but by the dramaturgical standards of public relations.

In a conversation with a *Washington Post* reporter on January 25, 1984, Jackson referred to New York as "Hymietown" and to Jews collectively as "Hymie." Jackson's words were not recognized as news right away. Not until February 18, five days after the story ran, did an editorial (written by Michael Barone, who was

Jackson's most dramatic campaign feat was traveling to Syria to get a captive U.S. Air Force lieutenant, Robert Goodman, released in January 1984. Goodman's plane had been bombing Syrian positions in Lebanon, and Syrian forces shot it down. The Reagan administration's efforts to persuade Hafez al-Assad's regime to release Goodman had failed. Jackson's freelance diplomacy probably did not disrupt the administration's relations in the region as much as some had feared. But it did steal a lot of attention from rival contenders for the Democratic presidential nomination.

Top: Barry Thumma/AP Images; bottom: courtesy of ronwadebuttons.com

not Jewish) call upon Jackson to apologize for his "degrading and disgusting" words. A major scandal took off from there.

At first, Jackson denied making the remarks, and he denied them more emphatically in a conference with *Washington Post* editors the following week.[25] On February 25, the Nation of Islam's Louis Farrakhan, standing next to Jackson in public, threatened anybody who harmed "this servant of Almighty God." The day after that, Jackson appeared at Temple Adath Yeshurun in Manchester, New Hampshire, and made an extraordinary speech. He admitted to the substance of the charge, adding that he was "shocked and astonished" that his "ethnic characterization" was overheard and also dismayed that it threatened "relationships long in the making," relationships he said he wanted to protect. "However innocent and unintentional, the remark was insensitive and it was wrong." He said, "In part I am to blame," and he was "deeply distressed." Some heard an apology here; others heard evasions and grudging rationalizations.[26]

Though the Hymietown incident did not end Jackson's career in the Democratic Party, or even appreciably change the rate of Jewish migration to the GOP, the memory of Jackson's revelation lingered as a kind of emergency brake, reminding Jackson supporters of their candidate's limits. Perhaps Jackson's followers, including his many white and Jewish followers, liked him and trusted him in some measure *because* they had no illusions that he would ever be purer than their private selves. They had no alternative national leader, at any rate, to uplift them with moral rhetoric, if they were even ready to be uplifted. At least Jackson could not surprise and disappoint them.

Campaign Successes

The 1984 campaign was marked by a series of amazing turns. On that year's Super Tuesday, when a large number of state primaries were held, Jackson's great achievement was to win 350,000 votes in the South, almost double Ronald Reagan's 180,000-vote margin of victory in five southern states in November 1980. Jackson's campaign stressed that his mobilization of new registrants and high black turnout alone could win the region back for the Democrats in 1984.[27]

Although Jackson prided himself on getting white votes, and emphasized his achievement as a nonracial candidate leading a new "rainbow coalition," his growing support among black voters was even more impressive. He'd won 79 percent of Illinois's black vote, 75 percent of Pennsylvania's (despite Philadelphia mayor Wilson Goode's strenuous work to deliver black voters to Walter Mondale), and 87 percent of New York's. Washington, D.C., set a new record for Democratic primary turnout, 108,000, of which Jackson won two thirds—crushing Mondale's 25 percent and Gary Hart's 7 percent. Jackson's other first-place finishes in 1984—South Carolina, Louisiana, and Virginia—were equally impressive.[28]

Over the whole primary season of 1984, black turnout in the Northeast and South soared over the levels of the 1980 primaries: by 19 percent in Illinois, 38 percent in Pennsylvania, 43 percent in Florida, 82 percent in Alabama, and 103 percent in New York.[29] Jackson knew he would not win the nomination, but also that he gained leverage and a grudging respect within the party. If he could do something similar for black turnout in November, he held the Democrats' key to victory.[30]

On the eve of the New York primary—which was the sixteenth anniversary of King's assassination—Jackson spoke: "Tomorrow we have a chance to roll the stone away. Then there can be a resurrection. Just as there was a crucifixion sixteen years ago. . . . The day of crucifixion in 1968 will be the day of resurrection in 1984."[31] Jackson said that his effort—to pull the party back in a "progressive" direction and to increase participation by minorities and the poor—was a continuation of Martin Luther King's work.[32] Certainly the 1984 primaries confirmed that Jackson could reproduce the local victories of black mayors and black members of Congress from isolated urban districts.

During the campaign, Jackson complained frequently that delegate selection rules deprived him of the influence that his vote totals dictated, and he challenged the party establishment to give black and poor voters a much greater voice. But at the convention in July, he dramatically apologized for his impatience and other sins, appealed to his supporters for Democratic unity, and pledged to support the nominee.[33] Black turnout did increase over 1980, and went 9-to-1 for Mondale.[34] But the hope that black voters could turn out sufficiently to swing key states back to the Democrats proved unrealistic: Reagan drew white voters away from the Democrats in unprecedented numbers, losing only Mondale's home state of Minnesota and the District of Columbia. There just were not enough black voters to offset that trend. Bill Clinton and other relatively conservative, southern Democrats read the results and set about carrying their party away from Jackson. In 1985, they set up the Democratic Leadership Council to redefine the center of the party. To them, the Democrats' future lay in winning back the masses of white voters who were disillusioned with the excesses of the "liberalism" that had defined the party in King's heyday.

Running again in 1988, Jackson far surpassed his 1984 performance. The most dramatic example was Michigan, which had been one of his great disappointments in 1984, when Detroit's black mayor, Coleman Young, and the United Auto Workers had delivered the state to Mondale.[35] But Jackson took Michigan outright four years later, with 55 percent of the total Democratic vote, despite Young's endorsement of Dukakis. This reflected his all-time high share of the white vote—at 20 percent. The result shocked the nation, much as Alabama's George Wallace had with his Democratic primary victory in that northern industrial state sixteen years before. And Jackson's victories in such odd states as Alaska and Vermont, where black votes were negligible, only heightened his achievement. He also won Delaware, which had only a 14 percent black population.[36] But the sheer power of Jackson's victories in five Deep South states on Super Tuesday made him look like a true champion, reversing the history of racism that had defined, and emanated from, the Democratic Party in those states. His victories were all the more impressive because Super Tuesday had been designed essentially to keep the party from nominating a liberal. From the perspective of later years, the most telling figure from the entire election was that every candidate in Super Tuesday finished in the same order they had spent on television advertising—except for Jackson, who came in first while spending less than the others. Jackson proved the power of radio to get out the black vote, which was a lot cheaper than TV.[37] It was not just the most memorable campaign in an otherwise dull season—the other Democratic candidates were called "the Seven Dwarves"—but the most cost-effective one.

Old Resentments Die Hard

One seminal event in Jackson's past haunted him throughout his career, and notably in the two presidential campaigns: King's assassination. Accusations that Jackson had launched his career with a dishonest and unseemly effort to exploit that event clung to Jackson and were never fully addressed.

The Washington Post, providing background for the likely presidential candidate in July 1983, explained that "the King mantle" was Jackson's "most precious possession," and also "his most controversial" one. "Within a few days of King's assassination, reports began circulating that Jesse Jackson said he was on the balcony of the Lorraine Motel with King when he was shot, that

Perhaps the most damaging story about Jesse Jackson centered on his allegedly unseemly behavior two decades earlier, in his reaction to King's assassination in April 1968. The surviving photographs, film, and eyewitness accounts of the assassination and its aftermath did not support accusations that Jackson had exploited the assassination and lied about it to enhance his reputation. This photograph shows that Jackson was on the balcony where King had fallen within minutes of the shooting. But other elements of the story about Jackson's post-assassination behavior could be neither corroborated nor refuted, which may help explain why the story flourished.

Joseph Louw/Getty Images

In 1983–88, Jackson's critics claimed, among other things,
that he had boasted to the media and to the Chicago City
Council, on April 4–5, 1968, that he literally had King's
blood on his chest. Some critics said that Jackson had actually
smeared his shirt with King's blood to achieve a mystical,
self-aggrandizing effect, and perhaps to demonstrate that he had
held or "cradled" the bleeding King as he heard his last words.
However, no stain is visible on Jackson's shirt in this photo, taken
by a Memphis news photographer shortly after the assassination.
Jackson is in the same clothes he had on the following morning
in Chicago. No stain is visible in the other known photos (also
partial, like this one), or in the film footage of the assassination
scene in Memphis.

Commercial Appeal/*Sam Melhorn/Landov*

he held the dying man, [and] that he wore his blood on his shirt."[38] Yet back in its 1968 coverage, neither the *Post* nor any other major paper reported that Jackson was on the balcony with King at the moment of the shooting. On the contrary, the *Post*'s own story, published the morning after the assassination, states in its first sentence that King had been shot "when he strolled alone onto the balcony of his hotel." Quotations of Jackson later in that story do nothing to contradict the point that King was "alone" when shot. No journalist then or in subsequent coverage of the assassination scene quoted Jackson *saying* he was on the balcony at the moment of the shooting: He indicates rather that he was in the parking lot below. Jackson did make one reference to King's blood on the record, but it was vague and might have been understood at the time as metaphorical. Only two papers quoted Jackson referring to King's blood, and they conflict. According to the *Chicago Tribune,* reporting on Jackson's statement to the Chicago City Council the day after the shooting, " 'I come here with a heavy heart,' the Rev. Mr. Jackson said to the council and audience, 'because on my chest is the stain of blood from Dr. King's head.' " But according to the *Chicago Sun-Times,* Jackson said: "The blood (Dr. King's) is on the chest and hands of those that would not have welcomed him here yesterday." Neither paper emphasizes this theme and neither indicates that Jackson emphasized it. At any rate, Jackson's recorded statements on what he did at the assassination scene were very few and fragmentary. They do not add up to evidence that Jackson sought publicity to aggrandize himself with some mystical connection to the dying man.

Though nobody in the 1980s produced a direct quotation from Jackson from April 1968 saying that he was on the balcony when King was shot, that he held the dying man, or that he wore a literally bloody shirt, the *Post*'s July 1983 story took off. Within a few months, other national papers were repeating the basic elements of this story, accepting them as true. Their purpose in the 1983–84 campaign season was to raise serious questions not only about Jackson's judgment and taste, but about his basic honesty.[39]

The principal witness against Jackson was Hosea Williams, who had also been an aide to King and present at the Lorraine in April 1968. Williams's most memorable accusation is that Jackson ordered other witnesses to stay off TV, then elbowed his way into the klieg lights to give his own dishonest, self-aggrandizing version of the event to the world.[40] Very little TV footage from that night survives. That which does survive has a brief segment from Jackson, which is very different in character from what Williams claimed to remember. On the videotape, Jackson says nothing about holding or cradling the dying King. He simply describes hearing the shot, and that all "we" could see was police coming. No blood (or other visible stain) shows on Jackson's shirt or hands. Nowhere does he say he was on the balcony at the moment of the shooting. Nowhere does he claim that King spoke to him after the bullet hit.[41]

Whenever a student does background research in newspaper and magazine accounts of Jackson's historic campaigns of the 1980s, these stories about his behavior in April 1968 have front-page prominence. The stories tend to begin on an invitingly positive note, with Jackson's unseemly grab at King's bloody mantle often as the *only* strongly negative counterpoint, the ballast that provides what twentieth-century American journalism strove so obsessively to convey: balance.

It turns out that this story of Jackson, repeated so unquestioningly in print in the 1980s, cannot be substantiated with the photographic record of the assassination scene and the eyewitness accounts laid down in print and videotape in the immediate aftermath of King's death.[42] Like so many historical beliefs, it gained much of its power from its unverifiability. The vigor with which a witness asserted it, and the dependence of the story itself on symbolic and mystical motives, gave the story a memorability with which no verifiable fact could compete.

Jackson himself denied the accusations: "This thing about holding him, I never said that I picked him up and held him in my arms," he told the *St. Petersburg Times* in January 1988. "That's not true. That's not what I said. He was laying there, we all reached out for him, urging him to please hold on." But the media did not follow up on the denials, or treat them with the credulity and emphasis they gave the accusations.[43]

On the other hand, Jackson was not particularly energetic or persistent in his denials. There is reason to suppose that Jackson thought it was in his interests to leave the damning story—which brought him tremendous publicity and may have damaged him little in the eyes of his adulating fans—unchallenged. Even had he wanted to challenge the story, the relevant evidence was so scattered and fragmentary that it might have done him little good. The safest bet may have been to hope the story would die of its own overplay. It did not die. But had Jackson fought it more vigorously, he may only have intensified the media's focus on it without planting substantial doubt in the public mind. Surely he would have lost the 1984 and 1988 nomination contests anyway, and it is hard to imagine his winning even his supporters over to the idea that he was trustworthy.

The Significance of Jackson's Campaigns

Jesse Jackson appeared to be as dissatisfied with his lineage to King as his critics were. Like most ambitious successors, worthy or not, Jackson looked like an impatient, disgruntled rival. After King died, Jackson tried to turn King's legacy to his own purposes. But he also strove to extend King's record of accomplishment. He was like King in one respect: He was never content to rest on the civil rights movement's laurels. Like King, he pushed quixotically for world peace, whatever that might mean, as well as freedom and dignity for black Americans and the poor.

Jackson's followers—substantial pockets of poor white south-erners as well as millions of black people who had familial connec-tions to poverty and orphanhood—had been told for centuries that their place was below and outside. Jackson's campaigns tee-tered like a high-wire act between unprecedented heroism and ill-prepared exhibitionism.

Perhaps the greatest difference between King and Jackson was that Jackson claimed credit—something King generally avoided doing. Partly for that reason, and partly because he lived, national memory has been unkind to Jackson. But it has also failed to grasp the real achievements of the 1980s in the struggle for black rights and black political power.

Whether achieved by an empty, self-serving egotist or not, the two campaigns add up to a remarkable achievement. Jackson's runs at the White House demonstrated the power of black votes within the Democratic Party, to which 87–93 percent of the black electorate became solidly loyal in the 1980s. For a brief shining moment, Jackson proved that he could also win disruptive num-bers of disaffected—and perhaps simply bored—white Democrats, particularly the 20 percent in Michigan. His ability to create that kind of volatility—to harness the desperation and frustrations of a majority of Democrats in several key states—led the Democrats under Clinton and Obama to build a new transracial centrism. The Democrats maintained the loyalty of black voters, despite turning away from the labor–New Deal agenda and toward the Democratic Leadership Council's program to remain competitive in the conservative white South. Even that—given Jackson's own pronounced conservatism in some areas and dalliances with the GOP in the 1970s—can be seen as a continuation of Jackson's impulses, or rather, a testament to how closely Jackson anticipated the drift of the party.

The rightward thrust of the GOP was blunted by the forces Jackson mobilized, however, in racial matters. Jackson led massive voter registration drives before and between his own 1984 and 1988 candidacies. In addition to making a case for greater Democratic attention to the poor and unemployed, these helped to consolidate the GOP's fear of the black vote. Black registration rose in 1984 to an all-time high of 66.3 percent of those eligible. (Barack Obama came close to matching that figure in 2008, but not quite.)[44] That fear kept southern Republicans from alienating the black electorate too much, lest they stimulate high black turnout. The fear helps explain some extraordinary legislative victories for civil rights in the 1980s, despite the conservative trend of those years on other issues.

Jackson's gravitational pull on the electoral tides cannot explain the legislative changes, but it almost certainly helped them along. Congress passed the Civil Rights Restoration Act in January 1988 and then overrode President Reagan's veto on March 22—some sort of proof that the most conservative administration since the New Deal did not have sufficient support in its own party, which still had enough votes to sustain a veto, to reverse the racial changes of the Second Reconstruction.

A more radical civil rights bill—a positive advance rather than a defense against judicial reaction—passed later the same year, in August: the amendments to the Fair Housing Act. The new Housing Act finally put "teeth" into the 1968 housing law, given that the original law turned out to be virtually unenforceable. This time there was hardly any opposition. The administration actually supported that bill, arguably the most radical civil rights law passed since the 1960s.

Whether Jackson deserved the credit he claimed for mobilizing supporters or not, the conservative effort—the preservation of previous victories—of the post-1960s civil rights coalition was startlingly successful in national politics. Jackson was at least a significant part of that effort, which was more successful than any other part of the dwindling liberal coalition. Even in foreign policy, where King was most overextended and frustrated, black elected officials triumphed when they overrode President Reagan's veto on comprehensive sanctions on South Africa, in 1986. Jackson had championed the anti-apartheid cause, too.

Jackson also claimed credit for the defeat of ultraconservative Supreme Court nominee Robert Bork in 1987. Had the Democrats not retaken the Senate in the 1986 elections—they picked up eight GOP-held seats, including in Florida, North Carolina, Georgia, and Alabama—they probably would not have been able to defeat Bork (who lost 58–42). Jackson's voter registration drives may have tipped close races, particularly in Alabama and Georgia.

Jackson was such a messy public figure, perhaps, because he tried to hold together in one personality all the strands of the fractured movement that King had been unable to put together again. Not only did he straddle the old divides of nationalism and integrationism, the impatient militancy of the Black Panthers and the pragmatic nonviolence of the original CORE, SCLC, and SNCC, he also reconciled the youthful streets of the 1950s and 1960s with the older, distinctly white-collar, work-within-the-system diplomacy and wheeler-dealerism of the NAACP—which, partly under Jackson's own influence in the 1970s, had been partly transformed into corporate wheeler-dealerism. When Jackson tested his own position, he was thus testing a synthesis, a certain effort at unity. The results had been for him an unprecedented demonstration of black power, or at least black power as tied to coalition politics and contained within the liberal wing of the Democratic Party.

For all its failures, Jackson's campaign did deliver stunning victories in Michigan, in South Carolina, and elsewhere. Those were more impressive than any civil rights leader's victories since the 1960s. Through all the disappointments and embarrassments of the candidate, there was something undeniably dramatic, something memorable about the campaign. Since King's death, it was the first instance of a charismatic leader mobilizing the black masses—and an impressive array of white supporters—nationwide. It was a vivid reminder of the momentum that had been lost since the 1960s, and of the sorts of high-profile, public things a charismatic leader could achieve. Jackson thrust back into people's faces the importance of the void left in people's memories by King's death: Though he could not fill the vacuum, he generated more excitement and publicity for the continued march of black power than any of King's successors. Charismatic leadership had not been the priority, the emphasis in black political life. It could not be ignored now.

Though Jesse Jackson did not run for president again, he had been for better or for worse at the center of a decade of renewed advancement and momentum in civil rights. Certainly the new civil rights laws of the 1980s consolidated the gains of Martin Luther King's movement—in contrast to the frustrations of the NBPC and the Humphrey-Hawkins campaign in the previous decade. The number of black elected officials, an incomplete but indispensable measure of black power, grew from 1,469 in 1970 (the first year data were collected) to 7,335 by 1990. The momentum appeared irreversible for the foreseeable future. But if Americans felt any sense of validation of the civil rights movement's achievements, that sense was soon tested.

CHAPTER SIX

Public Reckonings with King's Character

So far, the story of civil rights after King has taken its shape from efforts to finish King's own work. Battles were fought, historic questions decided: Congress mustered the will to ban discrimination from most of the private housing market in 1968. An independent black political force, however, could not be unified and sustained in the early 1970s. The old labor-liberal coalition gained recognition of full employment as a worthy and practical national goal but failed, in the late 1970s, to ratify that goal in policy. What King's legatees could ratify was the value of King's life and sacrifice—without defining what that life and sacrifice had been for. So King became part of the national landscape of civic celebration, with enactment of the holiday in 1983. By law, the holiday made King an official national hero, papering over if not transcending the ideological wounds and vendettas of his lifetime. His ghost appeared to rise to the level of Mount Rushmore, surprisingly aloof from further efforts to revive his work.[1] Jackson's presidential campaigns brought the most dramatic and disruptive reminder of the power of charismatic leadership and what it could achieve for the movement since King's death. The one thing Jackson did not disrupt was the settling of King's memory into the nation's rhythm of commemoration. Instead of a persistent goad and gadfly, King was becoming a fixture in the civic pantheon.

Suddenly, however, in late 1989 and 1990, controversies over King's extramarital affairs and his academic dishonesty threatened to dislodge King's reputation. Unlike the previous tests of the legacy, these controversies revealed real truths about his experience and moral choices.

The basic cause of the public controversy over King's adultery in 1989 was that, back in the early 1960s, FBI director J. Edgar Hoover made a record of King's affairs, through wiretaps and bugs. Hoover knew that King's enemies would gain from exposure of the evidence and spread its contents behind the scenes.

Many reporters and editors were aware of Hoover's charges. But some combination of doubts as to the relevance or accuracy of the charges, disgust with Hoover's methods, and fear of encouraging similar violations of privacy kept them from acknowledging or checking them. More to the point, perhaps, shame also held them back. No one wanted to be responsible for being the first to publicize this scandalous story—which would quite justifiably taint the messenger. To expose was to exploit. To exploit was to incur the disrespect of colleagues and readers.

Hoover had worked harder and more ingeniously than any radical of the late 1960s to prove that the personal is political. But in King's case, Hoover did not get his chance of vindication until twenty-one years after King's death—seventeen years after Hoover's own death. This most ruthless and determined of King's enemies did not get a full public hearing of his case against King until after the King holiday was secure and electoral politics had brought in a strong rightward reaction against the 1960s. Perhaps the country just was not ready to listen till then.

The story of how King's marital infidelities became a topic of heated public discussion in 1989, rather than long before, had little to do with King himself. The general appetite for personal secrets had been whetted by public revelations about the sex lives of televangelist Jim Bakker and Democratic presidential candidate Gary Hart, beginning in March 1987. Those scandals effectively ended the old taboo on reporting the sex lives of prominent political and religious figures. The pressure to break the taboo in King's case was significant: He had ripened into a national symbol of righteousness, despite the frequent if vague allusions in print over the years to rumors of his adultery. The question was, who had the authority and the audacity to make the public face up to the rumors?

As a new generation of post-movement black leaders gained unprecedented fame and influence, they blithely reaped what their often-unsung elders had sown at great peril. Some of the old black leaders felt left behind and passed over, if not used. How galling it must have been, for example, for King's chosen successor, Ralph Abernathy, to fall into obscurity. Jesse Jackson had passed him by within a few years of King's death and kept rubbing it in as the years passed. Now leaders like David Dinkins of New York City and Douglas Wilder of Virginia—elected as the first black mayor of America's largest city and the first black governor since Reconstruction, respectively, in November 1989—were even surpassing Jackson. King had died at Abernathy's side to make *their* successes possible. Abernathy had risked his life and suffered agonizing loss. Yet nobody paid attention to him anymore. If he was resentful, he had cause.[2]

So many commentators concluded, at any rate, when Abernathy published his memoir in October 1989. Like Abernathy, the book was unexceptional. But it contained two explosive passages—which Abernathy's publisher (Harper, which had also been King's publisher) and news reporters emphasized far more than Abernathy himself did in his 620-page book.

In the first passage, Abernathy described King's last night in Memphis, stating that King spent the night with a black woman, "a member of the Kentucky legislature" with whom King had a "close" relationship. (Abernathy did not name her, but this turned out to be Georgia Davis Powers, the first black woman in the Kentucky Senate, who in 1995 would publish a memoir about her affair with King.)[3] Another young woman had expected to see King that night, however, one whom "Martin knew well." In the morning, that second woman reacted angrily to King's explanation for his absence from his own hotel room, where Abernathy believed the young woman had looked for him and not found him the night before. She and King had a lovers' quarrel in front of Abernathy, which he described.[4]

The second passage began:

Much has been written in recent years about my friend's weakness for women. Had others not dealt with the matter in such detail, I might have avoided commentary. We all fall short of the mark, and an excessive preoccupation with one another's shortcomings is a form of pride that we should avoid. Hatred and a cold disregard for others are the besetting sins of our time, but they don't sell books or tabloid newspapers—and that's the reason why people have talked about Martin's failings and left the flaws of some others alone.

Altogether, Abernathy did little more than acknowledge and seek to explain, and to some extent excuse, what others had previously reported. As a Baptist preacher, Abernathy did not deny his fellow preacher's inescapable human sinfulness, as he knew King would never have denied it. King "understood and believed in the biblical prohibition against sex outside of marriage. It was just that he had a particularly difficult time with that temptation." Abernathy had once confronted King with the risk of exposure. Several reporters who had seen him in the company of one particular young woman would exploit the information, as Hoover's men would, too, he had warned. King replied, according to Abernathy, that he did not care. "The FBI can do whatever they please," he quoted King saying, "but I have no intention of cutting off this relationship." The two never discussed the matter again.[5]

The big surprise in the whole erupting controversy was that Abernathy's words were taken as news. Rumors of King's adulterous adventures had been nibbling around the edges of public discourse for years.

Chicago columnist Mike Royko, for example, reported in June 1969 that about three years earlier, an ex-FBI agent he knew told him that the FBI had bugged King's hotel rooms and tapped his phone. The ex-agent gave Royko examples from the resulting "very thick file" on King. "They were very personal things. Naturally, if you bug almost anybody's bedroom long enough, you would hear things that person didn't want anyone else to know about. . . . It was plain old mudslinging, on a level with the lowest scandal magazines and transom-peeking public actions." Royko did not question the credibility of the information, or its originating from the FBI. He was certain that this "was being leaked to me for the purpose of discrediting Dr. King." Other journalists made similar statements.[6]

Coretta King's memoir, published in 1969, is unsurprisingly mute on the subject of adultery. But it provides a view of the charged context, and the stakes, of his behavior. Reflecting on the early years of her marriage, Mrs. King observed, "A minister has to be constantly on guard morally, for he is on exhibition, being judged all the time; he has little freedom. Martin felt that to lead people requires that your own life must be an example to them." Baptists like her husband were stricter than her own Methodist people. To dramatize the seriousness of Martin's religious commitment—which in other contexts struck her as quaint—she noted that when he got the call to preach at age seventeen, "he stopped dating girls and stopped going to dances. He stayed in his room and prayed and read the Bible most of the time. I think he felt he had to purge himself."[7] She recalled the frequent phone calls that dogged their home life from the beginning of the Montgomery boycott in December 1955 on. "Often the women callers raved on about sex, accusing Martin and me of incredible degeneracies." Such calls were a small part of "the chaos of our private lives."[8]

Washington Post columnists Laurence Stern and Richard Harwood summed up the state of affairs in mid-1969. "For several years a piece of Washington apocrypha known as the 'Martin Luther King tape' was the subject of sly and ugly surmise among certain journalistic insiders," they wrote. Some reporters said they heard the tape. Some said they read a transcript. Others said they read a different transcript of a bugged gathering where "King and friends were present." This was "one of those repugnant but enduring stories that cling to controversial public figures."[9]

But the taboo on public discussion of King's sex life was not seriously breached until John A. Williams, a black novelist with a militant stance, published *The King God Didn't Save* in the summer of 1970. Williams claimed that six anonymous sources spoke to him of King's dalliances. One source said she had been photographed on a bed with King naked and had witnessed an orgy in King's Stockholm hotel, involving prostitutes and groupies.[10] A review in *Time* magazine dismissed Williams's book as an angry, intemperate attack on King, but civil rights leaders denounced the review for publicizing Williams's charges. Ralph Abernathy, in a joint statement with Andrew Young and Walter Fauntroy, said: "*Time* magazine discredits itself in seeking to throw mud on a man admired and loved by millions, black and white. It discredits itself in stooping to sensationalism through fiction and irresponsibility."

They emphasized *Time*'s inaccuracy in reporting on a meeting the three of them and King had had with J. Edgar Hoover in 1964: Hoover did not discuss King's personal life at that meeting, they wrote. Mrs. King also said *Time* was inaccurate about that meeting.[11]

The columnist Jack Anderson leapt in to publish information he said he and his partner had withheld in their earlier reporting on the FBI's eavesdropping on King, back in May 1968. Anderson explained in August 1970 that he had learned back then that one confidential informant had told the FBI that King had been having an "illicit affair" with "the wife of a prominent Negro dentist in Los Angeles" since 1962. King called and met her frequently. One drunken night in New York, King threatened to jump out a thirteenth-floor window if the woman would not declare her love for him. The FBI had already determined that the cuckolded husband was not the type who would kill or pay someone to kill his wife's lover.[12]

References to King's infidelities proliferated throughout the 1970s,[13] most notably during the Church Committee hearings in late 1975—the high-water mark of post-Watergate revelations of secret government eavesdropping, harassment, and outlandish plots to destabilize and/or assassinate foreign leaders. Many who read the coverage, and the tremendously popular volumes of published transcripts, found the hearings stranger than fiction. King figured in coverage of the hearings for a few days, when *The New York Times* ran the committee's discovery that the FBI tried to induce King to kill himself in 1964—among other things, to prevent him from accepting the Nobel Peace Prize thirty-four days later. The FBI did this by sending King a tape "of alleged unsavory activities engaged in by Dr. King." With the tape was an unsigned note, implying that the tape would be made public if King did not cooperate: "King, there is only one thing left for you to do. You know what it is. You have just 34 days in which to do it."[14]

Bayard Rustin gave an interview in 1986 in which he said he had read the FBI's reports on King and believed they were accurate.[15]

David Garrow added considerable confirmation to the published record in two books on King, most notably his 1986 biography, *Bearing the Cross*, which won a Pulitzer Prize.[16] Garrow did it with such understatement that no one could accuse him of scandal-mongering or sensationalizing the material. Indeed, Garrow's language tends to be restrained to the point of euphemistic, though overall he leaves no doubt that the "private" and "personal" problems King and his friends were "distressed" over involved frequent and sometimes careless extramarital sex. It is all reported in the same matter-of-fact tone as every other detail in Garrow's book.[17] Garrow's book confirms that people close to King knew about his extramarital sex and felt sufficiently alarmed—one might say threatened—by it to confront him. King ignored their pleas, up to the end.[18]

After all that, Abernathy's revelations in 1989 were a thin icing of incident and detail: nothing qualitatively new. But the reception revealed a great deal about a nation whose public leaders were still capable of surprise upon learning that the men who are honored with eternal flames may be haunted by old flames.

Coretta King, the papers noted from the start, had no comment. All her spokesman Stoney Johnson would say was that he believed that she and other family members had not read Abernathy's book.[19]

But King's other famous legatees reacted quickly and with amazing unity. Jesse Jackson, Atlanta mayor Andrew Young, NAACP president Benjamin Hooks, Georgia congressman John Lewis, D.C. congressional delegate Walter Fauntroy, SCLC president Joseph Lowery, former comedian Dick Gregory, and other prominent black leaders who had known King issued a statement:

"This is but another attempt to diminish the life and work of this spiritual genius. . . . It is time for detractors to cease their futile efforts to diminish this legacy that God has given to our time and to all time through Dr. King."

Hooks and Jesse Hill, chairman of the King Center board, also let reporters know they thought that Abernathy was "mentally impaired by two recent strokes," by "major brain surgery," and, Hooks added, by "more than 35 years of . . . beatings and physical abuse." (In fact, Abernathy had admitted to the "minor" strokes and the surgery in his memoir.)[20]

The signers also sent Abernathy a telegram. In the manner of Maoists, mobsters, McCarthyites, and ministers with arbitration training, they gave him an ultimatum with a face-saving way out: Since the words in his memoir sounded "foreign to your life," the signers were "driven to the conclusion that they were put into your mouth by others who needed a sensational story to sell books and slander the name of your martyred brother."[21] If Abernathy failed to retract his story, he would "retroactively repudiate" his "personal, private, inviolable relationship" with King.[22]

In most major black papers, the denunciation of Abernathy was the story, not the book or its revelations, despite the fact that the denunciations stemmed from the book. Spontaneous expressions of opinion came from far and wide. The Associated Press reported that the Colorado Springs, Colorado, chapter of the NAACP ritually burned Abernathy's book, saying it would mail the ashes to Abernathy. A letter to the *Los Angeles Sentinel* called Abernathy the "Benedict Arnold of our race. For a few dollars he has become our Judas."[23] The Rev. Al Sharpton announced that he and his lawyer Alton Maddox would go to Atlanta to seek a court order suppressing the publication.[24] Abernathy's bodyguard, a retired New York cop, told the press his client had had "three or four death threats."[25]

Famous black journalists contributed whole columns to the feud.[26] Juan Williams was the first national newsman—and the only prominent black writer—to defend Abernathy by considering the book as a whole. Williams tried to put the sex in perspective, giving it barely a paragraph. He found the rest "valuable," "charming," "beautiful," "a very human, realistic look," which includes an "elegant, sweet story of youth," along with a "fast-paced, roller-coaster ride" of intrigue and chance, with a unique "authoritative," "first-hand" perspective, which richly "deserves attention."[27]

Abernathy's own defenses were no more effective than his previous efforts at self-promotion and moral leadership. The media did him no favors by giving little attention to his defense—which happened to be truthful and far more germane to the substance of the controversy than most of the speculation targeted at him. He had revealed nothing new, he said: "[H]ad Martin's infidelity not already been the topic of discussion in other books, in the halls of Congress, and in the public forums, my decision would have been simple: avoid the entire issue." Who could dispute his own account of his decision? "If I hadn't written about what I saw," his critics "would have accused me of whitewashing history. . . . If I ignored the subject, then reviewers and readers would say, 'He's not telling the truth so the rest of his book is unreliable as well.' "[28]

Unfortunately for Abernathy, simple, plausible explanations like this were less dramatic than emotional conflicts over alleged motives and jealousies. His explanation was consistent with all the known facts and did not rely on speculation. If it had any meaning, there was nothing more to say—and no more story to feed the media. The author's lonely but cogent insistence that his book said nothing false and nothing new would deprive them of the scandal and of the pretense that it was news.

Abernathy fought back like a man with nothing to lose. He said the civil rights movement was in "splinters" because younger SCLC members lacked the self-sacrificial devotion that he and King had brought to it. After King's assassination, young staffers sought only political power and money. He named Jesse Jackson,

Andrew Young, and Hosea Williams. These "so-called leaders . . . don't have a movement. They're trying to become millionaires." The judgment applied retroactively to the movement days: "I was there, not because I was paid to be there like Andrew Young and Jesse Jackson and Hosea Williams[, who] were paid staff." He also criticized Coretta King, saying she built a $10 million monument to King rather than feed the poor.[29]

In the heat of the controversy, Abernathy's alma mater, Alabama State University, rescinded a decision to build a monument to him: Its trustees cancelled plans to name a dorm after him, one of a pair of buildings. The other was to be named after King.[30]

More galling was Abernathy's being turned away from the dedication of Maya Lin's great monument to the forty martyrs of the civil rights movement. Morris Dees, the white, southern executive director and cofounder of the Southern Poverty Law Center, told the press, "He was not asked to sit on the podium or make any comments." Before the scandal, Abernathy had been one of fourteen thousand invited to witness the dedication. But he now sent word he would not attend, and the center made clear its pleasure in his absence—till he showed up unannounced anyway. At the ceremony, as Abernathy approached the stage, Dees told him to leave the premises. Abernathy said he did not know he was not invited to the podium: "I am not a violent man. Mr. Dees pushed me. Mr. Dees had no right pushing me." The atmosphere grew "embarrassingly hostile," *The Boston Globe* reported. Johnnie Carr, transportation coordinator of the Montgomery bus boycott, "shook her finger at Abernathy" and, according to the *Globe,* "was visibly upset about his book." The center later issued a statement saying it "regrets that Rev. Abernathy chose to force himself onto the stage at the dedication. His ploy was simply a cheap effort to bring himself back into the fold of the civil rights community after selling out its most honored hero."[31]

The vilification turned into a kind of validation of Abernathy.

Sales of his book were faster than expected. The original printing of 30,000 sold out in the first week, and Harper quickly ordered a second run of 10,000 on the strength of all the publicity.[32] Surely all the news coverage and columns generated more reviews and sales than Abernathy would have inspired on his own.

Amid the heat of recriminations, a few tried to put matters in some historical perspective. David Garrow, who did not question Abernathy's motives, noted the irony that others missed: Abernathy seemed "far more certain of King's unshakable historical greatness" than King's defenders, who betrayed "a strange insecurity about the impact and durability of King's historic contributions"—as if those could be wiped away by revelation of his personal flaws.[33]

Garrow also joined many others in trying to create a new context in which the facts could be positively welcomed: All they could undermine were unrealistic deifications of King. The inflated popular memory of King—not his behavior and its moral or political significance—was the issue. The important thing was that people should remember King as no more virtuous or omnipotent than themselves. Their memory of him, after all, was a potential instrument in further political struggle.

This point about King's humanity soon became the generally accepted response for deflecting attention from his actions. Its use would grow in the next public discussion of King's moral failings. The point of both episodes would become: King's followers put him on a pedestal, and he needed to come down, for their sake. The more natural point—that King recklessly and irresponsibly put his followers and his cause at risk with his selfish lack of restraint—was all but lost. King's followers needed to have their own hero-worshipping habits checked, the argument went, so in a sense King did them and their cause a favor by erring and leaving enough evidence of it for his survivors to discover. Abernathy perforce did them a great favor as well though somehow explicit credit for that never extended to him.

Only one prominent commentator questioned this logic at the time. What bothered conservative columnist Cal Thomas most was "the instant absolution King gets from some black leaders." If adultery was so supremely excusable, why was talking about adultery so inexcusable? It was a good question—whatever Thomas's motives might have been in opening it up. Abernathy had not betrayed anyone. "If Abernathy's accusations are true, it was King who betrayed his wife and children, and who committed a grave disservice to the family, especially the black family." King was no superhuman saint, as his defenders hastened to assure everyone. "But to give King a free ride on the adultery issue by falling back on the excuse that he was 'human' is to betray those men who have remained faithful to their wives." It was also to devalue "commitment and fidelity," and the sacrifices and struggle these demand.[34]

The premise that King's followers had to choose—humanity or fidelity?—was absurd at other levels that Thomas did not get around to. The choice is as logically and historically bad as the choice that King greatly rejected: violence or passivity. To deny the significance of marital fidelity in the name of humanity is to cut humanity short—shorter than it is for many very real human beings who remain faithful to their spouses, and to the anguished strivings of many to overlook or overcome adultery.

In the second controversy over King's personal morality, his protectors and defenders had recourse to this same notion of humanity. This time the controversy concerned his intellectual honesty. Unlike the story of King's adultery, the information about his plagiarism came as a genuine surprise: It had not been published or significantly hinted at in the past. The controversy was intensified by its coinciding with a moment of intense questioning of the racial progress King had died for.

In a referendum on November 6, 1990, voters of Arizona re-jected a King holiday by 1 percent. Sixty-three percent of those who voted against the holiday told pollsters they had changed their votes at the last minute in a defiant reaction to outside intimidation—not from civil rights groups, but from the National Football League, which had threatened to withdraw the 1993 Super Bowl, scheduled for Tempe that year, if the holiday referendum failed.[35] The same day brought another setback in the progress of civil rights, in the North Carolina senatorial race: Republican incumbent Jesse Helms defeated black challenger Harvey Gantt, the nationally admired mayor of Charlotte.[36] Though Gantt had not fared a lot worse against Helms than previous white challengers, Helms's exploita-tion of racial fears—notably through provocative attack ads—offered fresh proof that white backlash was not defeated, or even in retreat. More proof came from Louisiana, where former Klansman David Duke—though he was repudiated by the Republican Party and indeed lost the election by a huge margin—still shocked the nation by winning 60 percent of the white vote in the state.[37] Duke would have won handily, that is, without the massive federal inter-vention that had restored black voting rights in the 1960s: 60 per-cent of white Louisianans had not progressed but were being held in check. Thus Arizona voters' rejection of the King holiday sym-bolized what some saw as a trend, a surging national reaction against the civil rights victories of the 1960s. That was the immedi-ate context in which *The Wall Street Journal* broke the story on November 9, 1990, that King had plagiarized repeatedly and ex-tensively in graduate school at Boston University, including in his doctoral dissertation. The evidence was clear. A typical example was the following passage from King's dissertation:

> But Tillich does not mean by creation an event which took place "once upon a time." Creation does not refer to an event, it rather indicates a condition, a relationship between

God and the world. "It is the correlate to the analysis of man's *finitude, it* answers the question implied in man's finitude and infinitude generally." Man asks a question which, in existence, he cannot answer. But the question is answered by man's essential nature, his unity with God. Creation is the word given to the process which actualizes man in existence. To indicate the gap between his essential nature and his existential nature man speaks of creation.

Researchers had found a nearly identical passage in a dissertation written by Jack Boozer, and approved by BU three years before King's:

But Tillich does not mean by creation an event which took place "once upon a time." Creation does not describe an event, it rather indicates a condition, a relationship between God and the world. It is the correlate to the analysis of man's *finitude, it* answers the question implied in man's finitude and in finitude generally." Man asks a question which, in existence, he cannot answer. But the question is answered by man's essential nature, his unity with God. Creation is the word given to the process which actualizes man in existence. To indicate the gap between his essential nature and his existential nature man speaks of "creation."

Though King footnoted Boozer in other passages, he did not footnote him for this passage and several others that are nearly identical to Boozer's wording.[38] The *Journal's* Peter Waldman quoted Clayborne Carson, director of the King Papers Project at Stanford University: "Several of King's academic papers, as well as his dissertation, contain numerous appropriated passages that can be defined as plagiarism." Carson calculated, and BU later admitted, that 45 percent of the sentences in King's second chapter were partially or wholly borrowed from uncited sources. In later chapters, King borrowed "only" 21 percent of his sentences.[39]

Even without taking the perceived backlash in Arizona and elsewhere into account, the revelation provoked powerful emotions. Carson's staff joined other King scholars in expressing "anguish and soul-searching" over the discovery. David Garrow said that "it's disconcerting, because it is fundamentally, phenomenally out of character with my entire sense of the man."

Some of the Papers Project staff resigned. An assistant archivist wondered angrily why King did not know better and why he didn't get caught. Another researcher faulted King's professors. "Their assumption was they were training someone to go teach in a predominantly black college in the South," said Penny Russell, associate editor of the project. "Were they setting up different standards?" One summer intern "broke down in tears."[40]

Carson and fellow researchers had first discovered serious lapses in King's use of quotation marks and footnotes three years earlier, in 1987. Word of their work leaked out and was referred to in print for the first time in the *London Sunday Telegraph* on December 3, 1989.[41] An obvious hot potato for the press, major newspapers and at least one magazine sat on the story for several months. *The New Republic,* according to editor Leon Wieseltier, had trouble getting a scholar to accept the assignment and declined, out of sentimentality and "correct politics," to pursue the story vigorously.[42]

Once revealed, the evidence for King's plagiarism was much more straightforward than the evidence of his adultery. The documentation was clear-cut and not in serious dispute. No one seriously questioned the motives of those who discovered and disclosed it. Controversy came, inevitably, but it proceeded on firmer ground.

Among the first to seize on the discovery were academic PR

men—anticipating hostile uses of the new information. A Boston University press release announced: "The stature of Martin Luther King Jr. as the pre-eminent leader of America's civil rights movement does not depend upon the truth or falsity of the charges now being raised."[43] It is not remarkable that a university found conflict between the general public's standards of greatness and its own standards. What is remarkable is that the university left the impression that it had nothing special to contribute to the public by insisting on its own, different standards. The famous black political leader and Boston mayoral candidate Mel King made the university spokesmen's point much more authoritatively than BU could: King's "reputation wasn't built on his Ph.D. or whatever."[44]

The New York Times clung to the idea that "academic experts will resolve the extent of the plagiarism and the validity of the doctoral degree."[45] The *Times* made the point again with unintentional humor a few days later: "[S]cholars are right to denounce plagiarism mercilessly."[46] In fact, no scholar had gone on record at that point to denounce King's plagiarism at all. Indeed several had defended or apologized for it in one way or another.[47]

BU did not encourage the *Times'* hope that academic experts would weigh in without fear or favor. Acting president Jon Westling told the press he had asked four professors—three from BU and one from American University in Washington, D.C.—"to make a prompt and careful examination of all the evidence." Westling added that BU would make no further comment until the committee was done.[48] *The New York Times* did not wait, however. It concluded, after speaking with BU officials that same day, that King's degree was unlikely to be revoked.[49] Others with a stake in King's greatness weighed in. The SCLC's president, Joseph Lowery, fired off a bit of wordplay worthy of Jesse Jackson, who indeed later repeated it: "The youthful Martin may have sidestepped footnotes, but thank God he stamped out greater foot prints for society later on."[50] Jesse Jackson, fixating on King's footprints "in the sands of time," brushed aside those who merely "deal with his footnotes." Jackson offered the most outlandish nonacademic defense of King: King wrote many of his papers during the heyday of segregation, Jackson told *USA Today,* when black people were not allowed to do scholarly work in many libraries. King "wrote his thesis, not at Boston University," Jackson said, "but in a war zone of civil rights demonstrations, bombings and protest marches." Jackson was not trying to understate the wrongness of plagiarism, he hastened to add. But "[a] lot of what Jesus said in sermons was from the Old Testament. A lot of what was in the Old Testament came from the Egyptian culture. The Ten Commandments came from a much longer list of commandments . . . that Moses grew up in. Much of it was oral tradition." The work of academic authorities "became internalized in [King's] talking rhythm."[51]

An academic expert from Arizona soon outdid Jackson and became King's most inventive and enduring apologist. Keith Miller, an English professor at Arizona State University, had done years of diligent, original work on the sources of King's rhetoric. He had in fact discovered some plagiarism on his own in King's published work, and reported it in his dissertation in 1984,[52] though nobody had paid much attention to that. Miller's work focused on King's published sermons, showing extensive "influences" from earlier preachers. There the question of honesty was clear to Miller: "With respect to King's language during his public career, he did absolutely nothing wrong."[53] But in context, Miller appeared to brush off academic rules as an occult obsession, alien to King. "He was trained in the black folk pulpit, which is an oral tradition. In this tradition, language was seen as common treasure, not private property. His sense of language comes out of that tradition, not out of his academic training."[54] Miller thus exoticized—and racialized—King's entire background. He made King immune to the white secular (or perhaps bourgeois) fetish of ownership. Miller's interpretation showed its own influences, especially from black nationalist theology.[55] His view was widely echoed in the controversy that followed.

Clayborne Carson, the editor of King's papers, knocked a little wind out of Miller's position. Carson pointed out that "the rules for academic writing at Boston University in 1955, and every other institution, clearly indicated that you were supposed to use footnotes in order to cite where it is you're getting your information." Asked whether King would have been expelled had he gotten caught, Carson answered, "If one of his teachers had raised a question about it, there would have been a hearing . . . and he might have ended up with no more than just a reprimand and have been told, 'Go back and be more careful.'" Asked whether it was fair to say that a black Baptist preacher like King "came from an oral tradition" and did not see ideas as property, Carson answered, "I'm sure he did. But the question becomes, at some level, he had to have known that he was in an academic environment and there were different rules. And clearly, when you look at his writings, he knew what footnotes were and he knew how to use them, and he used them extensively." He just didn't use them enough, Carson concluded.[56]

Professor Ralph Hill, a board member of the King Papers Project, stood out for a moment by squarely stating that King did a bad thing. But then Hill pulled his punch: "It certainly was not the ethical thing to do, and that's what makes him really very human."[57]

This idea of the human once again became a prominent theme in King apologetics, linking the discovery of his plagiarism to the discovery of his adultery. Hill embraced King's past turpitude as good news. Here was the long-overdue relief from the hagiography that constricted public memory. Most King apologists, quick as they were to accept King's dishonesty themselves, assumed the average King admirer was blinded by idolatry, in need of disillusionment. The problem, two *Boston Globe* writers opined, "is that

King has been built into such a towering figure that even the smallest failing becomes difficult to accept."[58] The *St. Louis Post-Dispatch* editorialized that King's plagiarism "comes as a surprise only to those who see the slain civil rights leader as a virtual saint, incapable of character flaws."[59] Thus the discovery at last brought King down from the pedestal that kept people from understanding him and carrying on his work themselves. His stolen words were not evidence of wrongdoing, but of approachability, of emulability.[60] Not to err was inhuman.

As in the adultery controversy, this shift of focus from King to his alleged worshippers substituted for any soul-searching or debate over what the news of King's actual and very specific failings meant. By drawing the circle of "humanity" around those who cheated, it left all the suckers who stayed up till 4 A.M. double-checking every citation and closing every quotation they opened, in some ill-defined limbo outside the circle—along with those who struggled to be faithful to their spouses. By letting King off the hook—with a boys-will-be-boys shrug—this consensus cheapened the rules that King violated, and the broader social and ethical purpose behind those rules.

An irony that went unremarked was that King would never have made—or tolerated—such excuses in cases when he deliberately violated rules for political and moral purposes. He expected to be held accountable for the laws he violated. Indeed, he insisted on it: If he paid no price for his disobedience, his disobedience had no persuasive effect. Moreover, King always supported the larger principle of a rule of law—a government of laws, not men—behind the peculiar laws he strategically violated. He saw clearly that the credibility of his protest—and that of millions who joined and supported him—depended on that.

Clayborne Carson's original and most enduring contribution addressed the question of King's motives. There were "instances of plagiarism" in King's work, Carson unswervingly told a reporter. But in "most" instances King was probably sloppy rather than deliberately deceptive. Carson noted that although significant portions of the copied material lacked footnotes and quotation marks, King did cite all of the sources from which he cribbed somewhere.[61]

That is a reasonable guess, though there are five obvious alternative explanations that the evidence does not rule out: In haste, King had simply forgotten how much he had stolen; he brazenly felt the rules did not apply to him, or that his violations were trivial compared to his other achievements; he believed that if he got away with cheating under close supervision, his guilt was unlikely to be detected later; like many a compulsive thief, he secretly or subconsciously wanted to get caught; or (as David Garrow suggested in passing later) by the time King bequeathed his papers, he was simply too busy to reflect much on his past.[62]

Carson scrupulously noted that his analysis was still tentative at that point. Still, it clarified the question of King's wrongdoing. Carson insisted that intentions—hard as they are to determine— had to be part of the evaluation of King's wrongdoing. A genuine appreciation of King's humanity demanded consideration of his motives, partly because that precarious human thing, moral responsibility, can rarely be resolved without taking motive into account. Yet nobody else took that question up in the public discussion.

A more immediate moral question was whether BU had held— and was still holding—King to special standards. If so, were the standards racial? David Garrow raised a relevant point that others failed to consider: King had gotten lousy grades—a C average—as an undergraduate at Morehouse, an all-black college.[63] At the very least, this suggested that resolving the question of racial standards would by no means be easy. A racial double standard could be unconscious, or, as many were arguing (and King himself once hinted, in his argument for affirmative action), might in some ways be justifiable.[64] The question came back to life later that year when the dean of Boston University's College of Communication, H. Joachim Maître, had to resign after he was charged with plagiarizing a speech—from a movie reviewer—that he gave to graduating students.[65]

The committee's ultimate refusal to hold King retroactively accountable also raised the question whether it feared it might expose a broader corruption of standards. How many graduates of BU or other institutions could withstand the sort of computer-assisted scrutiny to which King's work was subjected? The literature on plagiarism is full of such messy imponderables.

Though King's widow kept her counsel on this kind of cheating, as she had on the adultery, another widow made the headlines, one who had been married for forty-seven years to the scholar whose work King copied. Jack Boozer, who had gone on to teach theology at Emory, had finished his dissertation at BU three years before King.[66] King copied more from it than any other work. Boozer learned of King's theft two years before the rest of the world did. He died a year and a half later—in July 1990, three months before the story went public. The bereaved Ruth Boozer told *The New York Times* that her husband had hoped to avoid the sort of publicity the story was now getting. A native Alabamian who supported civil rights, Boozer had been inspired by King's leadership and had quoted him—with attribution—in his own book, *The Edge of the Ministry*. Living in Atlanta, Boozer and his wife became friends with the Kings, two of whose children stayed in the Boozer house for a few nights after King's death. When Jack Boozer learned years later that King had copied his work, "He wouldn't discuss it for two days," Ruth Boozer recalled. "He was a very careful scholar himself, and he respected scholarship, but he believed that this would be misinterpreted and used." She said,

"We were hoping it would just go away." Ultimately, Jack Boozer "was honored that he could have been of some help to Martin Luther." She implied it was improper to question the dead leader's integrity in a time of crisis (the Persian Gulf War was then brewing). "Martin Luther King's story is one that's more than footnotes," she said. "He had a prophetic voice, one of the first to speak out against the Vietnam War. Today, we're again on the brink of war. Instead, we're focusing on details and footnotes."[67]

Did ideological opponents of King prove Mrs. Boozer right by joining the discussion? The effect of the plagiarism revelations on the right wing, and on the right's appeal to a broader public, is hard to gauge. Five syndicated conservative columnists—Pat Buchanan, Ken Adelman, Cal Thomas, Joseph Sobran, and Jeffrey Hart—plus one major conservative paper, the Manchester, New Hampshire, *Union Leader,* used the plagiarism revelations as a weapon in the current battle over the holiday. In addition to Arizona, New Hampshire was also refusing to enact the King holiday. Anti-King rhetoric, if it made a difference anywhere at this point, mattered most in those two places.[68]

The BU committee filed its report in September 1991. As expected, it did not consider revoking King's degree, an option to which it said "no thought should be given." The committee did give the idea enough thought to cast it beyond the pale: To revoke the degree would be "absurd," "unheard of." This was not the same as explaining, or justifying, the refusal to consider that step.

The committee then offered the mildest possible sanction: "A letter should be placed with the official copy of Dr. King's dissertation in the Boston University Library, stating that improprieties have been discovered in the dissertation's citations, that these can be examined in detail in the forthcoming edition of his papers produced by the King Papers Project, and referring to his committee Report."[69]

By the 1980s, such a step was all but meaningless. Copies of the dissertation had circulated widely, including several in a microfilm edition. If the university did not dare revoke the degree, or recall all copies of the tainted document, why not send the committee's letter to all the known libraries that keep a copy—a feasible task? As it stands, no student would have any way of knowing that the integrity of the scholarship before him had been severely challenged: that it was a risky thing to quote or to cite—unless the student happened to remember the plagiarism dispute, which was increasingly unlikely with each passing year.

The letter itself is not terribly illuminating. It does not say King plagiarized or even that instances of plagiarism appear in his work. It only states two facts the committee could not conceal: "[T]his dissertation contains numerous passages that lack appropriate quotation marks and citations of sources consulted and used"; and "King fully understood that dissertations are to be properly documented." The word *plagiarism* only appears once, in the name of the committee that signed the letter. The letter exonerates more than it condemns: It claims narrowly that "in the matter of exposition, understanding, and criticism, King's dissertation is quite acceptable. Regrettably, however, it does violate the guidelines for proper documentation; and also regrettably the Author cannot answer for himself."[70]

The university thus shrank from a full public reckoning with King's plagiarism. It acknowledged only so much of his academic misconduct as it could not avoid, then apparently did its best to make sure that as few people as possible would know of its acknowledgment. It abdicated its duty to determine whether the credentials it had issued to its most famous alumnus were fraudulent—whether its own officers in some way encouraged or turned a blind eye to fraud—to the King Papers Project.[71] Years later, the project published the fullest record of King's cheating.[72] But a casual to moderately inquisitive student, seeking King's work in a library computer, would never see the committee's letter.

Conclusion

The controversy over King's plagiarism ultimately shed more light on Boston University, and the general state of higher education, than on King. King played a unique, unprecedented role in American history and in the historical struggle for human freedom. For that he will be remembered, regardless of academic pronouncements on his historical significance, *or* on his academic misconduct, let alone on his "humanity." That King the moral hero did not measure up to academic standards put the keepers of those standards—at a time when their self-confidence was at an all-time low—in an awkward position. They lacked the clearheadedness to affirm: King failed by our standards, and that is all we are qualified—and all we are asked—to say.

Academic authorities, including the guardians of King's graduate school, generally said that the standards of their professional expertise could not alter history's judgment of him. Logically, that should have given them room to go ahead and make their judgments without fear of their effects. But they did not do that. Their unwillingness to separate King's intellectual dishonesty from considerations of his later, larger role in history—a role that was primarily political and moral—left them adrift.

King's legacy either stands the historical test of survival in the nation's memory, or it doesn't. No one judging the newly revealed facts of his academic dishonesty could predict, let alone control, the nation's memory of King. Instead, Boston University officials and most other commentators predicted the worst effects of the new information and tried to control the memory out of a strange and faintly insulting belief that King needed their protection, and in the process they only belittled their own academic standards. Those who had confidence in King's legacy did not feel that they had to—or could—protect it, certainly not with such hasty and unconvincing assurances as Boston University, Keith Miller, Jesse Jackson, or the others insisted on making.

In any case, King had never been known as a particularly original writer. When *The New Yorker* eulogized him in April 1968, it sought to separate what was distinctive and great about him from what was not. As examples of the latter, it cited King's "florid plagiarisms" and "annoying plagiarisms." At the time, no doubt, the editor did not mean this literally; he was putting King's hackneyed phrases and notions in perspective with some rhetorical license. He took it to be self-evident that King, whose eloquence in delivery ranked among the most stirring in modern history, did not achieve greatness in composition.[73]

Most people—including many professional scholars who get paid to study civil rights—do not seem to remember that King cheated on his dissertation and other graduate school work. Everybody seems to remember that he cheated on his wife. They may not remember how or when they learned that. They may not have a definite opinion about its moral significance. But unlike his plagiarism, his adultery is part of nearly every American's ready pool of instant-access information about Martin Luther King. Many learn it in school. It has not dislodged him from his pedestal—any more than the things they don't remember have dislodged him. The comparisons are in one sense unfair. King did not seek the job of inspiring moral leader of world-historical significance. King did not ask for generations to name and otherwise try to model their children after him. But in another sense, national memory is too kind to King: Americans—his followers along with many of his former rivals and enemies—made him their great hero, putting him above politics and, seemingly, above self-interest. If King did not seek the job, he embraced it and often spoke of the importance of accepting the consequences of one's actions.

King's protectors and defenders emphasized that he had no chance to defend himself from the charge of plagiarism. His biographies, however, make one wonder whether it ever would have occurred to him to defend himself. For he insisted—in the teeth of lionizing, hero-worshipping praise from his followers—that he was just a sinner, like everyone else. More than that, he tortured himself with guilt, his friends said. He took responsibility for all the movement's failures, often for choices his rivals made against his counsel. His critics and enemies blamed him for many things he did, and many things he did not do and could not control. The two blameworthy patterns of his life that came into public view only after his death, his adultery and his plagiarism, were more unambiguously his fault, and also more shameful, than the things people knew about when he was alive. But for all his failures and sins, he has continued to go down in history as one of the great idealists of all time, as a great man who still symbolizes America's getting back in touch with two of its greatest founding principles— freedom and equality—and bringing those a great historic leap toward realization. That is an amazing achievement—all the more amazing in light of the unpredictable and often dispiriting revelations about him that have flowed since his death, along with the tangle of his unfinished business.

Conclusion

The struggles just traced in this book bring to mind a significant truth of the civil rights movement, one that has not received sufficient attention: People who honored King's memory carried on his work, though they generally did not speak about it as memorably. I have tried to trace the most ambitious of their often forgotten efforts. The history contained in these pages gradually discloses that deeds—however unglamorous and often unsuccessful—take more human energy, planning, and dedication than the sweeping rhetorical gestures that Americans all too easily remember. Deeds, thwarted and unthwarted, demand investigation—nonfiction prose—not merely poetic funeral orations and rousing sermons.

It will not do to remember King as the articulator of great American and human ideals. Sound bites on his commemoration days depict King as the riveting orator of his day, the spellbinder who had a stem-winding dream of a distant day to come. His words dazzle to this day. They shunt our attention away from the grim parts of the past and make us nostalgic for our predisillusioned picture of the future. Fifty years later, his dream still brings tears to hardened eyes.

His evocation of that distant, ideal day when brotherhood would reign did not make him exceptional, however. On any given Sunday, then as now, thousands of preachers warm their flocks with mellifluous visions of harmony and understanding. Some of them achieve heights of virtuosity, a few of them of genius. What made King exceptional by historic standards—what gave him the authority, the mass support, and the nerve, to mount the Lincoln Memorial, during the centenary year of Emancipation, and speak to eternity—was nothing aesthetic or idealistic. It was a record of accomplishment in the world of tangible deeds.

King delivered victories as well as lines. The first victory came seven years before the dream speech. It came at the end of a year-long nonviolent siege he led in Montgomery, Alabama, the first capital of the Confederacy. Economic coercion and a sympathetic federal court forced violently unwilling white southerners there to desegregate the transportation system they thought was theirs. They had to cry uncle, in public, to a black man who refused to play Uncle Tom. A year later, he organized the Southern Christian Leadership Conference, a moving target that could not be outlawed the way the NAACP had been in Alabama. The conference projected a new image of black America as unified behind a defiant demand for freedom now. It drew together the talents and intelligence services of like-minded boycott leaders from Baton Rouge, Tallahassee, and other southern capitals. It funded a youth initiative, soon to separate from its SCLC sponsors as the Student Nonviolent Coordinating Committee, which led sit-ins all across the South simultaneously. King's SCLC would not let the students' ambitions outperform his own generation's. In 1963, the SCLC organized and King led Project C, for "confrontation," to crack the spine of "Bombingham," where the Klan had terrorized the black population with impunity. There King played ingeniously—

Since King's death, presidents across the political spectrum have
found it worth their time to claim some allegiance to him.
Though King himself quickly became a lot less controversial after
his death than he ever had been during his public career—when
he was among the most hated and feared men alive—
efforts to finish his unfinished business have generally been
divisive, whenever they have been noticed at all.

*Top: Damon Winter/The New York Times/Redux; bottom: photo
by Eric Draper, courtesy of the George W. Bush Presidential Library*

and controversially—to the cameras. He suffered the little children to subject themselves to—and in a sense to provoke—the brutality of mobs and police. Together they achieved immortality, as seen on TV. The spectacle of dogs and fire hoses shocked enough of the northern white public, including President John Kennedy, out of its complacency. King and others sought to convert the momentum into revolutionary legislation against racial discrimination in public accommodations and employment. The most brilliant strategist of the movement, Bayard Rustin, brought the various generations and factions of the movement together for the largest civil rights demonstration in history, the March on Washington, the platform for the dream speech.

The dream speech made no sense—made no history and therefore no memory—except as the entr'acte in the Birmingham siege and the larger campaign to dismantle Jim Crow and restore black America's right to vote. We remember King's speech through the lens of the climactic victories that came on the heels of the speech. The demonstrations prodded a new, effectual president, Lyndon Johnson, to prod a sclerotic Congress to produce the most radical civil rights act yet, which in 1964 outlawed discrimination in public accommodations and employment, and empowered the federal government to enforce the Fourteenth Amendment's ninety-six-year-old equal protection clause more generally. The last great battle came later that year, in remote Selma, Alabama. It was probably the last place where activists could depend on local authorities to attack photogenically defenseless Christians at their prayers. The result of that outrage was the Voting Rights Act of 1965. In conjunction with the Twenty-Fourth Amendment (ratified in January 1964), and new interpretations of the Fourteenth and Fifteenth, it ended the near-complete disfranchisement that had settled on the South circa 1885 to 1908.

People remember King's words because the deeds of his followers, rivals, and critics in the mass movement before and after 1963 made those words indelible. Deeds call out for summary. They need a handle, a handy label stamped with a memorable new image—preferably a personal, human image. Post-Stalinists and modern academics may shun cults of personality, but frail humanity likes to personify epic achievements. That is one of humanity's ways to record complexity, to compress without removing the unpredictable and irreducible—to enliven the past. To personify is to vivify, and thus to preserve.

Today, the remembered record of the civil rights movement makes King's words—his ruminations and reflections on our common ideals—distinguishable from those of other dreamers and lesser doers. King fomented and fostered changes in laws, in institutions, in mass habits of public speech and behavior. The ideals, and the prettiest possible wordings of them, would be banal without the molding of reality that King represents. Where sentimental readers may still imagine that his ideas or his phrases are somehow monumentally outstanding, the critical and skeptical reader sees the painstaking process of reality-molding, which adds up to King's enduring and proper significance. That process—the civil rights movement—is what makes him memorable. The shredding and composting of memory turns this around, using King as a synecdoche, to make the movement memorable, and to evoke it.

It is beside the point to argue whether history is made by great individuals or by masses, since both are abstractions, comprehensible reductions of a fleeting, irreproducible series of incomprehensible moments that moved higgledy-piggledy in many directions beyond our ken.

The symbol that fit the moment of the civil rights movement's success came to be Martin Luther King, who believed its successes were barely begun. People who honored his memory tried to carry on his work after he died. It required some work—and some dispute, and some periodic recalibration—to discern what that work was. But in addition to being unfinished, that work was considerably more demanding than words of commemoration and remembrance. It was public, it was controversial, and it brought masses together in political and economic action to alleviate large-scale injustice and human suffering.

After King's death, his survivors in the movement had some lasting achievements that deserve recognition. The Fair Housing Act of 1968, for example, banned the most durable and insidious form of discrimination that had been left largely untouched by the civil rights movement up to that point. Eventually, the amended act empowered the federal government to enforce the ban. The Martin Luther King holiday indelibly reinforced the lesson that King's life's work—the cause of equality and social justice—had been set aside for the nation's highest honor. In the process of enacting the holiday—though they did it during a historic resurgence of conservatism—King's survivors pushed King's enemies to the margins of respectability, by lumping them together with hateful extremists and bigots.

These achievements may be unfairly diminished in national memory because they no longer had a recognized speaker with the authority and audacity to tattoo them with his memorable eloquence on national television. Even when King's survivors in the struggle fell short of their immediate political goals, however, they kept the struggle alive. They kept the unfulfilled promise of King's inspiring sacrifice on the nation's conscience, for days and weeks beyond his yearly birthday celebrations. They kept their own marching boots supple. They limbered up again and again for history's unpredictable opportunities to open wide once again, as they had for that rare moment of 1954 to 1965. And they aimed high—for national power to serve broad coalitions and to right historic wrongs. Even when they fell out of fashion and headline-worthiness, they kept themselves resilient and resourceful, by experimenting with an evolving range of plans and strategies. They prepared themselves to extend and revive the extraordinary record of achievement that King symbolized—and the larger promise he died without fulfilling. They kept on acting in a long period of history that, in its seeming aimlessness and inconclusiveness, was far more typical of history's openness to social change than King's own shining moment in the national spotlight. It was the sort of period for which humanity needs more constant and determined preparation. King's survivors expended themselves and often took great risks to fulfill the manifold promise that King articulated in memorable and also forgotten ways. Growing millions of Americans, from a growing distance, have admired the ringing sonority of King's words over the years. His striving survivors deserve more recognition for bringing America closer to a full recognition and realization of his meaning.

Acknowledgments

The debts I ran up in this project make me almost too self-conscious to criticize Congress. How humbling to think that that bedeviled body has a better chance of paying its debts than I. As a start, I thank the librarians and archivists who helped so much with the research: Alan Burns at the Strom Thurmond Institute, Carolyn Clark at the Auburn Avenue Research Library, Aaron Scott Crawford at the Howard H. Baker Center, James Cross at the Strom Thurmond Institute, Mike Duggan at the Ronald Reagan Presidential Library, Nancy Dylan at WGBH, André Elizee and Steven Fullwood at the Schomburg Center, Ed Frank at the University of Memphis, Angela Hand, the amazing Mikey King, Patrick Kirwin at the Library of Congress, Diana Lachatinere at the Schomburg Center, Tad Lewis at the National Archives at College Park, Keith Luf at WGBH, James Mathis and David Mengel at the National Archives at College Park, Sean Noel at the Boston University Libraries, David Roepke at the Ashbrook Center, Robin Roggio, Sam Rushay at the National Archives at College Park, Sarah Saunders at the Jimmy Carter Library, Laurie Scrivener, James Seikel at the Indiana Historical Society, Denise Strammel, Mary Evelyn Tomlin at the National Archives at Atlanta, Jeffrey Wilhite, and others. I thank others who gave their time and knowledge of the historical record so generously and helpfully: Glenn Eskew, John Frank, M.D., Louise Greaves, Kemper Kirkpatrick, Rick Kogan, Kenneth Mullinax, Chuck Osgood, Richard Reynolds, Amy Rosenblum, David Weir. I thank the hardworking, underpaid grad students who contributed so resourcefully and knowledgeably to my research: Tom Aiello, Kimmy Bess, Jeff Fortney, Michael Hammond, Lara Kelland, the late Matthew Kirkpatrick, Katrina Lacher, Mike LaCoste, Michael Martin, Stephen Mucher, Matthew Pearce, Mike Powers, Brent Riffel, Gene Vinzant, and the amazing Betsy Wood. I thank all my students, colleagues, and former colleagues at the Universities of Arkansas and Oklahoma, especially Ben Keppel, Patrick Williams, and David Wrobel, who read and criticized major portions of the manuscript, and Rob Griswold for the courage, ingenuity, and insomnia of his leadership. I also thank Shawn Alexander, Carol Anderson, Eric Arnesen, Ray Arsenault, Tony Badger, Pete Banner-Haley, Martha Bayles, Tim Boyd, Fitz Brundage, Evan Bukey, Stewart Burns, Sheryll Cashin, Jim Chase, Marcia Chatelain, Pat Conge, Joe Crespino, Jane Dailey, Ted Delaney, Dennis Deslippe, Angela Dillard, Glenn Eskew, Devin Fergus, Eddie Glaude, Allison Graham, Chester Hartman, Paul Harvey, Jonathan Holloway, Randal Jelks, Chris Lehmann, Jeff Littlejohn, Sharon Monteith, Bethany Moreton, Gwenn Okruhlik, Michael Pierce, Steve Prothero, Leigh Raiford, Renee Romano, Barbara Savage, Bruce Schulman, Daryl Scott, Jim Sleeper, Judith Stein, Randall Stephens, Robert Stepto, Ken Stout, Lindsey Swindall, Phil Tegeler, Cathy Tumber, Jack "Chip" Turner, Britta Waldschmitt-Nelson, Robb Westbrook, Stephen Whitfield, and others who read or listened to a hefty portion of the argument and saved me from God knows what. There remain others without whom I could not have finished this work. Some remain unnamed. My endless thanks go to Suzanne Wolk for lifelong friendship that surpasseth understanding, and for beating the hell out of my funny bone. I thank Kip McMillan, Cyndi Nance, and Fred Rotondaro for encouragement, understanding, and great dinners and stories, over many, many years, and also three who are gone but earned eternal thanks for teaching me and some of my greatest friends: Christopher Lasch, Betsey Fox-Genovese, and Gene Genovese. I thank my editor, Jonathan Jao, who pushed and pulled perfectly, his marvelous assistant, Molly Turpin, and others on the team at Random House. I thank my agent, Sandy Dijkstra, and all her crew for the miracles they worked, and for checking up on me. Closer to home, for the ferocity and tenacity of their love, I thank my brothers and my sisters, all over this land—Clay, Jaime, Jennifer, Jon, Bogie, Misa, Addison, and the latest addition, Steve—my father, Vere, my stepfather, Walter, and far from least my mother, Sally, to whom I dedicate the work at hand. A little closer yet to home, for enriching the present and enchanting the future beyond all I ever hoped, I thank Tony and Sanna.

Notes

Abbreviations used in the notes:

AP: Associated Press
BU: Boston University
CBC: Congressional Black Caucus
CD: *Chicago Defender*
CR: Congressional Record (as in CR-House, or CR-Senate, throughout)
CT: *Chicago Tribune*
JCL: Jimmy Carter Library and Museum, Atlanta
LAS: Los Angeles Sentinel
LAT: Los Angeles Times
NYT: *New York Times*
PPP: Public Papers of the Presidents
UPI: United Press International
WHCF: White House Central Files
WP: Washington Post
WSJ: Wall Street Journal

CHAPTER ONE: KING'S LAST VICTORY: THE CIVIL RIGHTS ACT OF 1968

1. At least people tended to view it as a private market. In fact, federal subsidies had vastly inflated the housing market, especially after World War II. The subsidies included the 1934 National Housing Act and amendments, which guaranteed mortgage loans for vast numbers who could never qualify for private credit; and the 1944 and 1952 GI Bills. The subsidies also included an incalculable amount of World War II and Cold War military spending, huge portions of which went into construction of military bases, which in addition to their own housing created demand for ancillary construction near the bases, not to mention the vast portion of military spending that flowed into demand for improved housing through civilian and military employees (some 6 million at the height of the Cold War).
2. King was present in the White House Cabinet Room in April 1966 when President

Johnson signed his message urging open-housing legislation. Johnson recalled King's presence two years later, when he finally signed the bill, saying few believed that the bill would become "the unchallenged law of the land." Johnson added, "And, indeed, this bill has had a long and stormy trip." Johnson in *WP*, April 12, 1968; and see *NYT*, April 29, 1966. See "King Demands Action on Fair Housing Law," AP in *WP*, Nov. 13, 1966.

3. The 1949 Housing Act had set an overall goal that remained unenforced: "A decent home and suitable living environment for every American family." Historical background in House Judiciary Committee, 89th Cong., 2nd sess., Hearings on Civil Rights, May 4–25, 1966, 1067.

4. King complained that the housing section of the bill had been "watered down": "I am very unhappy about the bill, and I do not think the bill is even worth passing like it is. . . . It will increase the despair, it will increase the discontent, and at the same time it will increase the possibility of violence." King quoted in CR-House, Aug. 9, 1966, 18725–26. King said that the final housing section "is virtually meaningless. It is so watered down that it will hardly do anything to undo the long-standing evil of housing discrimination." King quoted in *NYT*, editorial, Aug. 14, 1966. Title IV of the 1966 civil rights bill (passed by the House on Aug. 9, 1966) would have prohibited "discrimination on account of race, color, religion, or national origin, in the purchase, rental, lease, financing, use and occupancy of housing." But thanks to an amendment from Maryland's Charles Matthias, then a representative from the 6th District, it would apply only to brokers, bankers, and others in large-scale commerce—not to the roughly 60 percent of home sellers and lessors who traded as individuals. House Judiciary Committee Report, 89th Cong., 2nd sess., "Civil Rights Act of 1966," June 30, 1966, 9–10, 14–15. John Herbers in *NYT*, Aug. 10, 1966. The 60 percent estimate: Jack Nelson in *LAT*, Aug. 12, 1966, and editorial in *NYT*, Aug. 14, 1966. King accused President Johnson and the House of "immoral, unprincipled surrender" to racists and the real estate lobby: King quoted by Nelson, *LAT*, Aug. 12, 1966.

5. Filibuster: Herbers in *NYT*, Oct. 24, 1966; *LAT*, March 13, 1968; legislative history: House Judiciary Committee Report, 89th Cong., 2nd sess., June 30, 1966, 15–16; Paul Downing, "Civil Rights Legislation in the 90th Congress," Congressional Research Service, Feb. 19, 1969; and Herbert Danner, "Civil Rights Act of 1968: Brief Summary of Basic Provisions," Congressional Research Service, April 22, 1968.

6. Pessimism about the bill: Danner, "Civil Rights Act," i; Wilkins in *NYT*, Jan. 9, 1968; Alistair Cooke in *Manchester Guardian*, Jan. 17, 1968; *LAS*, Jan. 18, 1968; Herbers in *NYT*, Jan. 19, 1968; Bruckner in *LAT*, Jan. 19, 1968; Diggs Datrooth in *Pittsburgh Courier*, Jan. 20, 1968. Senator Sam Ervin summed up the case against the bill in Senate Judiciary Committee, Hearings, 90th Cong., 1st sess., Aug. 1, 1967, 59. LBJ made a renewed effort early in 1968 to push the bill through but deflated hopes by devoting only a single sentence to it in his State of the Union speech that January. Silence greeted that point, but loud applause came in response to his anti-riot proposals. The strong leadership Johnson had exercised in his first two years—producing the only serious civil rights legislation since Reconstruction—had passed. Now "Congress sat on its hands." *NYT*, editorial, Jan. 23, 1968; on State of the Union speech, Herbers, *NYT*, Jan. 19, 1968.

7. Despite growing pessimism, King still had some hope for Congress. David Garrow, *Bearing the Cross: Martin Luther King, Jr., and the Southern Christian Leadership Conference* (New York: Morrow, 1986), 595, 600–601.

8. Stephen B. Oates, *Let the Trumpet Sound: The Life of Martin Luther King, Jr.* (New York: New American Library, 1983), 437; Stewart Burns, *To the Mountaintop* (San Francisco: HarperSanFrancisco, 2004), 355, 381–83, 385–87, 394–97, 416–20, 431–33.

9. Bayard Rustin, "From Protest to Politics, *Commentary*, February 1965; King and Mar-

ion Logan's objections to planning the Poor People's Campaign and likely congressional reaction: Garrow, *Bearing the Cross,* 601. Logan was, sadly, vindicated, after King died and the Resurrection City encampment spun out of control. See Adam Fairclough, *To Redeem the Soul of America* (Athens: University of Georgia Press, 1987), 386–87.

10. King sees Jackson going off on his own, undermining the SCLC. Garrow, *Bearing the Cross,* 592–93, 616. Bevel's and Jackson's persistent opposition to the PPC: Fairclough, *To Redeem the Soul of America,* 358–59, 362, 378, 386–87.

11. Temple to LBJ, as quoted in Garrow, *Bearing the Cross,* 597.

12. King's fear of violence in planned April 22, 1968, protests in D.C.: See Garrow, *Bearing the Cross,* 594–618; he even worried the plan might have to be delayed or called off (597). King wanted the PPC to begin with a mule-cart procession from Mississippi (597–98). On March 29, 1969, King said he thought the D.C. demonstration was "doomed" (615); on King's persistent despondency, confusion, and doubt in this period, see below.

13. Harris poll; King on sick people and fascist takeover, plan to "plague Congress": Garrow, *Bearing the Cross,* 596–97, 618; Burns, *To the Mountaintop,* 395–96.

14. Pucinski in CR-House, 90th Cong., 2nd sess., Aug. 18, 1967, 22775. For similar examples, see, e.g., CR-House, 89th Cong., 2nd sess., Aug. 28, 1966, 20724–25; CR-House, 90th Cong., 1st sess., Aug. 15, 1967, 22674–86, 22690–91, and 27815–27 (Ashbrook); CR-Senate, 90th Cong., 2nd sess., Feb. 2, 1968, 1968; CR-Senate, 90th Cong., 2nd sess., Feb. 7, 1968, 2495–96; CR-House 90th Cong., 2nd sess., March 28, 1968, 8247–48; CR-Senate, 90th Cong., 2nd sess., March 28, 1968, 8263–66, 8222, 8244, 8327–28; CR-House, 90th Cong., 2nd sess., April 1, 1968, 8380–81 (Kuykendall); 8509–10; CR-House, 90th Cong., 2nd sess., April 4, 1968 (Brock); CR-Senate, 90th Cong., 2nd sess., April 4, 1968, 8946, 8981; Rep. Jimmy Quillen (R-Tennessee), in House Rules Committee, 90th Cong., 2nd sess., Hearings on H.Res. 1100, April 4–9, 1968, 21–22.

Though a few congressmen came to King's defense—see Augustus Hawkins on the House floor, April 4, 1968, for example—these voices are few and far between. For example, John Conyers criticized the association of rioting with the housing legislation under consideration, without defending King: CR-House, Aug. 15, 1967, 22690. Robert Nix of Philadelphia also rejected the wave of condemnation of rioters, pointing to the conditions that caused them, but also criticized King for poor administrative work in Memphis, implying King might have been partially responsible. Nix in CR-House, April 4, 1968, 9092–9093.

15. See on Clarence Mitchell, UPI in *NYT,* March 24, 1968; on the Urban Coalition, *NYT,* Feb. 25, 1968; on Urban Coalition and A. Philip Randolph, UPI, Jan. 13, 1968.

16. Wilkins in Oates, *Let the Trumpet Sound,* 437. See Burns, *To the Mountaintop,* 334–35, 360; Garrow, *Bearing the Cross,* 97–98, 100–101, 103, 121.

17. So *The Wall Street Journal* suggested: "Liberals would like to placate King by pushing through civil rights legislation before his April rally in Washington." *WSJ,* March 1, 1968.

18. These executives included Walker Cisler, of Detroit Edison; John Connor, Allied Chemical; Donald Chook, American Electric Power; Edgar Kaiser, Kaiser Industries; James McCormack, Communications Satellite; Graham James Morgan, US Gypsum; J. Irwin Miller, Cummins Engine; James Roche, General Electric; Herbert Silverman, James Talcott; Charles Thornton, Litton Industries; Sidney Weinberg, Goldman Sachs; Ben Heineman, Chicago & Northwestern Railroad; David Kennedy, Continental Bank; Gaylord Freeman, First National Bank of Chicago: *CT,* March 4, 1968. On lobbyists' pressure for bill: UPI in *NYT,* Jan. 13, 1968; Herbers in *NYT,* Jan. 19, 1968; and see David Broder in *WP,* Feb. 27, 1968.

19. President Johnson throws weight into battle for housing bill: UPI in *Atlanta Daily World,* March 28, 1968; Reed in *NYT,* March 28, 1968.

20. On Republican governors lobbying for open housing: Broder in *WP,* Feb. 27, 1968.

21. The head of the RNC, Ray Bliss, wanted to appeal to older black voters who fondly remembered the party of Lincoln and had never been comfortable in a party with George Wallace and Lester Maddox, and increasing numbers of upwardly mobile black voters who worried about taxes and inflation as much as did upwardly mobile white ones. *WP,* Feb. 2, 1968; Broder in *WP,* Feb. 21, 1968; *CT,* Feb. 25, 1968; *CD,* editorial, Feb. 29, 1968; *WP,* March 13, 1968.

22. The Senate approved Dirksen's compromise on March 4, 1968, achieving cloture. All witnesses seem to agree that that was the point when the tide turned in favor of the bill in the Senate, and passage of a relatively strong bill became inevitable. *NYT,* March 5, 1968; Lyons in *WP,* March 6, 1968. Had the filibuster not been beaten on that fourth attempt to end it, Majority Leader Mike Mansfield indicated that "he would drop the civil rights measure and turn to other legislation." *LAT,* March 10, 1968. Despite this, prospects for House passage of the bill were "gloomy": *NYT,* March 5, 1968, 1. Mansfield said this was "the most difficult period" in the nation's history: *NYT,* editorial, March 5, 1968.

23. The Senate on March 8 approved additions to the housing bill that made it "[f]ar stronger than its sponsors once thought possible." "Opposition Collapses" was the *New York Times* subtitle. The senators voted 61 to 19 to lower racial barriers in about 52.6 million housing units, including millions of single-family homes. Only sixteen Democrats and three Republicans voted against the revised compromise. In the Senate debate, "opposition [had] centered largely on open housing." *NYT,* March 9, 1968, 1. Downing, "Civil Rights Legislation in the 90th Congress," 17–27. The 80 percent figure: *LAT,* March 10, 1968; *NYT,* March 9, 1968.

24. Ervin for Indian rights "almost at the last minute," in *NYT,* March 9, 1968, 20.

25. The anti-riot provisions had been considered in previous versions of the bill. Though popular, they were perceived as anti-black, and moved more swiftly, some thought, for that reason. The success of those amendments to the bill initially contributed to pessimism over the housing bill. See Harvey Johnson, Jr., "Reading the Riot Act," *Norfolk Journal & Guide,* July 1, 1967. Among "all Afro-Americans . . . [t]he general feeling is that the actions of Congress have been just as criminal as those of the looters and arsonists rampaging in the streets." Editorial, *Amsterdam News,* July 29, 1967. *The Wall Street Journal* saw the anti-riot bill as "squirting at the riot flames with mere eyewash." There was "an ugly new race war at home," which would strengthen "[s]ociety's machinery for repression" in the form of "more money and muscle for the police, stricter gun controls and perhaps more riot training for the National Guard. Money channeled into devastated neighborhoods may be directed increasingly to storekeeper victims of riots, rather than for improvement of the living conditions of rioters." Arlen Large in *WSJ,* July 27, 1967.

26. Garrow on King's deepening depression, *Bearing the Cross,* 600.

27. On King's despondency, confusion, and growing self-doubt in this period, see esp. ibid., 592–617.

28. Young in ibid., 602. Biographer Stewart Burns observed that by 1963, King's "fear of death had become a companion, a soul mate," and by the end he had become "fixated on his own death." Burns, *To the Mountaintop,* 170, 436; and see ibid., 82–83, 89, 125–26, 150–51, 167–68, 177, 179, 215, 227, 345–48, 391, 394. One thing, however, lifted his spirits: LBJ's announcement he would resign: Garrow, *Bearing the Cross,* 618. King had reiterated recently to the press, "I cannot support President Johnson," and in private said he strongly favored Robert F. Kennedy. (On March 16, RFK threw his hat into the ring.) Ibid., 604.

29. Ashbrook was delighted that King was doing to himself what Ashbrook tried to do to him before; CR-House, 90th Cong., 2nd sess., April 1, 1968, 8509–10. Ashbrook had

delivered himself of his thirteen-page philippic against King in CR-House, 90th Cong., 2nd sess., Oct. 4, 1967, 27814–27.

30. Unlike Thurmond and other colleagues on the extreme right, Ashbrook had a devotion to unmasking King that only grew: Only Jesse Helms (then still a radio editorial jockey little known outside his home market) rivaled Ashbrook for the persistence of his anti-King vituperation long after King's death. As chapter 4 will reveal, Helms did not throw himself into the latter-day anti-King effort nearly as frequently or conspicuously as Ashbrook.

31. Johnson on piddlin' and excuses: Reed in *NYT*, March 28, 1968; Averill in *LAT*, March 28, 1968; UPI in, e.g., *Norfolk Journal & Guide*, March 30, 1968, and *Atlanta Daily World*, March 30, 1968.

32. Nixon, Rockefeller push for open housing: *WP*, March 21, 1968. Ford had hinted he might "switch over to support of a national open housing statute," in *WP*, March 13, 1968. Ford dramatically announced that he refused Nixon's invitation to join the bill's supporters: he would not bow to pressure to move the bill through to passage. Its provisions were too strong. *Norfolk Journal & Guide*, March 30, 1968, and *Atlanta Daily World*, March 28, 1968.

33. Clarence Mitchell letter to Nixon, and context: UPI in *NYT*, March 31, 1968.

34. Representative Robert Sikes of Florida was complaining by 1966 of "the annual civil rights confrontation," which would tie Congress up for weeks. "First, there are marches and demonstrations in the South . . . that produce racial tensions. The[s]e are picked up by the northern papers, which build up a crescendo of condemnation, and presto—a new civil rights bill miraculously appears from one of the administration offices. Sometimes over-eager congressional committees report the bills so quickly, the ink barely has had time to dry. . . . It is alleged that Members do not even bother to read the bills. Possibly this is to keep their hands clean." Sikes in CR-House, July 26, 1966, 17116.

35. Senator Proxmire stands out for acknowledging the change in tone: "If we are honest, we will recognize that in his life King's protest was not popular in white America, or in this body, or in Congress. By his own measure, he had failed to achieve his goal." Proxmire prayed that white Americans would understand and "support his dream, so that we can swiftly bring full American citizenship to the American Negro." Proxmire in CR-Senate, April 5, 1968, 9137.

36. For example, Senators Brooke, Symington, Young of Ohio, and Hart all spoke in some way for action, but did not specify what action. Senators Mansfield, Kuchel, Baker, and Church spoke more generally of Americans' (and others') duty to dedicate themselves anew to peaceful realization of King's goals, without putting themselves or their colleagues on the spot. Senator William Spong of Virginia spoke even more blandly about the imperative "to resolve the problems of lawlessness and crime, and to end the divisiveness and polarization which threaten the American dream of peace and tranquility, and opportunity for all." Ibid., 9136–37, 9138.

37. Clark also included the rest of King's agenda: "Let us pass the open housing bill. Let us pass the emergency job bill. Let us provide the funds to carry on the war on poverty. Let us pass the equal employment opportunity bill. Let us appropriate whatever is needed to bring meaningful educational opportunity to the deprived children of the slums. Let us not cut back on Head Start programs. Let us now, for God's sake, before we are visited by national tragedy again, pass the Federal gun control bill. In this way, we in Congress can build a living memorial to one of the greatest Americans of our generation." CR-Senate, 90th Cong., 2nd sess., April 5, 1968, 9137.

38. Javits, like Clark, put the housing bill first, but like Clark, he had other goals and noted that King had other goals, too: "There is much work for us to do. The civil rights bill now in the other body is one unfinished task. We will shortly be debating the supplemental appropriations bill, either today, or Monday or Tuesday next, which

contains another kind of cause to which Martin Luther King was deeply dedicated. There are other memorials which will keep his memory alive. There are schools, there are bridges, there are airports, and there are many other things in our Nation which should be used to remind our children that there was a Dr. Martin Luther King and how he served and how he loved his country. . . . His life of nonviolence will overcome, provided we take the appropriate lessons from his life and tragic death, as I have tried to outline, under the grief of the moment. . . . So let us not just speak words of memorial and pass the issue, but let us be deeply impressed by Dr. Martin Luther King's death as by his life, with the determination that we have it within our power to bring about a realization of the things for which he gave his life. Our greatest tribute to his memory will be to make them come true." Javits in CR-Senate, April 5, 1968, 9137–38.

39. Three mere sentences from Byrd in CR-Senate, April 5, 1968, 9138.

40. Frankfurter served on the Supreme Court from 1939 to 1962. Byrd also said that, given the violence in Memphis, King "must have known" that there was "such an atmosphere of tension as to make his presence in that city dangerous to himself and others." Remaining agnostic as to whether King's cause was just, Byrd added: "even in fighting for a just cause, one must pursue his course with reason, with due regard for the public welfare and good order, and with due respect for the law." King had had ample warning: he "usually spoke of nonviolence. Yet, violence all too often attended his actions." Byrd in CR-Senate, 90th Cong., 2nd sess., April 5, 1968, 9139–40. It may be of some interest that another segregationist senator, J. William Fulbright of Arkansas, had nothing but praise for King at this point in his career—lauding him for recognizing "clearly that the tragic war in Vietnam, contributed to the growth and acceptance of violence here at home." Countering Byrd, Fulbright said King "was an influence for the restoration of respect for law and order." Ibid., April 8, 1968, 9214.

41. King and his comrades believed that violence inhered in America's racial system. They often said they merely brought the tensions of that degrading, unjust system to the surface, a cleansing step toward honesty that would benefit white as well as black America. As King put it in his Letter from the Birmingham Jail, "we who engage in nonviolent direct action are not the creators of tension. We merely bring to the surface the hidden tension that is already alive. We bring it out in the open, where it can be seen and dealt with. Like a boil that can never be cured so long as it is covered up but must be opened with all its ugliness to the natural medicines of air and light, injustice must be exposed, with all the tension its exposure creates, to the light of human conscience and the air of national opinion before it can be cured." In King, *Why We Can't Wait* (New York: Morrow, 1963), 85.

42. Thurmond made the point more obliquely than Byrd, sandwiching it between reflections on the riots that by then were the top news story.

43. Thurmond in CR-Senate, 90th Cong., 2nd sess., April 8, 1968, 9226.

44. Without blaming King for his own murder, the following five representatives took the occasion to denounce the pending civil rights bill as an irrational capitulation to rioters: Republican Jack Edwards of Alabama (not willing to legislate "with a gun to my head"), Robert Lee Fulton Sikes (D-Florida), Clarence Watson (R–South Carolina), Basil Whitener (D–North Carolina), and, more vaguely Earle Cabell (D-Texas, who had been mayor of Dallas when Kennedy was shot there).

45. Joseph Waggoner (D-Louisiana), along with Watson and Abernethy, complained on behalf of innocent people who did not get national rites of mourning. Watson specified an "innocent white man." He did not mention that most riot victims were black. Concerns about victims who merited as much recognition as King were expressed in segregationist publications. See, e.g., William Douglass, lead letter to *Charleston News & Courier*, April 9, 1968.

46. Even the unassisted single-family-dwelling owner fell under the act's coverage if he or

she used discriminatory advertising. This is a summary of the act's coverage as of Jan. 1, 1970. The act went into effect in stages, expanding till its final form became effective after Dec. 31, 1969. Herbert A. Danner, "The Civil Rights Act of 1968: Brief Summary of Basic Provisions," Congressional Research Service, April 22, 1968, 5. The estimate of the 80 percent left after these exemptions (as of Jan. 1, 1970) is in *WP,* April 14, 1968, which also summarizes the 154 existing state laws.

In June 1968, in *Jones v. Alfred H. Mayer Company,* however, the Supreme Court eroded these exemptions, on the basis of the 1866 Civil Rights Act, which affirmed that black citizens had "the same right . . . as is enjoyed by white citizens" to buy and sell property. *Jones v. Alfred H. Mayer Company, 392 U.S. 409 (June 17, 1968). NYT,* June 22, 1968. Sex was added to the list of illegal bases of discrimination in 1974; physical handicap and familial status were added in 1988.

47. PL-90-284, 82 Stat. 73, secs. 804 and 805; U.S. Code, *Congressional & Administrative News,* 90th, 2d (St. Paul, Minn.: West, 1968), vol. 1, 101–102. On the new enforcement provisions of 1988, see "After 20 Years, Fair Housing Teeth," *NYT* editorial, Aug. 8, 1988.

48. Ramsey Clark on blockbusting in Senate Banking Committee, Hearings, Fair Housing Act of 1967, 90th Cong., 1st sess., Aug. 1–Sept. 27, 1967, 21. The anti-blockbusting goal ranked high—second paragraph—in the Senate Banking Committee's six-paragraph summary of the laudable purposes of the act: Senate Banking Committee, Hearings, Fair Housing Act of 1967, 90th Cong., 1st sess., Aug. 21–23, 1967, 3. Blockbusting also was discussed in the first series of Senate hearings, in May–August 1966. On Aug. 4, 1966, King was marching in Marquette Park in Chicago, where he famously said he had "never seen as much hatred and hostility on the part of so many people." The practice, common in northern cities, came up for special attention. The head of the New York Human Rights Commission, for example, testified that it was the "greatest obstacle" to racial balance in neighborhoods in his city. It was created "by the wily real estate people who have seized the situation as a means to exploit the white home-owners." Senate Judiciary Committee, Hearings on Civil Rights, 89th Cong., 2nd sess., July 13–Aug. 4, 1966, 1512–13.

49. Senator Walter Mondale of Minnesota (also one of the sponsors) discussed blockbusting with Clark in the Senate Banking Committee, Aug. 1–Sept. 27, 21–22. Mondale also described blockbusting vividly—he wanted to make it a crime, not simply a civil wrong, as the bill aimed to do—at the close of the hearings (437–38).

50. *Pittsburgh Courier,* April 20, 1968.

51. *Charleston News and Courier,* April 12, 1968. William Colmer in CR-House, April 10, 1968, 9528, H. R. Gross in ibid., 9540.

52. Taft in CR-House, April 10, 1968, 9552, Anderson in ibid., 9557–58. UPI in *CD,* April 11, 1968, 4.

53. PL-90-284, 82 Stat. 73, secs. 804 and 805; U.S. Code, *Congressional & Administrative News,* 90th, 2d (St. Paul, Minn.: West, 1968), vol. 1, 101–102. There was no significant public discussion of the weakness of the bill's enforcement provisions at the time it was debated. See "After 20 Years, Fair Housing Teeth," *NYT* editorial, Aug. 8, 1988. It is important to add that all civil rights victories, legislative and other kinds, have been limited—and dependent on the will of African-Americans and other protected classes to claim their rights under them, and of judges and other political officers to respect and enforce the laws, which were always hard won and controversial.

54. See Sheryll Cashin, *Failures of Integration* (New York: PublicAffairs, 2004); Douglas S. Massey and Nancy A. Denton, *American Apartheid* (Cambridge, Mass.: Harvard University Press, 1993); Arnold Hirsch, *Making the Second Ghetto* (Chicago: University of Chicago Press, 1998); Thomas Sugrue, *Origins of the Urban Crisis* (Princeton, N.J.: Princeton University Press, 1996); Bill Bishop, *The Big Sort* (Boston: Houghton Mifflin, 2008).

CHAPTER TWO: CAN A MOVEMENT BE INSTITUTIONALIZED?
THE NATIONAL BLACK POLITICAL CONVENTIONS

1. Manning Marable called the Gary convention "the largest black political convention in U.S. history." Marable also said that Gary was "the zenith not only of black national- ism but of the entire black movement during the second reconstruction." Marable, *Race, Reform, and Rebellion,* 3d ed. (Jackson: University Press of Mississippi, 2007), 120. Common in convention coverage were statements like that of delegate John Roy Harper, founder of the United Citizens' Party of South Carolina: The NBPC was "the most significant event to happen to black people since 1619, when our ancestors were first brought to the colonies as slaves." Harper in Thomas A. Johnson, "Black Dele- gates Seek More Contacts," *NYT,* March 19, 1972, 42. Amiri Baraka—one of the un- likely troika of cochairs, with Detroit congressman Charles Diggs and Gary mayor Richard Hatcher—wrote that the NBPC was "the most forceful demonstration of mass motion toward the realization of Black Power of that period." Baraka, *Autobiography of LeRoi Jones* (New York: Freundlich, 1984), 296. Vincent Harding, among other historians sympathetic to black nationalism, uses similar superlatives, quantitative and qualitative. See Harding, *The Other American Revolution* (Los Angeles and Atlanta: IBW/UCLA, 1980), 213–19. Steven Lawson, in *Running for Freedom,* 2nd ed. (New York: McGraw-Hill, 1997), 141, says the NBPC was "the most ambitious attempt to unite black leaders." Peniel Joseph, in *Waiting 'Til the Midnight Hour* (New York: Holt, 2006), 276, says the NBPC was "perhaps the most important political, cultural, and intellectual gathering of the Black Power era."
   I do not know of a single scholar who has challenged these judgments. Many other accounts of the era repeat the unquestioned belief that the NBPC was a huge, defining event—without adding any new research or fresh analysis. Many just as blithely ignore the NBPC or give it breathtakingly short shrift. There remains precious little historical scholarship to flesh out the picture, or to test the convention's significance from a fur- ther distance. The best effort at an overall analysis is a chapter in Robert C. Smith, *We Have No Leaders* (Albany: SUNY Press, 1996); see also Komozoi Woodard, "The Making of a New Ark: Imamu Amiri Baraka (LeRoi Jones), the Newark Congress of African People, and the Modern Black Convention Movement" (Ph.D. diss., University of Pennsylvania, 1991); Cedric Johnson, "Dilemmas of Black Power Politics: The Na- tional Black Assembly, Race Leaders and Radicalism in the Post-Segregation Era (Ph.D. diss., University of Maryland, 2001); David L. Chappell, "The National Black Political Conventions and the Quest for Racial Unity," unpublished paper presented at Southern Historical Association, Nov. 8, 2009; and Derrick E. White, *The Challenge of Black- ness: The Institute for the Black World and Political Activism in the 1970s* (Gainesville: University Press of Florida, 2011). The superlatives, repeated by many at the time and since, appear accurate. There were several national black political conventions during Reconstruction, for example, in 1869 (D.C.), 1871 (Columbia, South Carolina), 1872 (New Orleans), and 1876 (Nashville), not to mention the Pan African Congresses, in 1919 (Paris) and 1921 (London), and later.

2. Robert Norrell's otherwise excellent overview of racial history in the twentieth century, *The House I Live In* (New York: Oxford University Press, 2005), has exactly one sen- tence on the NBPC. James Patterson, in his fine book on the legacy of school desegrega- tion, also devotes a single sentence to the convention. Patterson, *Brown v. Board of Education: A Civil Rights Milestone and Its Troubled Legacy* (New York: Oxford University Press, 2001), 174–75. The NBPC does not come up at all in Dona Cooper Hamilton and Charles Hamilton, *The Dual Agenda: The African-American Struggle for Civil and Economic Equality* (New York: Columbia University Press, 1997).

3. Abernathy proclaims himself the Joshua: quotation in Betty Washington, *CD,* April 9, 1968, and in University of Memphis Library's film footage and film log (102–103),

April 8, 1968, reel 66, 6 min. 20 sec. to reel 67, 10 min. 50 sec.; and 107–109, April 8, 1968, reels 70–72. The *LAT* added: Abernathy proclaimed, "We are bound for the promised land. I am not going to lead a short distance, I am going to lead all the way." He also said, "God said to me, 'Martin Luther King didn't get there,'" and then apparently implied that God told Abernathy to carry on. *LAT,* April 9, 1968. Joshua story echoed in Rev. Milton A. Galamison, Siloam Presbyterian Church, Brooklyn, in *Amsterdam News,* April 13, 1968. Rev. Charles Billups supported Abernathy as the Joshua in: Betty Washington in *CD,* April 17, 1968; so did His Holiness Prophet Jones of Los Angeles: "[G]od ordained and sent Martin Luther King to earth to lead his people, as he did Moses. His job was completed here, he did what God sent him here to do. Moses le[d] the people, but he didn't finish the job, Joshua took up where Moses left off. Mrs. King will lead the people like Joan of Arc. . . ." Jones admitted, however, that "God didn't ordain or appoint [Abernathy] to lead the people as he did Dr. King," in *LAS,* July 25, 1968. King's former aide Wyatt Tee Walker (then special assistant to New York governor Nelson Rockefeller) also supported Abernathy's succession to the leadership role as a Joshua, in *NYT,* Aug. 17, 1969.

4. Abernathy's general efforts are reported in Paul Good, "'No Man Can Fill Dr. King's Shoes'—but Abernathy Tries," *New York Times Magazine,* May 26, 1968. Before the emergence of Jesse Jackson, Abernathy is the focus of stories about possible successors of King. Abernathy had become president of the SCLC. At a Memphis rally in April 1969, on the first anniversary of King's death, Abernathy was still vowing a second phase of the Poor People's Campaign. Nixon's assistant labor secretary, James Farmer, the founder of CORE, brought greetings from Nixon and promised to work with those present to make King's dream a reality. Joseph Lowery held an umbrella to keep Abernathy dry while he spoke. Jesse Jackson held an umbrella for him later (film log, University of Memphis). Jesse Jackson still appeared to be playing a minor role in *Newsweek*'s "Report from Black America," June 30, 1969. *The New York Times* noted that Jackson had felt a "rebuff and 'humiliation'" in the Resurrection City disaster and said he was emerging from "a period of self-doubt and a loss of public confidence." But it also pointed out that the Nixon administration—which had added to Abernathy's humiliation by refusing to speak to a group of eighty to whom Abernathy had promised a presidential audience—believed that Abernathy "lacked an important following." *NYT,* Aug. 17, 1969.

5. Jesse Jackson found it prudent on that occasion to flatter Abernathy. As one black southern weekly rendered Jackson's speech, "Our (Joshua) Abernathy stood by Moses (King) when he could have had a movement of his own." As the UPI story in the *Norfolk Journal & Guide* put it, Jackson's speech was "a move obviously designed to pull the SCLC solidly behind Abernathy and show his own loyalties." This at SCLC's twelfth annual convention, held that year in Charleston, South Carolina. "Many come in as meteors, lasting for a day," Jackson also said of Abernathy. "Compare that with the sun, which has given off its warmth for thousands of years." UPI on Abernathy (and Jackson speaking about Abernathy) in *Norfolk Journal & Guide,* Aug. 23, 1969. See somewhat different version by Jack Nelson, *LAT,* Aug. 15, 1969.

At that point, Abernathy was sick and had recently served jail time on behalf of the Charleston workers, "adding to his role of martyrdom at a time when his own position is threatened by the Rev. Jesse Jackson of Chicago." *CD,* July 12, 1969. Joel Weisman led off his story "Jesse Jackson Seeks Economic Initiative" this way: "He was the man standing next to the Rev. Martin Luther King Jr., when Dr. King was gunned down on a Memphis motel balcony in 1968. But now he threatens the organization Dr. King so carefully crafted. . . . He is Jesse Louis Jackson, 30, the charismatic colorful former national director of Operation Breadbasket, economic arm of the SCLC." Jackson split with the SCLC. "And he took his well oiled Chicago civil rights machine with him away from King's old organization. The entire boards of SCLC and Breadbasket stepped down with Jackson. His resignation brought tears of joy and wild cheers from his 3,000 supporters in Dr. King's workshop, an old movie theatre in Southside Chicago." Jackson claimed he would not be in competition with Breadbasket and SCLC, but "my programs will be chiefly economically oriented" in the future. Jackson said: "For years the civil rights movement has been viewed in social or moral terms: right and wrong; good and evil; in guilt and innocence. I think black people should be thought of in terms of dollars and cents. We've simply got to show it isn't profitable for the country to have poor schools, poor housing and poor minority programs." *WP,* Dec. 13, 1971. By January 1972, *The New York Times* identified Jackson and Abernathy both—and only those two—as "spiritual heirs of Dr. King." Both had, however, "adopted different methods of carrying on his work." *NYT,* Jan. 7, 1972, caption of photo of King, flanked by Abernathy and Jackson, on Lorraine Motel balcony, "a day before he was shot—at nearly the same spot."

6. Reed, and Abernathy quoted in Reed, in *NYT,* Jan. 7, 1972. Abernathy often appeared at events without appearing to be responsible for them. The press reported tension and friction among the restless staff. Andrew Young left in 1970 to run for Congress—unsuccessfully. (He then became, in 1972, the first black person elected to Congress from the South since 1900.)

7. UPI on Jackson in *Norfolk Journal & Guide,* Aug. 23, 1969.

8. Jackson founded his own PUSH on Martin Luther King Drive in Chicago. He built it on the structure of the SCLC's economic action wing, Operation Breadbasket, to which King had assigned him—and which remained SCLC's beachhead in Chicago after King's disastrous defeats there in 1966. Jesse Jackson quit the SCLC at the end of 1971 in a dispute over policy with Abernathy: *CT,* Dec. 19, 1971; *NYT,* Dec. 12, 1971, and Dec. 19, 1971. Jackson's $28,000 in initial funding included donations from George Johnson of Johnson Products and Roberta Flack. His new organization would not only "picket, boycott, march and vote, but if necessary will engage in civil disobedience." Faith Christmas in *CD,* Dec. 20, 1971. Jackson pulled together elements of "street gangs, the middle class and the business and professional people, . . . nationally known black entertainers, businessmen, politicians and intellectuals." Thomas Johnson in *NYT,* Dec. 21, 1971. "There is no doubt . . . Jackson is a forceful, charismatic man. . . . Black Expo in Chicago was the finest black commercial exposition and festival of economic, political, and cultural awareness ever produced in this country. But the birth of Operation PUSH may hasten the death of the Southern Christian Leadership Conference. At the least, it seems, SCLC is now severely diminished. The race cannot afford any such loss." Doc Young, in *LAS,* Dec. 23, 1971. See editorial, "Abernathy vs. Jackson," *Norfolk Journal & Guide,* Dec. 25, 1971.

9. Though Mrs. King's life story, on display in a photo essay at the Martin Luther King Center, described her role in Local 1199 as gathering the civil rights coalition together for the first time since the 1963 March on Washington, she let union officials, or Abernathy and other King successors, make the decisions and get the publicity. Though she had well-developed ideas of her own, in public she generally played the role of a living symbol. Exhibition at Martin Luther King Center, Atlanta.

The new Martin Luther King Jr. Labor Center in New York opened in November 1970—New York mayor John Lindsay and Newark's new, black mayor, Kenneth Gibson, were scheduled to attend the ceremony. According to the *Amsterdam News,* the $3 million, fifteen-story building was headquarters for the fifty thousand metro-area hospital, nursing home, and drugstore employees—Local 1199 of the Drug and Hospital Workers Union. King had been a strong ally of the drive to organize workers in voluntary hospitals in New York in the 1960s. King called Local 1199 "my favorite union" in his last public appearance in New York. Coretta Scott King was honorary chairman of the National Union of Hospital and Nursing Home Employees, AFL-CIO, which was an outgrowth of Local 1199's fast national organizing campaign among

2.5 million "underpaid & primarily black hospital workers." Their new July 1970 contract with the League of Voluntary Hospitals won higher pay and an additional paid holiday on King's birthday. They had fought bitter strikes for such gains in 1959 and 1962. The union displayed a bronze bust of King in its lobby. *Amsterdam News,* Nov. 21, 1970. Mrs. King's book was serialized in the *Washington Post.* See Coretta King, ten-part series, *WP,* April 5, 1970, through April 14, 1970, and *My Life with Martin Luther King* (New York: Holt, 1969).

10. Rustin in *Amsterdam News,* March 22, 1969.

11. Abernathy, trying to visit Angela Davis in jail, only managed to speak with her briefly. UPI in *WP,* Sept. 11, 1971. Jackson announced he was "spiritual adviser" to Angela Davis, then in the San Rafael County Jail: *Pittsburgh Courier,* Jan. 16, 1971.

12. On Rustin, David McReynolds wrote: "We do not know why he left his old comrades and coworkers of decades to seek his way into the Establishment," which was "a profound tragedy." David McReynolds of War Resisters' League letter to *NYT,* March 30, 1969. Other inklings of growing fear that Rustin was insufficiently "radical," one writer noted, stemmed from Rustin's goal that "black people have their just share of the goods of this society and are able to exercise their due proportion of power. . . . Mr. Rustin seems to think along the old liberal lines of class struggle and conflicts of economic interest as explanations for social unrest. But we turn the pages and find the sons and daughters of well-to-do whites rejecting that very style of life Mr. Rustin wants to make a reality for the have-not members of his race." Robert Strouse to editor, *NYT,* March 9, 1969. On Rustin's position in the 1970s and its provenance, the best guides are Daniel Levine, *Bayard Rustin and the Civil Rights Movement* (New Brunswick, N.J.: Rutgers University Press, 2000), and Jerald Podair, *Bayard Rustin: American Dreamer* (Lanham, Md.: Rowman & Littlefield, 2009). Rustin's more celebrated biographers shrink from reckoning fully with this period in his life.

13. Fifty thousand march in Memphis: *CD,* April 9, 1968; 19,000–42,000, in *NYT,* April 9, 1968; Rustin's role: *WP,* April 8, 1968, and April 9, 1968; *LAT,* April 8, 1968; *NYT,* April 9, 1968.

14. CBC's original nine founders wanted to fill void left by King: a retrospective story on the CBC in the *WP,* Sept. 26, 1980. Robert Singh also sees a "disturbing leadership vacuum in the black community" as one of the major reasons for the caucus's founding: Robert Singh, *The Congressional Black Caucus: Racial Politics in the U.S. Congress* (Thousand Oaks, Calif.: Sage, 1998). The Democratic Select Committee, founded in January 1969 by three newly elected black members and six black House incumbents, renamed itself the CBC in 1971, by which time it had thirteen members. On the CBC see also: Norman Miller, "Negroes in the House Join Forces," *WSJ,* March 31, 1970; "Women Criticize Black Caucus Men," *NYT,* July 29, 1973; Alan Ehrenhalt, "Black Caucus: A Wary Carter Ally," *Congressional Quarterly,* May 21, 1977, 968–69; Marguerite Ross Barnett, "Congressional Black Caucus," reprinted from "Congress Against the President," *Proceedings of the Academy of Political Science* 32, no. 1 (1975): 35–36; Michael Preston, Lenneal Henderson, Jr., and Paul Puryer, eds., *The New Black Politics: The Search for Political Power* (New York: Longman, 1981); "Congressional Black Caucus May Be a Victim of Success," *WP Weekly Edition,* Oct. 12, 1987; Beth Donovan, "The Wilder-Dinkins 'Formula' Familiar to Blacks in the House," *Congressional Quarterly Weekly Report,* Nov. 11, 1989; Bruce Ragsdale and Joel D. Treese, *Black Americans in Congress, 1870–1989* (Washington, D.C.: U.S. Government Printing Office, 1990); William Clay, *Just Permanent Interests* (New York: Amistad, 1992); and esp. Carol Swain, *Black Faces, Black Interests,* enlarged ed. (Cambridge, Mass.: Harvard University Press, 1995); and Richard Fenno, *Going Home: Black Representatives and Their Constituents* (Chicago: University of Chicago Press, 2003).

15. Rustin prophetically struck the keynote, moving away from King, with his famous call

to arms, "From Protest to Politics," *Commentary*, February 1965. The Urban League convened a wide array of leaders and found consensus among them not on ends but means: *When the Marching Stopped* (New York: National Urban League, 1971). Some of the most astute observers of black political life have organized their chronicles and analyses around this theme. See esp. Smith, *We Have No Leaders*, and Katherine Tate, *From Protest to Politics* (Cambridge, Mass.: Harvard University Press, 1993).

16. Ossie Davis here as quoted by Chisholm in *Essence*, November 1972, 41–43. A twelve-page post-convention report by the CBC, which tried to put Gary and other attempts at black political coalescence in perspective, also emphasized Davis's "It's not the man it's the plan, it's not the rap it's the map" speech as a fundamental principle. "Black Declaration of Independence and the Black Bill of Rights" (CBC report), copy in Robert S. Browne Papers, Schomburg Library, Box 19. Vincent Harding (on staff of the Institute of the Black World, originally set up under the auspices of the Martin Luther King Center in Atlanta), who evidently had a hand (with William Strickland) in drafting the proposed "agenda" of the convention, wrote to the Urban Coalition's Carl Holman just before the convention that "with you, we were convinced that *program* is more crucial than who 'our leader' is right now." Harding to Holman, March 1, 1972, on IBW letterhead, copy in Robert S. Browne Papers, Schomburg Library, Box 19. This repudiation of leadership was also strongly voiced by Carl Stokes, the former mayor of Cleveland, a firm advocate of integration and coalition politics. To get over their "voluntary political servitude," Stokes said that "black voters" must "concern themselves with issues, not personalities." "Carl Stokes Spe[e]ch," typescript mimeo, in NBPC collection, Indiana Historical Society, Burton Collection, SC2643, f. 1.

17. Roy Reed's lead, *NYT*, Jan. 7, 1972.

18. Martin Luther King Jr. Labor Center press conference, Feb. 23, 1972: *CT*, Feb. 24, 1972. The center had also hosted a meeting on Jan. 29 of the Coalition of 100 Black Women, with invited speakers Robert J. Brown (Nixon's special assistant), Constance Baker Motley, and Shirley Chisholm, "to discuss the goals and objectives" of the NBPC and other gatherings, according to an *Amsterdam News* column, Feb. 5, 1972. Other meetings and announcements had been made as to plans for the NBPC (for example, announcements reported in *NYT*, Nov. 21, 1971, and Jan. 31, 1972), but the one in New York on Feb. 23, 1972, appears to have been the biggest effort to attract mass support and participation.

19. Stokes was elected Nov. 7, 1967, and inaugurated Jan. 1, 1968.

20. Charles V. Hamilton, Foreword (dated June 1970) to Alex Poinsett, *Black Power, Gary Style* (Chicago: Johnson, 1970), 9. Hatcher embraced a go-it-alone strategy in his speech to the First Modern Pan-African Congress, in 1970: "I do not feel very much hope about coalitions. The experiences of Black America with other segments of our society have most often been disappointing." Hatcher speech in Baraka, ed., *African Congress: A Documentary of the First Modern Pan-African Congress* (New York: Morrow, 1972), 64–72. Hatcher (67) also approvingly quoted King's words: "There is more in socially organized assets on the march than there is in guns in the hands of a few desperate men. All history teaches us that like a turbulent motion beating great cliffs into fragments of rocks, the determined movement of people excessively demanding their rights always disintegrates the old order." Hatcher went on: "And this too is a form of Black Power though we didn't call it that at the time. But this form of power in and of itself we also found inadequate to meet our needs." Rustin, however, believed that the successes of coalition-building black elected officials like Charles Evers, Howard Lee, Carl Stokes, and Tom Bradley were "proving that black separatism is an obstacle to black political power." Rustin, "Myths of the Black Revolt," in Rustin, *Three Essays* (New York: A. Philip Randolph Institute, 1969), 12.

21. Significantly, in pre-convention planning documents, evidently written by Amiri Baraka or nationalists aligned with him, "nationalists" were repeatedly listed as a discrete

category. In the mind of the Baraka faction of nationalists, that is, nationalists were distinct from: "activists," "community organizers," elected officials, and "national black organization representatives." See, for example, William Hart and Baraka in "Habari gani," Feb. 10, 1972, and "Statement of Political Strategy," Nov. 20, 1971, both in IBW Papers, Schomburg Library, unprocessed papers—box is currently (March 2009) marked "Strickland-NBPC."

22. The range of arguments for black political independence can be seen in Stokely Carmichael and Charles Hamilton, *Black Power* (New York: Vintage, 1967) and Harold Cruse, *The Crisis of the Negro Intellectual* (New York: Morrow, 1967).

23. Most black members of Congress represented black-majority districts—11 of 17 in 1976. Similarly, most black mayors—110 of 152 in 1976—represented black-majority cities: Joint Center for Political Studies, *National Roster of Black Elected Officials, 1976* (Washington, D.C.: Joint Center for Political Studies, 1976), xxvii, xxxix.

24. "Unity without Uniformity" became a quasi-official motto. For example, it is the title chosen by one of many young BEOs who came to the convention and later went on to great fame and national influence: Mervyn Dymally, *Unity Without Uniformity* (May 1972; pamphlet distributed by his office, then in the California Senate), 96 pp. This is an extensive and very good selection of news and magazine clippings on the NBPC. Hatcher noted in his keynote that the banner overhead emphasized unity. "Without that unity, all is lost." Hatcher speech, 19 pp., copy in Robert S. Browne Papers, Schomburg Library, Box 19. Other announcements of "unity" as the NBPC theme appear in: Robert McClory, "Stop Rapping Each Other Now," *Pittsburgh Courier,* Jan. 8, 1972; Carlos Russell: "The cry was unity, and at times this cry seemed unattainable," in Russell, "A Journey We Must Make," *Amsterdam News,* March 18, 1972. Baraka attributed the concept of unity without uniformity to Maulana (Ron) Karenga. Baraka, "Introduction" to Baraka, ed., *African Congress,* viii. The old movement goal of black-white unity had largely evaporated.

25. Most estimates have roughly 3,400 delegates attending, plus another 4,000 to 4,500 visitors observing, including about 500 newspeople. Some enthusiasts in the black press went ahead and rounded it on up to 10,000—for example, *Amsterdam News,* March 18, 1972.

26. Diggs to National Black News Service, in *Kansas City Call,* March 10–16, 1972, 2. A Bay Area black weekly led with what was "unique" in the NBPC: "[T]his gathering brought together representatives of groups with such divergent views as the Black Muslims, the NAACP, and the Black Panthers[. T]he convention was designed to consolidate the heretofore unorganized blo[c] comprised of about 7.5 million Black voters." *San Francisco Sun Reporter,* March 18, 1972.

27. *Gary American,* March 11, 1972, and March 16, 1972, front-page editorial and top story headline. The *Los Angeles Herald-Dispatch* also gave Chisholm's candidacy higher and more enthusiastic billing (headlines in larger type, etc.) than the Gary Convention—which is somewhat surprising, in that the *Herald-Dispatch* was much more sympathetic to go-it-alone nationalism than its local rival, the *Los Angeles Sentinel,* and indeed than most of the major black weeklies. (In November, the *Herald-Dispatch* ended up endorsing McGovern; it does not appear to have endorsed a candidate in the primaries.) See *Los Angeles Herald-Dispatch,* Jan. 20, 1972, March 16, 1972, Aug. 17, 1972, Nov. 2, 1972. For more coverage of the convention by nearby black papers, see *Indianapolis Recorder,* March 11, 1972, and the *CD,* as cited below.

28. Chisholm in *Essence,* November 1972, 41–43.

29. Bond told an interviewer that people in the National Black Political Assembly (a spin-off of the NBPC) "have a tendency" to "question the validity of my existence as an elected official. . . . Not me particularly, but with black elected officials generally." Bond "frankly didn't want to go to a meeting with people" like that. Though Bond is by this point speaking primarily about 1974, his generalization seems to suggest that

the NBPA and its forerunners had the same attitudes in 1972, when he avoided their big convention. Julian Bond, interview by Trevor Chandler, Nov. 7, 1974, transcript in Bond Papers, Auburn Avenue Public Library, Atlanta, 21–22. See also Bond pushing a strategy that diverged from the independent-party initiative that seemed to dominate early convention planning in *NYT*, Sept. 20, 1971.

30. The press missed the confiding widows almost entirely—redolent though their dialogue was of the Malcolm-Martin reconciliation so many wished for after King's death. The one mention I have seen is a reference buried deep in Ethel Payne's *Defender* column of March 13, 1972. The press's omission repeats the pattern from Martin Luther King's 1968 funeral: Nearly every paper, black and white, made a big deal of Jackie Onassis's spending time alone with the freshly bereaved Mrs. King. A few noted Mrs. Medgar Evers's commiserating with her. But I have yet to find a single paper that commented on Betty Shabazz's presence, though she was certainly there.

31. We have no idea what the two are saying to each other. But the silent discussion of the two widows is one of the most striking scenes in the whole movie, and Greaves prolongs his focus on it. *Nationtime: Gary* (1972), produced and directed by William Greaves. Greaves's movie remains I think the best single source on the convention, at least among those that are readily tracked down.

32. Her enigmatic silence was prophetic of her later career, for instance when she refused to say anything on abortion—though she sat, for example, on the stage again twelve years later, when Catholic vice presidential nominee Geraldine Ferraro proclaimed her own hedged pro-choice position—just as Mrs. King's own niece was using her martyred husband's name to advance the anti-abortion cause, and just as King's protégé Jesse Jackson was repudiating his own ten-year commitment to that same cause. She makes you think it took considerable courage and vision to keep out of that controversy, as though she refused to countenance either side's dehumanizing oversimplifications.

33. Jackson on cover of *Time*, April 6, 1970. The substance behind the picture went as follows, in an article that began with King's absence and possible irreplaceability: "One who is more articulate and arresting than most is Rev. Jesse Jackson, an intense, passionate advocate of using black economic power to force white-run businesses to provide more and better jobs for blacks and to open chain-store shelves to black products. . . . Jackson fully recognizes the uses of diversity in black leadership, and is the first to put down anyone who attempts to fit him for the mantle of Martin Luther King or even label him first among his peers in local organizing. He has chosen to work within the system and manages to twist it against itself into grudgingly granting black demands, but he does not disparage other voices, other tactics. 'No man can tell a man who is hurting how to holler,' he argues." *Time*, April 6, 1970.

34. Richard Levine in *Harper's*, March 1969; *Ebony*, November 1969; *Ebony*, March 1972; "Jesse Jackson: A Candid Conversation with the Fiery Heir Apparent to Martin Luther King," *Playboy*, November 1969.

35. Quotations of Jackson speech are from the film *Nationtime: Gary*, cited above. Greaves devoted nearly a third of his airtime (just under sixty minutes) to Jackson's speech. In the dramatic structure of Greaves's editing, at least, it is the climactic event of the convention.

The Los Angeles radio personality and guest columnist, the Gary-bred Booker Griffin, had anticipated Jackson's birth figures. Griffin was active in the Southern California caucuses that sent delegates to Gary. Griffin wrote: "Missing [from those caucuses] were the old-line political hacks and hustlers and those who have dominated the political scene. The whole affair was a reflection of a new day and a new political order." The new faces "will not suddenly and with a bang take over the political direction of the community." But "[i]t is inherent in the most basic laws of the universe that when the water bursts in a pregnant mother the baby will come. All the might and resistance of that mother cannot hold that baby back when its time has come." Griffin had hoped this change was going to come for a long time "through a lonely vigil." He riffed further on the birth pangs metaphor at some length. Griffin, "Black Convention and Chords of Auld Lang Syne," *LAS,* March 2, 1972. One witness emphasized that Jackson addressed the unity question directly. "Mr. Jackson, in his remarks at the gathering, criticized press coverage of the convention, saying, 'The white press has described us as having dissension and diversity here, but you see we have come from different families across the nation, and this is the first time many of us have met.'" Walter Lowe in *Chicago Sun-Times,* March 12, 1972.

36. That month, the *Pittsburgh Courier* observed that Jackson "is on his own at last. But not quite. Upon his chest he wears a medallion as big as a medium-sized pie pan bearing the image of Dr. Martin Luther King." Following his departure from SCLC in December 1971, Jackson had said, "I have a new sense of independence." But what with "the silver King medallion bobbing," the *Courier* noted, he "does not let you forget" King. His master of ceremonies at PUSH—on Martin Luther King Drive—exhorted the crowd to "follow the leadership of Jesse Jackson in the image of Martin Luther King." The evocation of King "seems to be about the Rev. Mr. Jackson always." *Pittsburgh Courier,* March 11, 1972.

37. Jackson speech to First Congress of African People, quoted in *Baltimore Afro American,* Sept. 15, 1970; and in *WP,* Sept. 7, 1970.

38. New York was the largest, Michigan the second. NBPC "Delegate Apportionment," and NBPC "Meal Ticket Schedule," Indiana Historical Society, Burton Collection, SC2643, f. 1.

39. Young told a hometown reporter that Baraka's Agenda made reckless, outlandish charges. He said the delegates had come to Gary "to unite black people, not to have shoved down our throats [a] lengthy document we had not seen until Saturday afternoon." Nadine Brown quoting Young in *Michigan Chronicle,* March 25, 1972. The convention chair agreed to convene a special committee to work out a compromise on Young's proposal. The compromise was simply to print Michigan's "Minority Report" along with the agenda. But then Baraka "reneged on his commitment," according to Young, and Young had "no choice" but to walk out. Coleman Young, press release, March 18, 1972, in Young Senate Papers, Detroit Public Library, Box 3. On the Illinois delegation: *Los Angeles Herald-Dispatch,* March 16, 1972, 1.

For background on the political and social divisions in black Detroit, see Angela Dillard's superb book, *Faith in the City: Preaching Radical Social Change in Detroit* (Ann Arbor: University of Michigan Press, 2007). Roger Wilkins noted in his three-part series on the convention that suspicions abounded in the convention hall that the Michigan delegation, and much of the Illinois delegation, were infiltrated or dominated by the United Auto Workers (UAW). Roger Wilkins in *WP,* March 16, 1972. Ethel Payne reported that one of the Michigan delegates who remained in the convention said, "Michigan didn't walk out. The UAW did." Payne in *CD,* March 18, 1972. On the nationalists who remained, see Representative David Holmes, "commentary," and Riley Smith, motion to steering committee, March 24, 1972, in Young Senate Papers, Box 3.

Coleman Young saw Republican maneuvering behind much of the nationalist opposition to his delegation in the convention. See note 47, below.

40. Knotty questions remain as to what happened. For example: What proportion of the delegates were actually present when the controversial resolutions against busing and Israel were "approved"? Was there no quorum rule, or quorum call—no challenge in the post-convention deliberations to the procedural laxness that may have determined the controversy? What about the procedures by which the post-convention steering committee repudiated what had been presented as approved on the floor? Were any sort of procedures followed in rewriting the resolutions and then releasing them to the

press in the name of "the convention"? Was there any fallout from rank-and-file delegates about the committee's evident nullification of a resolution without authority from the delegates?

41. "Full Text (Resolutions adopted at Steering Committee meeting, March 24, 1972)," and Wilkins's notes on same, in Wilkins Papers, Library of Congress, Box 27. See note below on administration use of the convention.

42. Baraka to Wilkins, May 15, 1972, in Wilkins Papers, Library of Congress, Box 27.

43. The original plan had been to release the convention's final resolutions on a holiday— "either on the Martin King assassination anniversary or on some other date which would permit the cadre of experts and writers to complete a truly representative final document." "Some Notes on the Platform Committee Meeting," Feb. 16, 1972, in Robert S. Browne Papers, Schomburg Library, Box 19.

44. "The Gary Mayor [Richard Hatcher] deemed it unfortunate that a resolution passed late in the convention when there were only a few delegates present, that called for the 'dismantling of Israel.' . . . Hatcher said: 'The resolution was passed late in the session when there were few people on the floor, and I did not think it reflected the sentiments of the majority. I didn't see any strong anti-Israeli sentiments on the floor. In my judgment, it was a very unfortunate resolution." *Pittsburgh Courier,* March 25, 1972. Hatcher, Diggs, Fauntroy, repudiate National Black Political Agenda: Delaney in *NYT,* May 20, 1972. Wilkins officially withdrew the NAACP from the NBPC the previous Tuesday. *NYT,* May 20, 1972, which was a Saturday, so Wilkins's withdrawal was made public on May 16, 1972. Fauntroy had helped coordinate the 1963 March on Washington. The thirteen members of the CBC rejected the Israel resolution: *WP,* March 24, 1972.

45. Mrs. King may have been provoked by a front-page story in the *Chicago Tribune,* "'Black Parley' Comes Out Against Busing," which ran a big photo of her, arms triumphantly raised, implying that she endorsed the convention's position. (She did not.) *CT,* March 13, 1972.

46. Mrs. King did allow that parts of the platform/agenda could be preserved. The "call for Black vanguard leadership, Black peoplehood and oneness" could work—if the authors would get their heads out of the clouds and roll up their sleeves for action. (Her examples ran from mass civil disobedience, boycotts, and strikes, to electoral coalitions.) She was most withering when she got to the foreign policy section. There the agenda's authors were out of their depth. Embarrassingly, they held up China as a model of freedom and social justice. (Interestingly, her observations echoed the stinging criticism that so many had leveled at her husband when he had ventured into Asian politics, late in his career.) "Unless we are to develop an unthinking cult of Mao," Mrs. King wrote, the agenda's authors could not put their version over on the masses of black Americans. Those masses, after all, knew as little about China as the authors themselves did. Coretta King to Walter Fauntroy, April 21, 1972, in IBW Papers, Schomburg Library, unprocessed box marked "Strickland/NBPC."

Similarly thoughtful and lengthy critiques of the agenda's content—notably those by G. J. Eddy Gouraige and Sherry Ann Suttles—can be found in the same box: IBW Papers, Schomburg Library, unprocessed box marked "Strickland/NBPC."

47. Coleman Young stated in a press release, "The convention reeked with overtones of anti-religion, anti-elected officials, anti-labor, and anti–Democratic party sentiments. Its pro-Nixon thrust was obvious with Black Republicans in key positions in the convention and the adoption of an anti-bussing resolution, designed to make more palatable Nixon's anti-bussing stance." [Punctuation altered from the original for clarity.] Young press release, March 18, 1972, Young Senate Papers, Detroit Public Library, Box 3.

On White House efforts to infiltrate the convention: Nixon's aide Ken Clawson described a "foul-up in communications" between two of his "operatives" who were attempting "a Black Caucus counterattack." This counterattack depended on what Clawson described as "four or five versions of the attached Xerox"—pro-Nixon boilerplate, attacking CBC member Congressman William Clay for calling Nixon a "racist," etc. Clawson said the language was "delivered in speeches by our operatives at the Black Convention in Gary." He did not name the operatives. It was no secret—indeed the administration publicized the fact aggressively—that Nixon's black appointees attended, choosing thereby in effect to challenge Roy Wilkins's skepticism about the convention, though perhaps ultimately vindicating it. Clawson to Richard Howard, cc. Herbert Klein, Charles Colson, Stan Scott, and Noel Koch, re: Black Caucus, March 18, 1972. (I have not been able to track down Richard Howard's previous memo, March 15, 1972, to which this is a response.) (Scott was Nixon's special assistant for minority affairs.) Stanley Scott Papers, Gerald Ford Presidential Library, Ann Arbor, Mich., Box 4.

Nixon papers released to the author under the Freedom of Information Act in June 2008 show a much more extensive campaign to recruit and retain black spokesmen than I think historians have previously understood. (They also show considerable hand-wringing over criticism of the administration by black spokesmen. See, for example, John Ehrlichman to Bob Brown, April 24, 1972, and Leonard Garment letters to Bayard Rustin, Roy Wilkins, Vernon Jordan, Carl Holman, and Ralph Abernathy, April 27, 1972, regarding the administration's exploitation of the NBPC's anti-busing resolution.) Administration officials, black and white, discussed the problem that Nixon's black spokesmen were seen as Uncle Toms: It was a big public-relations problem, they said, but a manageable one. See, for example, the nine-page letter on busing from Nixon's Council of Black Appointees, stamped Feb. 28, 1972. These papers were all at National Archives and Records Administration, College Park, Md., WH Special File— Confidential File, CF HU 2-1, Box 35—though they have been or will soon be moved with the rest of the Nixon presidential materials to the Nixon Library in California. One Office of Economic Opportunity official attacked and threatened Rustin personally because Rustin opposed the separatist "soul courses" promoted by the official. The official had been dismissed the day before launching his attack on Rustin, according to the apology to Rustin offered by his boss, Donald M. Rumsfeld. See Billings to Rustin, Jan. 16, 1969, et seq., in Nixon Ex HU-2, Box 2, also newly declassified for me in June 2008.

48. Polls showed that large numbers of black respondents opposed busing nationwide—on occasion outnumbering the black respondents who favored busing—though never an absolute majority. See *WP* and *NYT*, Sept. 12, 1971; *WP*, Nov. 1, 1971; *NYT*, March 6, 1972; *CD*, March 7, 1972; *LAT*, March 17, 1972; *NYT*, Sept. 9, 1973. *The New York Times* was often less forthright in reporting the black opposition to busing than the *WP*.

49. "Black Parley Comes Out Against Busing," *Chicago Tribune*, March 13, 1972.

50. Among the many who emphasize the convention's honoring Daisy Bates: Sala Udin Saif Salaam, in *Pittsburgh Courier*, March 2, 1974; Stanley Williford in *LAS*, March 21, 1974; *CD*, March 19, 1974.

51. Little Rock's Central High School 45 percent black, with a black principal, teachers: *CD*, March 19, 1974. Ethel Payne commented, "The school is nearly half black, with a black principal. Whites are fleeing to the suburbs. The problem is still with us. Only the characters and tactics have changed." Payne in *CD*, March 23, 1974.

Shortly after the second NBPC, the papers were flushed with reflections on the twentieth anniversary of the Brown decision. See, for example, "Twenty Years After Brown," the *Chicago Tribune*'s informative editorial trying to support Brown while giving "considerable latitude" to local school districts in choosing busing—which should neither be "required nor prohibited by federal law." "Busing for consolidation has been accepted with hardly a whimper, and to date only 3 percent of public school busing has been for desegregation." *CT,* editorial, May 17, 1974. Among others emphasizing the symbolic importance of Little Rock for the second NBPC: Ethel Payne in *Tri-State Defender,* March 30, 1974, and in *Pittsburgh Courier,* April 6, 1974. Baraka and Hatcher, in a joint letter to the editor, praised Little Rock's vice mayor, Charles Bussey, saying his support was "very significant in a city like Little Rock which still has a lingering reputation for its repressive attacks on black students in 1957." Hatcher and Baraka letter in *CD,* April 2, 1974. Gloster Current, NAACP director of branches, defended his organization from the criticisms of " 'black leaders including our own Roy Wilkins for failure to attend the Black Political Convention in Little Rock. It is ironic,' he said, 'that the attack was delivered from the platform of Little Rock Central High School in the presence of Daisy Bates and some of the original Little Rock Nine who desegregated that high school in 1957 under the aegis of the NAACP.' " Current quoted in *Atlanta Daily World,* April 11, 1974.

52. Bradley won 56 percent to 44 percent in a city with black population of 15 to 18 percent: *LAT,* May 30, 1973. Atlanta's population was 51 percent black, but white voters still outnumbered black ones by about four thousand: UPI in *LAS,* Oct. 18, 1973.

53. Modeste: no superstars; *CT,* reprint in *Arkansas Gazette,* March 11, 1974.

54. "national reputation": These were Paul Delaney's words in *The New York Times.* Diggs was one of three co-organizers of the 1974 convention, with Hatcher and Baraka. *NYT,* Feb. 13, 1974. Speaking of black elected officials, who were consumed after Gary with "tough, time-consuming fights in the Democratic National Convention and subsequent election," Austin Scott observed: "With few exceptions, they have been largely absent from the state and local assemblies that were supposed to carry on the organizing begun at Gary. Without the presence of black elected officials, control of the ongoing, independent black political structure set up at Gary fell to the next best organized coalition at the Gary convention, groups and individuals that fit under the broad heading of Pan-Africanist. They are seen as more interested in working out a black political structure than in figuring out ways to move within the established political structure. And they are often lumped loosely under the heading 'Black Nationalist,' although they are really more diverse than that, and they have frequent disagreements among themselves. The Little Rock meeting was put together largely by the Pan-African caucus, and its agenda is designed to minimize ideological disputes at the same time it emphasizes the need to get busy building those state and local assemblies. It is expected to be smaller, with only a portion of one morning given over to resolutions, all of which must be cleared through a resolutions committee appointed by the Pan-African caucus. Its public emphasis is a day-long series of workshops Saturday intended to give practical how-to courses in local economic, political and cultural organizing in black communities. The hidden agenda, however, is expected to play at least an equally important role: will the assembly machinery continue to be dominated by a Pan-African caucus, or can it be turned over to a coalition that included black elected officials? Some of the black elected officials who are still deeply involved, like Gary Mayor Richard Hatcher, president of the council, feel Little Rock will be a test. The issue, they say, is whether politically active blacks are ready to support an independent political force which tries to encompass a broad spectrum of widely differing black views." Austin Scott in *WP,* March 15, 1974.

55. Diggs drops out of 1974 NBPC: *NYT,* March 15, 1974. Stanley Williford reported that many felt that "elected officials stayed away because they learned the convention was too radical and would alienate both black and white voters; that the more radical elements did not have a sound understanding of the practical side of electoral politics; that basically it was a convention for grassroots people, rather than major political figures. Possibly the most painful backset to the convention was the absence of Cong. Charles Diggs (D-Mich.), president of the National Black [Political] Assembly, who at the last

minute opted to stay away." He noted that "[n]either Baraka nor Hatcher would comment on Diggs's absence." Williford in *LAS,* March 21, 1974.

56. Bradley had little connection to Arkansas, though Alex Haley, famous then as Malcolm X's ghostwriter, attended Bradley's inaugural and, in 1986, wrote the foreword to Bradley's biography, with its King-like title, *The Impossible Dream.* Black and white papers traced Bradley's reluctance to his multiracial constituency, Diggs's to his need to work in an interracial United States Congress.

57. Bradley out and Hatcher threatening out: *NYT,* March 15, 1974. Hatcher threatening out if convention did not return to "a more middle-of-the-road stance," Hatcher quoted in *Norfolk Journal & Guide,* March 23, 1974. Black nationalists had already succeeded in preventing any white-owned businesses from displaying goods at the convention. *NYT,* March 15, 1974. Hatcher told Walter Morrison of the *Chicago Daily News* that the Little Rock convention had "screening" procedures to insure no resolutions like the Israel and busing resolutions of 1972 would pass this time. Hatcher to Walter Morrison in *Chicago Daily News,* reprinted in *Arkansas Gazette,* March 15, 1974.

58. Coleman Young on NBPC disorganization: *Arkansas Gazette,* March 11, 1974.

59. Nationalists almost succeed in disinviting Maynard Jackson: *NYT,* March 15, 1974.

60. Coretta King and Farrakhan "indicated" they would attend. (Farrakhan was then billed as "second in command to Elijah Muhammad"): *Arkansas Gazette,* March 11, 1974, 7A. According to Stanley Williford of the *Los Angeles Sentinel,* however, the National Welfare Rights Organization did have some representation in the Little Rock convention: "The NAACP, CORE, and SCLC were not represented, while the National Welfare Rights Organization (NWRO), the National Office of Black Catholics, the National Conference of Black Churches and others were." *LAS,* March 21, 1974.

61. Ted Watson, "Black Pols See Hope in Caucus at Little Rock," *CD,* March 16, 1974.

62. Modeste insists rumors of NBPC death are greatly exaggerated, renounces fingerpopping: *Arkansas Gazette,* March 14, 1974.

63. Maynard Jackson in *Atlanta Daily World,* March 19, 1974, and *Norfolk Journal & Guide,* March 19, 1974. He continued: "If we can prove during these 48 hours here, in the old stubble-ground of hate and prejudice, slavery and segregation, black men and women of discipline, tolerance, wisdom and strength can create a new way out of the old, then we shall offer to our people a model of possibility and hope in the midst of distrust, anxiety and conflict." "One of the few black politicians who did attend, Mayor Maynard Jackson of Atlanta," in *Norfolk Journal & Guide,* March 23, 1974.

64. Hatcher's speech to NBPC: *NYT,* March 18, 1974. The *Tri-State Defender* gave a fuller account, March 23, 1974. A "very disgruntled reader" objected to "Hatcher's criticizing black leaders who were absent from the second National Black Political Convention (in Little Rock)," as did *Amsterdam News* editor James L. Hicks, but the reader thought Hicks should have gone further. "He should have cited the disenchantment of respected, courageous Blacks like Mr. Roy Wilkins (God Bless him!) with the 'leadership' of the NBPC, namely that jive Black poet, LeRoi Jones, forever preaching his separatist policies. The absentees had only to look at the shambles in Newark to know that Jones' kind of 'leadership' is for the birds, and self defeating for the Black man. (I really feel for Black investors in that defunct housing project in Newark). . . ." Letter to *Amsterdam News,* April 13, 1974. Other coverage of Hatcher's speech: *LAS,* March 21, 1974; Clarence Page and James O. Jackson in *CT,* March 17, 1974; and *CD,* March 19, 1974.

65. Hatcher's accusation that Wilkins was "defending our grandfathers" rather than children: *CD,* March 25, 1974. Hatcher's defense, citing King, claiming "conciliatory" intent: *CD,* March 25, 1974.

66. Baraka "said he would like to see a 'unified black front' that would 'attack those who have been attacking us.'" Merriweather in *Arkansas Gazette*, March 17, 1974.
67. Dellums confronting separatism: Merriweather in *Arkansas Gazette*, March 16, 1974.
68. Dellums on black officials who know why they are in office: in AP in *Arkansas Gazette*, March 16, 1974.
69. That Sunday happened to be Men's Day at the church. Jackson was special guest speaker. *Arkansas Gazette*, March 16, 1974, 12A, tiny item with Jackson photo, captioned "Chicago Man to Talk."
70. The biggest Jackson story, with interviews and observations about the press conference, was Merriweather's in *Arkansas Gazette*, March 17, 1974. Merriweather speaks of at least one other reporter being present for this post-press-conference interview with Jackson, but no other paper seems to have reported Jackson's presence that day. (Though see postmortem by Sala Udin Saif Salaam, below.)
71. One of the few mentions of Jackson in the coverage came from a black columnist whose main purpose was to defend the convention, as an "orderly constructive" event, from the general wash of criticism in the black press: "The Right Rev. Jesse Jackson made an impromptu appearance at the school and called an instant press conference outside on the front steps. The press who were inside covering the workshops, etc., left [e]n masse to check out the Country Preacher who 'just happened to be in the neighborhood.'" Sala Udin Saif Salaam, "Afrikan View," in *Pittsburgh Courier*, March 30, 1974. Another, buried deep in the *Los Angeles Sentinel*'s report by Stanley Williford, speaking of absences, said, "Among the civil rights figures" who were absent from Little Rock, "the Rev. Jesse Jackson, head of Operation PUSH, was clearly the most prominent. But Rev. Jackson later privately voiced doubts as to whether the convention was broad enough." Williford in *LAS*, March 21, 1974. A *Chicago Defender* gossip columnist noted, "Rev. Jesse Jackson was the speaker last Sunday morning at the Mount Pleasant Baptist Church in Little Rock, Ark. Incidentally, Jesse is urging that leaders of the national civil rights organizations, the Congressional Black Caucus and the National Newspaper Publisher's Association meet with leaders of the National Black Political Convention to try and settle their differences." Charlie Cherokee in *CD*, March 20, 1974.
72. Addressing some who were downcast, he said, "You read the white press and you are depressed. You see a mirror reflection of something strange that doesn't look like you. If somebody has told you blacks haven't made political progress, let's look at the record." Jackson also said black people should own their own banks, and he reminded the crowd of the need to improve job security, increase employment, and organize workers. About the crowd and Jackson's sermon, *Arkansas Gazette*, March 18, 1974; sermon title: *Arkansas Gazette*, March 16, 1974, 12A. The *Gazette* billed Jackson distinctly lower, however, than comedian Dick Gregory, who closed the convention that evening. A lesser story, on the delegates' failure to answer the call they had issued earlier to form an independent party, was also placed more prominently in the paper than Jackson. That lesser story, subheadlined "Few in Attendance as Convention Ends," noted that the final session (at which Gregory spoke) drew only three hundred delegates. The only delegation that appeared to be full by then was Pennsylvania's, which wanted to resolve a credentials dispute; half of the delegation walked out when it couldn't. *Arkansas Gazette*, March 18, 1974.
73. The quoted words are the *Gazette*'s paraphrase of Gregory, which continued: "some said the obsession was the media's and not the convention's, and there was some evidence to support that theory." Gregory speech in ibid.
74. Vernon Jarrett, "The Disruptive Concept of 'Unity,'" *CT*, March 24, 1974: "Racial, religious and political unity is a fragile, illusive thing." The quest for it had threatened the second NBPC at Little Rock. Unity should be "confined to the realm of inspirational oratory. Otherwise, it becomes an impediment to the development of the most

elementary planning for collective action. The absence of unity can become a disheart-
ening experience to a disadvantaged people—when they don't have it."

75. General disillusionment of delegates, reported by *NYT,* March 24, 1974.

76. Early reports predicted a slight growth in attendance over the Gary convention: "4000
to Attend National Black Convention," *Amsterdam News,* March 9, 1974. Vernon
Jarrett spoke of "the expected 8,000 observers and delegates," including "near 2,800
black elected officials." *CT,* March 10, 1974. On the scene at the start of the convention, Jarrett predicted: "Over 3,000 delegates from throughout America will converge
on this city." He admitted that "[f]rom a public-image point of view, this convention
may not live up to the expectations generated two years ago. . . . 'We'll be happy to
exceed 3,000 official delegates this time,' Gary Mayor Richard Hatcher told me last
week. 'For one thing, this is not a presidential election year and at Little Rock the
delegates represent a uniform method of selection at the state level.'" Jarrett in *CT,*
March 14, 1974.

The 1974 organizers, after announcing expectations that 4,375 would attend (*Arkansas Gazette,* Jan. 20, 1974), downgraded that to 3,000 (*Chicago Daily News,*
March 11, 1974, and *CT,* March 11, 1974), then to 2,000 (AP in *NYT,* March 16,
1974). In the event, they appear actually to have hosted about 1,700, though it is impossible to be sure. Reports on actual attendance varied considerably. On one day at
the 1974 convention, Little Rock's *Arkansas Gazette* reported 599 delegates actually
attended meetings, along with 215 observers, mostly press: James Merriweather in
Arkansas Gazette, March 16, 1974. On another day, "of the 1,718 registered delegates, no more than 300 attended." *Arkansas Gazette,* March 18, 1974. Two hundred
reporters attended the convention's press conference on March 15, 1974 (*Arkansas
Gazette,* March 16, 1974). "[A]pproximately 1,000" attended the second NBPC at
Little Rock": *Tri-State Defender,* March 16, 1974. *The Washington Post* reported there
were "1,718 registered participants": Austin Scott in *WP,* March 23, 1974. Charles
Kenyatta, who attended, said the attendees numbered 1,600. Kenyatta in *Amsterdam
News,* March 30, 1974. The western Pennsylvania delegation reported, after the convention, that attendance at Little Rock was 1,800 (down from 8,000 at Gary). *Pittsburgh Courier,* April 13, 1974. The conservative Little Rock paper, the *Democrat,*
relying on the AP, reported a higher attendance figure (2,000 on March 16, 1974;
2,600 on March 17, 1974) than the liberal *Gazette.* Like the *Gazette,* the *Democrat*
ran a sympathetic though noncommittal editorial. *Arkansas Democrat,* March 19,
1974.

77. The black *Michigan Chronicle* was typical. In its two-year life, the convention was
"still searching for a place in the political hierarchy and for a formula to counter the
inertia of the two major parties." But it made "no measurable headway" in Little
Rock. Like the first convention, the second was marked by a "continuing pattern of
irrational preachment that borders on hysteria, improbable resolutions and unreach-
able dreams [that] transformed the convention into a quagmire with danger signals
that have driven away . . . the NAACP and the National Urban League. Without the
support . . . of these two centers of power, the Black Convention cannot attain national
importance or influence the course of political thought and action in the black community." At any rate, "The public deserves more than vacuous poolroom arguments."
The *Michigan Chronicle* compared the NBPC to "the old National Negro Congress,
which gave warrant of a promising future in the early 20s, but petered out for lack of
unity, organization and a sense of history." "The Black Convention: A Dismaying Ex-
hibit," *Michigan Chronicle,* April 13, 1974. See other postmortems, in *Norfolk Journal
& Guide,* March 23, 1974; Stanley Williford in *LAS,* March 21, 1974; Charles
Kenyatta in *Amsterdam News,* March 30, 1974. Particularly interesting were complaints about the treatment of the black press, who, some said, were not treated as well
or granted as much access as white reporters and cameramen: See esp. *Tri-State De-*

fender, March 23, 1974; and *Pittsburgh Courier,* April 13, 1974; Sala Udin Saif Salaam, "Afrikan View," in *Pittsburgh Courier,* March 30, 1974; Robert Sengstacke in *CD,* March 30, 1974.

78. Editorial, *Tri-State Defender,* March 30, 1974. The paper recommended the convention "redirect its energy and emotional zest toward an unflagging drive for registration of some seven million of unregistered voters, that would give it a needed political tool to accomplish much in the context of power. It would by the same token become an irresistible force to be reckoned with by politicians of any hue or creed. That would insure its identity as a gadfly stinging both Republicans and Democrats in particular and the American electorate in general to a recognition of the black leadership as a solid entity that must be given its slice of the melon together with its share of responsibility in the conduct of America's national affairs." *Tri-State Defender,* March 30, 1974. A similar editorial ran in *Pittsburgh Courier,* March 30, 1974.

79. Jackson was not mentioned in that summary. *The New York Times* had last reported Jackson as absent from the convention. Jackson not mentioned in *NYT* analysis, March 22, 1974; listed as absent from convention, *NYT,* March 18, 1974. Other post-convention analysis: "Arkansas Blacks Call Convention 'Failure,' 'Mockery,'" *Arkansas Gazette,* March 19, 1974; "Arizona Delegate Calls Convention a Success, Hits 'Petty Jealousies,'" *Arkansas Gazette,* March 31, 1974.

80. Minimalist defenses—that the convention could have been a lot worse but concluded peacefully, etc.—include: "Nearly three thousand people, no fights, no arrests, no Nationalist take-over. Just us Black folks takin' care of business, Organizing for Political Power." Salaam, "Afrikan View," cited above.

"Baraka said he felt the convention accomplished a number of things, including the fact that 'two years later there is still a viable and very energetic political movement.'" Williford in *LAS,* March 21, 1974. Vernon Jarrett puts an interesting twist of his own on all the attention "given to the absence of most black elected public officials at the recent national Black Political Convention in Little Rock." Black folk had held several important conventions in the past—he briefly recounted examples from four State Conventions of Negroes in 1865—from back "before blacks had any elected officials anywhere in America." They could still accomplish a great deal and make their concerns felt. Jarrett in *CT,* March 29, 1974.

81. Harold Cruse, "The Little Rock National Black Political Convention," *Black World,* October 1974, 10–17, 82–88, and *Black World,* November 1974, 4–21. He described the 1974 convention as "weak kneed." It squandered the "Black militant potential" that built up in the 1960s. To Cruse this was a tragic lost opportunity, at a time when "the enemy *itself* was floundering in the Watergate disasters, with its flanks openly exposed to further ambush." Cruse in *Black World,* October 1974, 13.

82. Ibid., 88. Cruse referred to the decision at Little Rock to table, after "lengthy debate," the Georgia delegation's motion to form a national black political party. The tabling motion was approved by voice vote on the convention floor, after proposals from the Louisiana and Ohio delegations to reject the motion outright. Spokesmen from the contending delegations "said ideological differences among Blacks made formation of [a] third major party impractical. . . ." *Oakland Post,* March 24, 1974. On the black political party motion, also Austin Scott in *WP,* March 23, 1974.

83. Cruse in *Black World,* November 1974, 20–21. Italics are in original.

84. As mentioned earlier, Jackson told a crowd of 1,200 people in Norfolk "that the civil rights movement is dead." Jackson said: "yes it is dead, because now we have our civil rights. We have the right to go to any school, but we can't pay the tuition. We have the right to move into any neighborhood, but we can't make the payment on the note. We have the right to buy any car we want, but after two months it's repossessed. We got our civil rights, what we need now is silver rights, we need some money." Jackson in *Norfolk Journal & Guide,* May 4, 1974. Jackson was one of the civil rights leaders on

the list of people targeted for assassination by Marcus Wayne Chenault, Jr., who killed Martin Luther King's mother and a deacon in her church, and wounded another parishioner in the chest, during their recitation of the Lord's Prayer, on June 30, 1974. Also on Chenault's list were Martin Luther King, Sr., Ralph Abernathy, and Hosea Williams, among others. A second list named Rev. James Cleveland, Aretha Franklin, Reverend Ike, and others. *LAS,* July 18, 1974.

CHAPTER THREE: A COALITION FOR FULL EMPLOYMENT

1. *Pittsburgh Courier,* April 15, 1978.
2. Humphrey in House Education and Labor Committee, Hearings on Equal Opportunity and Full Employment Act of 1976, 93d Cong., 2nd sess., Oct. 8, 1974, 24. Humphrey emphasized the practical and general social benefits of the universal rights that had been articulated, thanks in large part to Eleanor Roosevelt, in the Universal Declaration of Human Rights, which included a right to work. He hoped that both progressives to his left and conservatives to his right would see that "action along these lines transcends mere economics. By dealing with one of the most fundamental human rights, a guaranteed job program goes to the very heart of America's most complex social problem: the hopelessness and alienation, even drug addiction and crime, that often arise when human beings—no matter what their sex, age or ethnic background—are told that they are not needed." Ibid., 24. He quoted from the Beveridge report, Full Employment in Free Society, a landmark in the history of social democracy, which was thirty years old that year: "A person who has difficulties in buying the labor he wants suffers inconveniences or reduction of profit. A person who cannot sell his labor is in effect told that he is of no use." Ibid., 28, 36. He elaborated by quoting John Stuart Mill: "Let a man have nothing to do for his country and he shall have no love for it." Ibid., 31.
3. Humphrey in ibid., 29, 36, 28. As Humphrey noted, the inalienable rights had been updated by Franklin Roosevelt's 1944 Economic Bill of Rights, by the 1946 Employment Act, and by the United Nations' 1948 Universal Declaration of Human Rights.
4. Background on Hawkins mainly from Hawkins, interview, January 1988 and December 1988, California State Archives, State Government Oral History Program, transcript in University of California, Los Angeles, library, and at http://www.content .cdlib.org/view?docId=hb5870096f&brand=calisphere, 47–48, 57–58, 131–32.
5. Despite expressing discomfort with the racially exclusive Black Caucus, Hawkins joined it. Smith, *We Have No Leaders,* 193. It should be noted that Hawkins attended the Northlake, Illinois, meeting in September 1971, where Hatcher and Baraka began planning what became the National Black Political Convention, and he remained a member of the CBC, though he never served as its chair, which changes every two years. He remained in Congress through 1990.
6. Hawkins, California State Archives interview, 135–36. Two recent histories—the best yet done on the forces that shaped the 1970s—restore the battle over Humphrey-Hawkins to its central role in the politics of the decade. Judith Stein, in *Pivotal Decade: How the United States Traded Factories for Finance in the Seventies* (New Haven, Conn.: Yale University Press, 2010), juxtaposes the Humphrey-Hawkins bill with the more comprehensive Humphrey-Javits bill. The GOP—let alone the Democrats—had not yet forsaken the Keynesian heritage of the post–World War II boom, and the GOP was still courting working-class and lower-income voters with fiscal and monetary policies. Jefferson Cowie, in *Stayin' Alive: The 1970s and the Last Days of the Working Class* (New York: New Press, 2010), juxtaposes Humphrey-Hawkins with labor reform proposals that seemed viable in the first few years of the decade. Other important works on the topic include the special issue of the *Annals of the American Academy of Political and Social Science* 418 (March 1975); Andrew Levison, *The Full*

Employment Alternative (New York: Coward-McCann, 1980); Barry Bluestone and Bennett Harrison, *The Deindustrialization of America* (New York: Basic Books, 1984); Philip Harvey, *Securing the Right to Employment: Social Welfare Policy and the Unemployed in the United States* (Princeton, N.J.: Princeton University Press, 1986); Gary Mucciaroni, *The Political Failure of Full Employment Policy, 1945–1962* (Pittsburgh: University of Pittsburgh Press, 1990); Margaret Weir, *Politics and Jobs* (Princeton, N.J.: Princeton University Press, 1992); Guian McKee, *The Problem of Jobs: Liberalism, Race, and Deindustrialization in Philadelphia* (Chicago: University of Chicago Press, 2008); and Anthony Chen, *The Fifth Freedom: Jobs, Politics, and Civil Rights in the United States, 1941–1972* (Princeton, N.J.: Princeton University Press, 2009).

7. Though critics later faulted the bill for lacking specific mechanisms to achieve its goals, the original bill required "creation of an actual structure to provide jobs for all." This began by expanding the functions of the U.S. Employment Service and changing its name to the "United States Full Employment Service," and by expanding the planning councils under section 104 of the 1973 Comprehensive Employment and Training Act. Hawkins explained how the new system would work: "An individual desiring a job would go to the Job Guarantee Office of the local office of the US Full Employment Service. He would be promptly interviewed and a three step process carried out": First, the agency would refer him "to available openings offering a high probability of success in the private sector or in that part of the public sector which is not directly dependent upon this Act for funding. If such openings are not immediately available, then the individual is referred to a contracting agency or organization or other entity funded under this Act (Subsection 5 (e)) for placement in a job on a project from the Reservoir of Public Service and Private Employment Projects." The Reservoir would consist of "public service projects and . . . private sector projects with public impact planned and proposed by the Local Planning Councils (the CETA Prime Sponsor Planning Councils) and approved by the Job Guarantee Office. . . . These projects would include ones that provide 'expanded or new goods and services that reflect the needs and desires of the local community, such as social services, community health services, day care facilities, legal aid, public transit, housing, recreation, cultural activities, sanitation and environmental amendment' (Section 4 (b)(1)) and other projects such as 'infrastructure construction, repair and maintenance,' compensation, repair, and maintenance of public buildings and projects for 'charitable and educational purposes.' . . ." Through CETA, local governments would have "overall control" of the local planning councils. If these first two methods failed, the applicant would register for the Standby Job Corps, which would employ the applicant immediately on "a project drawn from the Community Public Service Work Reservoir" established by the Community Board, and begin paying the applicant an amount that "bears a positive relation to his or her qualifications, experience, and training" but "will encourage him or her . . . to advance from the Corps to other employment" and is at least equal to the local minimum wage. The secretary of labor would be the overall administrator of the act. Hawkins, statement in CR-House, 93rd Cong., 2nd sess., June 26, 1974, 21279.

Hawkins quoted Henry Ford II, Chairman of Ford Motor Company, saying he had never felt "so uncertain and so troubled about the future of my country and my company." House Education and Labor Committee, 94th Cong., 1st sess., Hearings on Equal Opportunity and Full Employment, Feb. 25, 1975, 10.

On the intellectual background of full employment, see John H. G. Pierson, *Full Employment* (New Haven, Conn.: Yale University Press, 1941); John H. G. Pierson, *Essays on Full Employment, 1942–1972* (Metuchen, N.J.: Scarecrow, 1973); William Henry Beveridge, *Full Employment in a Free Society* (London: Allen & Unwin, 1941); and esp. Leon Keyserling, *Progress or Poverty: The U.S. at the Crossroads* (Washington, D.C.: Conference on Economic Progress, 1964). See W. Robert Bazelton, "On the 'Orthodoxy' of Leon Hirsch Keyserling," *American Economist* 51 (Spring 2007):

15–28. Keyserling's testimony is in, inter alia, House Education and Labor Committee, 94th Cong., 1st sess., Hearings on Equal Opportunity and Full Employment, Feb. 25, 1975, 11ff.

8. Poll on concern for domestic over foreign policy for the first time in forty years: *The Gallup Poll: Public Opinion, 1972–1977* (Wilmington, Del.: Scholarly Resources, 1976), cited by Cowie, *Stayin' Alive*, 271.

9. Barbara Reynolds, "I Am Acting in the Name of Dr. Martin Luther King: Coretta Scott King Strives to Complete Phase 2 of the Dream," *CT*, Jan. 11, 1976. Perhaps the most fascinating thing about Mrs. King was her refusal to comment on an amazing range of questions into which people tried to drag her, including abortion. The great exception came near the end of her life: gay marriage, which she supported, and said her husband would have as well, had he lived.

   Later in the campaign, Mrs. King used very similar language about how the crusade for full employment was not really new: "This is not a new crusade for us. When Martin Luther King, Jr., left us in 1968, he was leading the struggle for jobs and income for every American. . . . I fear the civil rights legislation we struggled for, and some died for, is about to be repealed by the harsh reality of high unemployment and persistent poverty." She emphasized that "joblessness threatens far more than Black Americans, in fact, most of the unemployed in this country are white." Coretta King in Senate Committees on Human Resources and Banking, Housing and Urban Affairs, Joint Hearing on Full Employment and Balanced Growth Act of 1978, 95th Cong., 2nd sess., Feb. 2, 1978, 169, 175.

10. Coretta Scott King, testimony in House Education and Labor Committee, Subcommittee on Equal Opportunities, Hearings, 94th Cong., 1st sess., "Equal Opportunity and Full Employment," April 4, 1975, 253–60.

11. The Joint Economic Committee held hearings on Humphrey-Javits in November 1975. See *Policy Studies Journal* 8 (December 1979), esp. articles by Ginsburg, Schantz and Schmidt, Keyserling, and Humphrey, interview in *Challenge* (May–June 1976). On Humphrey-Javits, see esp. Judith Stein, *Pivotal Decade*.

12. Full Employment Act of 1946, S. 380, 79th Cong., 2nd sess. (1946), P.L. 304.

13. Parren Mitchell attributed the troubles of the full employment bill, and the Carter administration's failure to endorse it and other needed social measures, to a new conservative trend in Congress and "Proposition 13 fever." Mitchell, in Barbara Reynolds, *CT*, Sept. 27, 1978.

14. Humphrey, daring to dream a little, in *WP*, Jan. 16, 1975.

15. Humphrey-Hawkins introduced to Congress June 1974: See House Education and Labor Committee, Hearings, Equal Opportunity and Full Employment Act of 1976, 93d Cong., 2nd sess., Oct. 8, 1974. See also Hawkins's column in *Norfolk Journal & Guide*, March 30, 1974; *Pittsburgh Courier*, April 20, 1974. The bill was endorsed by the first Black Economic Summit: *CD*, Sept. 26, 1974. The hearings that year appeared pro forma. Smith, *We Have No Leaders*, 193. Recession dates and figures from V. Zarnowitz and G. H. Moore, "The Recession and Recovery of 1973–1976," *Explorations in Economic Research* 4 (National Bureau of Economic Research, October 1977): 471–557; monthly unemployment data from Bureau of Labor Statistics, http://data.bls .gov/timeseries/LNS14000000.

16. *The New Republic* supported strong intervention to remedy unemployment and saw no alternative to Humphrey-Hawkins, though it did not express a great deal of faith in the bill, which it said was "a statement of intent and a list of suggestions, not a final plan." *The New Republic*, March 27, 1976. *The New Republic* also supported full employment on April 28, 1973, Feb. 7, 1976, and May 17, 1975, when it gave space to William Lucy, secretary-treasurer of the American Federation of State, County and Municipal Employees, president of the Coalition of Black Trade Unionists, and chairman of the Democratic Party in the District of Columbia. On June 12, 1976, contribut-

ing editor Melville Ulmer argued that a tax increase and price controls could save Humphrey-Hawkins from its flaws.

17. Quotations of revised bill from CR-House, 94th Cong., 2nd sess., Sept. 21, 1976, 31703. The critics of inflation weighed in with particular force in the House Education and Labor Committee, Report, Full Employment and Balanced Growth Act of 1976, 94th Cong., 2nd sess., May 15, 1976, 33–73. The revised version is in CR-House, Sept. 17, 1976, 31021–28. Hawkins explained the revised version (revised in response to inflation critics) in CR-House, Sept. 21, 1976, 31702–05. On the March 1976 version, see Humphrey, interview in *Challenge*, May–June 1976. For the full legislative history, see Peter Henle, "Proposed 'Full Employment' Legislation (HR 50 and S 50): Summary of March 1976 Bill and Comparison with Original Version," Congressional Research Service, March 1976; Dennis Roth, "The Revised Humphrey-Hawkins Bill . . . ," Congressional Research Service, Feb. 7, 1978; and U.S. Senate Committees on Human Resources and Banking, Joint Report, "Full Employment and Balanced Growth Act of 1977," 95th Cong., 2nd sess., Sept. 6, 1978.

18. Coretta King, testimony in Senate Committee on Labor and Public Welfare, 94th Cong., 2nd sess., Labor Subcommittee, May 14, 17, 18, and 19, 1976, 638–39. Portions of her testimony were quoted in *Atlanta Daily World*, May 21, 1976. Also on reality's repeal of the Phillips curve: Vernon Jordan wrote later that the goal of getting people back to work "may not happen unless the link between inflation and unemployment is broken. Most people still think the two are related, that you can't have low inflation and high employment. That's not true—we've had runaway inflation along with intolerable unemployment but convincing people will be hard." Vernon Jordan in *Oakland Post*, Nov. 14, 1978.

19. The push is reflected in increased news coverage both for the bill and for association of King's name with the bill: seven hits for "Humphrey-Hawkins" and "Luther King," June 1974 through April 1976; fourteen hits for May 1976–January 1977; sixty-three hits for May 1976–December 1978. (Scanned ProQuest for eleven historical newspapers: *Amsterdam News, Atlanta Daily World, Chicago Defender, Chicago Tribune, LAS, LAT, Norfolk Journal & Guide, NYT, Pittsburgh Courier, WSJ, WP*.)

20. Sponsors pushed the bill hard, but conceded to the press that they expected President Ford to veto it: *NYT*, May 8, 1976.

21. See Jackson's endorsement of Bob Dole, campaign ad in *Kansas City Call*, Oct. 31, 1980; see also Paul Delaney in *NYT*, June 12, 1974, Louis Martin in *Tri-State Defender*, Feb. 11, 1978, and *Washington Post*, July 21, 1980. On Jackson's flirting with RNC chairman Bill Brock, speaking at Republican National Convention, and Brock's broader efforts to recruit black voters, see Bill Brock Papers, Baker Center, University of Tennessee Knoxville, Boxes 57–58; and the Mississippi GOP Papers, Mississippi State University, Starkville, Box C-7 (subject files on Urban Policy, Welfare, and Jimmy Carter; typescripts of Bill Minor's analyses—"we're going to have quite a few blacks voting for Reagan in Mississippi, judging from what some have told me," etc.); Box K-16 esp. f.1, f.9; Box Y-23; and esp. ser. XXI, Box W-1, on the Mississippi Black Republican Council.

22. Charles Hucker, "Blacks and the GOP: A Cautious Courtship," *Congressional Quarterly*, April 29, 1978. The 95 percent overall figure, widely repeated at the time, appears for example in the *Routledge Atlas of Presidential Elections*. The electoral votes of each of these states in 1980 were: Alabama, 9; Florida, 17; Louisiana, 10; Maryland, 10; Mississippi, 7; Missouri, 12; New York, 41; North Carolina, 13; Ohio, 25; Pennsylvania, 27; South Carolina, 8; Texas, 26; and Wisconsin, 11. The total is 216. The thirteen states initially targeted in Operation Big Vote were: California, Florida, Illinois, Indiana, Maryland, Mississippi, Missouri, New Jersey, New York, Ohio, Pennsylvania, Tennessee, and Texas: *NYT*, Aug. 22, 1976. "90 percent of Blacks are voting Democratic; that's the gold dust for voter registration—for a Democratic candidate":

Basil Patterson, chairman, National Caucus of Black Democrats and vice chair of the DNC, in *Amsterdam News,* Aug. 21, 1976. Sponsors of "bipartisan" drive—including Coretta Scott King—repeatedly denied an intention "to give covert support to the Democratic national ticket, citing participation by at least two Republican party aux-iliaries": *NYT,* Aug. 25, 1976. Despite its Republican partisanship, the *Atlanta Daily World* supported Operation Big Vote: *Atlanta Daily World,* Aug. 31, 1976.

Pat Buchanan, using Louis Harris's data, claimed, however, that Carter received "the identical 82 percent of the black vote that George McGovern carried" in 1972. Carter's victory "resulted, almost exclusively, from raising the Democrats' share of the *white* vote from 32 percent in 1972 to 48 percent in 1976." Buchanan in *NYT,* April 5, 1977.

23. Urban League officer quoted in Philip A. Klinkner, *The Losing Parties* (New Haven, Conn.: Yale University Press, 1994), 146.

24. Faith Christmas in *LAS,* July 28, 1977; "Carter Criticism Grows," *LAS,* Aug. 11, 1977. In his Urban League convention speech, Jordan continued: "We have no welfare reform policy. We have no national health policy. We have no urban revitalization policy. We have no aggressive affirmative action policy. We have no national solutions to the grinding problems of poverty and discrimination." In Tom Wicker in *NYT,* July 29, 1977. See also Ernest Holsendolph, "Carter's Record Assailed by Head of Urban League," *NYT,* July 22, 1977; editorial, *NYT,* July 27, 1977; Ethel Payne column, "Stinging Carter," *Pittsburgh Courier,* Aug. 13, 1977; and editorial, "Who's a Dema-gogue," *Amsterdam News,* Aug. 6, 1977.

25. Samuel Evans to Martha Mitchell, March 2, 1978, and Vernon Jordan to Landon Butler, with attachments, April 19, 1978, both in Vernon Jordan Name File, Jimmy Carter Presidential Library (JCL), Atlanta. These materials were closed to researchers until June 2006, when, at the author's request, the Carter Library opened them up. To grasp the context, see: Samuel Evans to Martha Mitchell, March 2, 1978, with attach-ment, and Bunny Mitchell memo re: Black Leaders' Forum, Dec. 14, 1977, both in Ex HU, Box 5; Coleman Young to Carter, Sept. 23, 1977, in Coleman Young Name File, JCL; Frank Raines to Stu Eizenstat, Feb. 9, 1978, in Ex HU, Box 5; Louis Martin to Carter, Nov. 13, 1978, and March 12, 1979, both in Ex HU, Box 6; transcript of press briefing by Drew Days, July 11, 1978 (attachment to Adamson to Powell, July 12, 1978), in Ex HU, Box 6, JCL; Frank Moore to Valerie Pinson, July 26, 1977, in Bunny Mitchell Papers, Box 19, JCL; Moore memo re: Parren Mitchell, Sept. 20, 1978, the Congressional Black Caucus's "Review of the Carter Administration," Sept. 29, 1978, and Pinson to Moore, Sept. 4, 1979 ("the political climate in the black community is hostile and at its lowest ebb. There is a deep sense of disappointment and hurt," etc.), all three in Louis Martin Papers, Box 22, JCL. The newly released materials vindicate the analysis of Elizabeth Drew—that a public appearance of discord between Carter and Jordan served the interests of both: *New Yorker,* Oct. 10, 1977, 156–73.

26. Congressman Hawkins, in his newspaper column, tried to find "a middle ground" be-tween Jordan and Carter. *LAS,* Aug. 13, 1977.

27. First major civil rights strategy session since 1963, unemployment figures, and quota-tions from Vernon Jordan and Carl Holman are in Charlayne Hunter-Gault in *NYT,* Aug. 31, 1977. The new NAACP leader, Benjamin Hooks, was at the meeting, as were Jesse Jackson and Mrs. King. Figures from the Census Bureau were slightly different. Unemployment of "Negro and other races" in 1962: 10.9 percent; unemployment of "black and other" in 1975: 13.9 percent female, and 13.6 percent male. *Statistical Abstract of the United States, 1982–83* (Washington, D.C.: U.S. Census Bureau, 1982), 376; *Historical Statistics of the United States,* I (Washington, D.C.: U.S. Census Bu-reau, 1975), 135.

28. "Organized labor, already embroiled in bitter battles on Capitol Hill over labor-law reform and the minimum wage, plans nationwide rallies next week to move an equally

controversial proposal onto the front burner of Congressional attention: its call for a 'decent job at a decent wage' for every American willing and able to work." The aim of Full Employment Week is to move Humphrey-Hawkins forward. "President Carter has said that he considers the principle underlying the bill 'admirable' and that two revisions approved by its sponsors in March and September of last year have brought it 'closer and closer to consonance' with his own beliefs." A. H. Raskin in *NYT*, Aug. 31, 1977.

29. *WP*, Nov. 10, 1977; Dennis Roth, "Major Revisions in the Compromise Humphrey-Hawkins Bill," Congressional Research Service, Nov. 18, 1977, and Roth, "The Revised Humphrey-Hawkins Bill," Congressional Research Service, Feb. 7, 1978, 6–31. Roth noted, 6–7, that the 1946 act had also established that it was "the continuing policy and responsibility of the Federal Government to promote maximum employment, production, and purchasing power."

30. See, for example, the Sept. 8, 1978, letter signed by leading economists (Gardner Ackley, Robert Eisner, Walter Heller, Leon Keyserling, Charles Killingsworth, Lawrence Klein, Robert Nathan, Arthur Okun, James Tobin, and Lester Thurow) supporting Humphrey-Hawkins, particularly the goal of an unemployment rate of 4 percent, and deploring the Senate Banking Committee's changes to the bill (adding stringent inflation targets and decreases in federal spending), copy in Higgins-Spring (Domestic Policy Staff) files, Box 22, JCL. The chairman of Carter's Council of Economic Advisers, Charles Schultze, and his domestic policy adviser, Stuart Eizenstat, stated that these amendments from the Banking Committee were also "unacceptable" and "absolutely unacceptable" to the administration. Schultze and Eizenstat to President, Aug. 5, 1978, and Eizenstat memorandum re: "Meeting with Humphrey-Hawkins Bill Supporters," Aug. 18, 1978, WHCF Box Ex LA-2, JCL.

31. Parren Mitchell calling for rallies, *Norfolk Journal & Guide*, Oct. 1, 1977; Mrs. King leads rally: *Amsterdam News*, Dec. 17, 1977; *LAS*, Dec. 22, 1977. Mrs. King described the King birthday rally and the connection to King's work in her testimony in Joint Hearings, Senate Committees on Human Resources, and Banking, Housing and Urban Affairs, 95th Cong., 2nd sess., on "Full Employment and Balanced Growth Act of 1978," Feb. 2, 1978, 168–69, 175.

32. For more on corporate sponsorship of civil rights events, see chapter 5, below; Frank Dobbin, *Inventing Equal Opportunity* (Princeton, N.J.: Princeton University Press, 2009); Jennifer Delton, *Racial Integration in Corporate America, 1940–1990* (Cambridge, U.K.: Cambridge University Press, 2009); and Dennis Deslippe, *Protesting Affirmative Action* (Baltimore: Johns Hopkins University Press, 2012). In his autobiography, Barack Obama described his application for a job at a "prominent civil rights organization" in New York: "The director's office was furnished with Italian chairs and African sculpture" and "a bust of Dr. King." Obama quoted the organization's director saying that he particularly liked "the corporate experience" recorded on Obama's résumé. "That's the real business of a civil rights organization these days. Protest and pickets won't cut it anymore. To get the job done, we've got to forge links between business, government, and the inner city." Looking at a photo of the organization's board of directors, Obama observed, "There was one black minister and ten white corporate executives." Future civil rights work would rely on people like Obama, the director explained: "Educated. Self-assured. Comfortable in boardrooms." Obama, *Dreams from My Father* (New York: Three Rivers Press, 2004), 138–39.

33. Others who favored Humphrey-Hawkins were Stuart Eizenstat, adviser on domestic policy, and Joseph Califano, secretary of the Department of Health, Education, and Welfare. Opposition to the bill within the administration is well summed up by Charles Schultze, memorandum re: "Administration Position on the Humphrey-Hawkins Bill," March 14, 1977, and twenty-page attachment, in Bunny Mitchell Papers, Box 11, JCL.

34. See John Kenneth Galbraith, *American Capitalism* (Boston: Houghton Mifflin, 1951); Robert A. Dahl, *A Preface to Democratic Theory* (Chicago: University of Chicago Press, 1956); cf. Theodore Lowi, *The End of Liberalism* (New York: Norton, 1969); Robert A. Dahl, *Polyarchy* (New Haven, Conn.: Yale University Press, 1971); Charles Lindblom, *Politics and Markets* (New York: Basic Books, 1977).

35. People forget that in the deregulation movement of the 1970s, Ralph Nader and Ted Kennedy joined forces with many business leaders to fight for deregulation because Nader and Kennedy, like many liberals, tended to believe that regulation only served the interests of monopolists—it helped them dominate markets and bar the path of potential competitors. Pro-labor books like Derek Bok and John Dunlop, *Labor and the American Community* (New York: Simon & Schuster, 1970), and Richard Freeman and James Medoff, *What Do Unions Do?* (New York: Basic Books, 1984), were aimed largely at liberals who saw so much union corruption exposed (by Bobby Kennedy, among others) in the 1950s and 1960s, so much hostility to black workers and other minorities, and so much militant support for the Vietnam War and military spending in general.

36. Hatcher as quoted and paraphrased in "Tribute to Dr. M. L. King Jr. Focuses on Importance of Jobs/Matter of Jobs Linked to Human Rights Issue," *Atlanta Daily World*, Jan. 15, 1978, 1. *Atlanta Daily World*, Jan. 15, 1978, quoting statement by Roger Smith (on behalf of Thomas Murphy, businessman who received the King Center's Management Award).

37. On Humphrey's not dying in vain, etc.: *LAS*, Jan. 19, 1978. Other outlets also linked Humphrey to King in big front-page tributes—see, for example, Woodrow Taylor, "Did Martin Luther King, Humphrey Die in Vain?" *Pittsburgh Courier*, Jan. 21, 1978.

38. Riegle in Senate Committees on Human Resources and Banking, Housing and Urban Affairs, Joint Hearing on Full Employment and Balanced Growth Act of 1978, 95th Cong., 2nd sess., Feb. 2, 1978, 166–67.

39. Brooke in ibid., 160.

40. Ashbrook's balanced budget amendment defeated, and bill passes House: *NYT*, March 17, 1978; John Fisk, "Legislation to Limit Federal Expenditures," Congressional Research Service, Jan. 18, 1979, 13. House Majority Leader Jim Wright also said that the amendments that passed had made the bill "more palatable." *NYT*, March 17, 1978. The vote was "mainly" on "partisan lines" with Republicans saying the bill was inflationary and a step toward government planning of the whole economy; "Republicans and their supporters, including most of the major business groups," also said the bill was an "empty promise." Ibid. *The Wall Street Journal* said: "the entire nonsensical premise of Humphrey-Hawkins is to repeal economic cycles." *WSJ*, editorial March 9, 1978. On the recent amendments, which the *Journal* opposed along with the original bill, see *WSJ*, March 10, 1978.

41. Coretta Scott King defending watered-down House-passed bill, *Atlanta Daily World*, March 26, 1978.

42. Vernon Jarrett in *CT*, April 2, 1978. See also Barbara Reynolds in *CT*, Sept. 27, 1978, and Sept. 30, 1978. Vernon Jarrett on Carter and other southerners for Humphrey-Hawkins in *CT*, April 2, 1978. Edith Austin in *San Francisco Sun-Reporter*, July 10, 1976.

43. Ossie Davis, Muriel Humphrey, Coretta King, and others rally on King legacy: in *Amsterdam News*, March 25, 1978, April 1, 1978, and April 8, 1978. Also appearing in the last story was Al Sharpton, still known in those days as Alfred.

44. Jarrett on football versus full employment, *CT*, Sept. 22, 1978. Incidentally, Vernon Jarrett's son, Dr. William Robert Jarrett, married Valerie Bowman in 1983. Valerie Jarrett went on to become cochair of Barack Obama's transition team and at this writing is senior adviser to President Obama in the White House.

45. Fivefold increase in spending 1976–77: Bob Wright, in GOP Papers, Mississippi State University, Starkville, Box W-1, 3, attachment to Jackson speech. That was part of a larger GOP effort that year—$640,000 according to *The New York Times*—to recruit black support. The RNC retained the black-owned consulting firm Wright-McNeill to lead the effort and paid $140,000 to establish the Black Republican Council. Klinkner, *The Losing Parties*, 147; Clymer in *NYT*, Jan. 21, 1978, and Hucker, "Blacks and the GOP: A Cautious Courtship," 1045–51. And see Herbert Alexander, *Financing the 1980 Election* (Lexington, Ky.: D.C. Heath, 1983). Klinkner notes that this is when the GOP first became "a financial powerhouse, raising unprecedented amounts of money for Republican party-building and campaign activities and dwarfing the efforts of the DNC" (141).
46. Martin Schram, "They Helped the GOP to Help Itself," *WP*, Oct. 19, 1978.
47. Barbara Reynolds in *CT*, Sept. 27, 1978. Other accounts of meeting emphasizing Conyers's dramatic exit include: *LAT*, Sept. 27, 1978; *WP*, Sept. 27, 1978, Sept. 28, 1978, and Oct. 5, 1978; *Amsterdam News*, Sept. 30, 1978. See Frank Moore memo re: "Meeting with the Congressional Black Caucus," Sept. 25, 1978, in WHCF Box LA-3, JCL. The previous month, SCLC leaders had denounced Carter at their annual meeting. *Newsweek* reported that the Carter administration had "dropped the bill from its top-priority list," but the next week, Carter staff member Stuart Eizenstat wrote to the magazine "for the record that Humphrey-Hawkins remains a key part of our list of priority bills and that the president is fully committed to do all he can . . . to secure its passage in this Congress." *Newsweek*, Aug. 7, 1978, and Eizenstat to Editor in *Newsweek*, Aug. 16, 1978. Internal correspondence bears out the latter claim: "The bill is on the priority list we recently presented to Senator Byrd, and he is expected to be helpful in handling of the bill on the floor." Schultze and Eizenstat to President, Aug. 5, 1978, and Eizenstat memorandum re: "Meeting with Humphrey-Hawkins Bill Supporters," Aug. 18, 1978, WHCF Box Ex LA-2, JCL. The Black Caucus's stinging review of Carter's first eight months ranked the administration's "failure to make any significant dent in the structural unemployment problem . . . [including] a still extraordinarily high Black unemployment rate" as its "most serious shortcoming." "Review of the Carter Administration by the Congressional Black Caucus," Sept. 29, 1978, and see Frank Moore memo re: Parren Mitchell, Sept. 20, 1978. (A year later, things had not improved. A White House staffer concluded, "the political climate in the black community is hostile and at its lowest ebb. There is a deep sense of disappointment and hurt." Valerie Pinson to Frank Moore, Sept. 4, 1979.) All in Louis Martin Papers, box 22, JCL.
48. Silent protest outside Capitol and march led by Coretta Scott King for full employment bill; under pressure Carter agrees to make bill a priority before recess: Barbara Reynolds in *CT*, Sept. 30, 1978.
49. Carter at CBC dinner, Jacqueline Trescott in *WP*, Style, Oct. 2, 1978; Vernon Jarrett in *CT*, Oct. 4, 1978.
50. The Senate approved weakening amendments and passed Humphrey-Hawkins bill without filibuster, "decisively": Schram, "They Helped the GOP to Help Itself."
51. On final amendments: *WSJ*, Oct. 16, 1978.
52. Lugar led the fight for a strong anti-inflation provision: *LAT*, Oct. 14, 1978. In the final version that passed, the goal was to reduce inflation to 3 percent by 1983 and zero by 1988: *WSJ*, Oct. 16, 1978. The language of the previous anti-inflation goals had not had a specific target number: See Joint Report on Full Employment and Balanced Growth Act of 1978, Senate Human Resources Committee and Senate Banking, Housing, and Urban Affairs Committee, 95th Cong., 2nd sess., Feb. 2, 1978, 21–22.
53. Coretta Scott King on final passage of Humphrey-Hawkins: UPI in *Atlanta Daily World*, Oct. 19, 1978.

54. *WP,* editorial, Oct. 4, 1978. For similar reasons, *The New York Times* denounced the final bill as "A Cruel Hoax." *NYT,* editorial, Feb. 21, 1978.

55. *Atlanta Daily World,* Oct. 19, 1978; also see Mrs. King's fuller, unbridled statement, in *Seattle Skanner,* Nov. 22, 1978.

56. Hawkins in *Daily Labor Report* (Bureau of National Affairs), March 27, 1979, copy in Higgins-Spring (Domestic Policy Staff) files, Box 22, JCL, and in *WP,* Oct. 28, 1978.

57. Conyers and Rangel in *Amsterdam News,* Oct. 21, 1978. Conyers said it was "the most important piece of economic legislation I've ever worked on" because it made reducing unemployment a major national goal. *WP,* Oct. 14, 1978.

58. Roy Wilkins on the 1957 act, quoted in Steven Lawson, *Black Ballots* (New York: Columbia University Press, 1976), 196.

59. *Amsterdam News,* Oct. 21, 1978.

60. See, for example, *Amsterdam News,* editorial, Oct. 7, 1978, and Annette Samuels in *Amsterdam News,* Oct. 14, 1978. Gus Hawkins in *Norfolk Journal & Guide,* Nov. 3, 1978. The *Atlanta Daily World* (generally not pro-union) did not rejoice in the bill's passage, but it did praise it as an illustration of the all too rarely practiced "art of compromise" in Congress: *Atlanta Daily World,* Oct. 29, 1978. Other support for the final version of Humphrey-Hawkins came from Harold Ford in *Tri-State Defender,* Nov. 25, 1978. Skepticism and disappointment dominated other reactions, for example, William Raspberry, "Ho-Hum(phrey-Hawkins)," *WP,* Oct. 20, 1978.

61. Vernon Jordan in *Oakland Post,* Nov. 14, 1978.

62. Annette Samuels in *Amsterdam News,* Oct. 14, 1978. On the purpose of the CBC weekend, to provide "a focal point for involving the Black community and recognizing the persons who have made great sacrifices for global human and civil rights": Parren Mitchell, quoted in *Portland Skanner* (Oregon), Oct. 5, 1978.

63. Hawkins aide on how a lack of sufficient pressure on key liberal senators explains their failure to support Humphrey-Hawkins: Jarrett in *CT,* Sept. 22, 1978.

64. Samuels in *Amsterdam News,* Oct. 14, 1978.

65. See John A. Garraty, *Unemployment in History: Economic Thought and Public Policy* (New York: Harper, 1978); Alexander Keyssar, *Out of Work: The First Century of Unemployment in Massachusetts* (New York: Columbia University Press, 1986); Bruce Laurie, *Working People of Philadelphia* (Philadelphia: Temple University Press, 1980); Edward Pessen, ed., *Most Uncommon Jacksonians* (Albany, N.Y.: SUNY Press, 1967); Joel Blau, ed., *Social Theories of Jacksonian Democracy* (New York: Hafner, 1947); Nick Salvatore, *Eugene V. Debs: Citizen and Socialist* (Urbana, Ill.: University of Illinois Press, 1982); Stephen Hahn, *Roots of Southern Populism* (New York: Oxford University Press, 1983); Leon Fink, *Workingmen's Democracy: The Knights of Labor and American Politics* (Urbana, Ill.: University of Illinois Press, 1985); Roy Rosensweig, *Eight Hours for What We Will* (New York: Columbia University Press, 1983); Matthew Hild, *Greenbackers, Knights of Labor, and Populists* (Athens, Ga.: University of Georgia Press, 2007); Anthony Chen, *The Fifth Freedom: Jobs, Politics, and Civil Rights in the United States, 1941–1972* (Princeton, N.J.: Princeton University Press, 2009).

66. Humphrey, interview in *Challenge,* May–June 1976. Ten years after its passage, Hawkins did not say the act was a failure and did not express too much disappointment in it. What weakened its implementation, he said, was the loss of the penalties for violations. He remained "optimistic that eventually we will get someone in the White House who will say that this is the way to balance the budget, this is the way to restore the leadership of the country to its rightful place." To Hawkins, full employment meant full production. Hawkins, interview, January 1988 and December 1988, California State Archives, State Government Oral History Program, transcript in University of California, Los Angeles, library, and at http://www.calisphere.com, 131–37.

67. Coretta King and Murray Finley, joint testimony, in Senate Human Resources Commit-

tee, and Senate Banking, Housing, and Urban Affairs Committee, Joint Hearing, on Full Employment and Balanced Growth Act of 1978, 95th Cong., 2nd sess., Feb. 2, 1978, 169, 189.

68. Thomas Fleming, column in *San Francisco Sun-Reporter,* Oct. 5, 1978.

69. *Statistical Abstract of the United States, 1992* (Washington, D.C.: U.S. Census Bureau, 1992), 399.

CHAPTER FOUR: LEGALIZING THE LEGACY:
THE BATTLE FOR A MARTIN LUTHER KING HOLIDAY

1. Holiday bills introduced: CR-House, April 8, 1968, 9187; also in 1968: CR-Index, 1968, 527; CR-Index, CR-Senate Joint Resolutions, 1101; CR-House Bills, 1185; CR-House Joint Resolutions, 1263. In 1969: CR-Index, 782. In 1970, CR-Index, 646. In 1971, CR-Index, 830. In 1972, no holiday bill, see CR-Index, 593. In 1973, CR-Index, 911. In 1974, CR-Index, 845, etc. The introductions continue every year through 1979, when the bill that eventually became law in 1983 was introduced.

2. James Brown meeting with Nixon and aides, Nixon Presidential Materials Staff, National Archives, College Park, Md.: audiotape of Conversation No. 795-8, Oct. 10, 1972, discussion of holiday begins around 6:44 mark of a ten-minute discussion. Similar conversation among Nixon's aides is in audiotape of Conversation No. 793-14, Oct. 6, 1972, beginning around 5:38 mark.

3. House Committee on Post Office and Civil Service, 94th Cong., 1st sess., Hearings, "Designate the Birthday of Martin Luther King, Jr., as a Legal Public Holiday," Sept. 10, 1975.

4. *WP,* Jan. 15, 1979.

5. *Birmingham World,* Jan. 20, 1979.

6. Now in 1979, Conyers specified that "scores of cities" and "Fifteen States now regularly observe" King's birthday as a holiday. Perhaps he betrayed a fear that this luck would not last: "Ironically and wonderfully, the support for Dr. King grows each year," but now "the anvil is hot" and he urged colleagues to support what was so popular outside Congress. CR-House, Jan. 15, 1979, 59–60. This same point had been aired in the House's halfhearted hearings on the holiday back in 1975. See House Committee on Post Office and Civil Service, 94th Cong., 1st sess., Hearings, "Designate the Birthday of Martin Luther King, Jr., as a Legal Public Holiday," Sept. 10, 1975, 1–27.

7. On Ted Kennedy and Martin Luther King, Sr., at Ebenezer Baptist Church on King's jubilee: *WP,* Jan. 15, 1979. The speech is in CR-Senate, Jan. 15, 1979, 234–35.

8. King holiday attributed to Carter's initiative: *U.S. News & World Report,* June 18, 1979, and May 5, 1980.

9. CR-House, Jan. 15, 1979, 59–63, 234–35.

10. See House Committee on Post Office and Civil Service and Senate Judiciary Committee, Joint Hearings, 96th Cong., 1st sess., "Martin Luther King, Jr., National Holiday, S. 25," March 27, 1979, and June 21, 1979, 1–169. Bob Michel (R-Illinois) in CR-E (H), Jan. 25, 1983, 309.

11. See House Committee on Post Office and Civil Service, 94th Cong., 1st sess., Hearings, "Designate the Birthday of Martin Luther King, Jr., as a Legal Public Holiday," Sept. 10, 1975, 1–27.

12. Michael Barone et al., eds., *Almanac of American Politics 1980* (New York: Dutton, 1979), 213–14 (on McDonald), and 702–703 (on Ashbrook); and *Almanac of American Politics 1982* (Washington, D.C.: Barone & Company, 1981), 884–86.

13. See House Committee on Post Office and Civil Service and Senate Judiciary Committee, Joint Hearings, 96th Cong., 1st sess., "Martin Luther King, Jr., National Holiday, S. 25," March 27, 1979, and June 21, 1979, 3–4.

14. Office of Management and Budget on the cost of lost work, etc., in ibid., 93–94.

15. Kennedy claiming credit: ibid., 77.
16. Senators Bayh and Kennedy, in ibid., 6, 18.
17. Coretta Scott King in ibid., 18–20, 21, 23, 22.
18. Danforth in CR-Senate, June 4, 1979, 13279. As the only ordained minister in the Senate, and heir to the philanthropic Ralston Purina fortune, Danforth was to establish a somewhat unusual brand of moralistic yet pragmatic conservatism: for free trade though also for the huge military contractors of his state, for the starving masses of sub-Saharan Africa but via "market" economics, and opposed to both capital punishment and abortion. *Almanac of American Politics 1980*, 90.
19. Danforth in CR-Senate, Oct. 19, 1983, 28370; Connally and Anderson in AP, Jan. 5, 1980; and *Christian Science Monitor*, Oct. 10, 1980.
20. Stang's tract was owned by 447 of the major libraries in the Online Computer Library Center as of July 21, 2008.
21. Stang in House Committee on Post Office and Civil Service and Senate Judiciary Committee, Joint Hearings, 96th Cong., 1st sess., "Martin Luther King, Jr., National Holiday, S. 25," March 27, 1979, and June 21, 1979, 41–42.
22. Julia Brown and Karl Prussion in ibid., 42–45.
23. McDonald had implied earlier, in the March hearing, that someone had denied him a hearing on this issue. See ibid., 17–18. Now in the June hearing reserved for opposition witnesses, McDonald took up more pages (twenty-five) by far than any other witness: ibid., 17–18, and 51–74.
24. Quotations from this paragraph: House Committee on Post Office and Civil Service and Senate Judiciary Committee, Joint Hearings, 96th Cong., 1st sess., June 21, 1979, 38–59. McDonald statement: 51–59, 66–74.
25. Ashbrook, prepared statement, in ibid., 90.
26. Though Gingrich would later oppose affirmative action and identity politics, he added that a statue would show "our commitment to make this a country in which every American can walk through this Capitol and have a sense of identity and a sense of belonging. I very strongly support this resolution." Indeed, Gingrich was a sponsor, along with every member of the CBC. Many who had opposed and would later oppose the holiday voted for the statue. So did both Cranes, Dick Cheney, Trent Lott, Dan Quayle, Bob Dornan, Henry Hyde, and House Minority Leader Bob Michel. Ashbrook's company in opposing the King statue was the thinnest ever, consisting only of McDonald, Collins of Texas, Hansen, Ichord, Kelly, Paul, Rousselot, Stump, Symms, and Young of Florida. See: Gilman, Nezdi, Ashbrook, and Gingrich, in CR-House, July 31, 1979, 21594; list of statue sponsors, 21595–96; roll call on 21610. There were further delays before a bust of King was finally placed in the Capitol on January 16, 1986. See the Architect of the Capitol website at www.aoc.gov/capitol-hill/busts/bust -martin-luther-king-jr, and *United States Statutes at Large, 96* Stat. 2697, Dec. 21, 1982. The legislative history is summarized in: Senate Committee on Rules and Administration, "Authorizing the Joint Committee on the Library to Procure a Bust or Statue of Dr. Martin Luther King, Junior, to Be Placed in the Capitol" (Report No. 97-677), 96th Cong., 1st sess., Dec. 9, 1982.
27. Lester Kinsolving, "Atlanta's MLK Center: 'Where's the Money Going?,'" *Washington Weekly* (n.d.), inserted by Ashbrook, and Ashbrook in CR, Sept. 27, 1979, 26569–70.
28. House Committee on Post Office and Civil Service, "Designation of the Birthday of Martin Luther King, Jr., as a Legal Holiday" (Report No. 96-543), 96th Cong., 1st sess., Oct. 23, 1979. The minority report had five signers, all Republicans: Derwinski, Taylor, Corcoran, D. Crane, Dannemeyer. It is significant that the minority's objections centered on the cost to the taxpayer—which it broke down as $173 million for a day's basic pay, "which the Administration does not recognize as having any budget impact," and $23 million in premium pay, and additional unspecified costs, which, the minority insisted, were sure to be "substantial" (8). The minority firmly avoided any

aspersions on King's character. Indeed, rather than question King's worthiness for such an honor, the minority took it for granted that his worthiness had been established, and only questioned whether "a legal public holiday is the most appropriate way to honor him and recognize his contributions to our Nation." To honor any private citizen, it observed, "would be contrary to our country's longstanding tradition" (7–8).

29. CR-House, Dec. 5, 1979, 34751–53; data on Beard's district in *Almanac of American Politics 1980*.

30. Cardiss Collins in CR-House, Dec. 5, 1979, 34751.

31. CR-House, Dec. 5, 1979, 34761–64.

32. Coretta Scott King said the circus echoed those who "vilified and slandered" her husband while he was alive, and emphasized that King had been a more effective anticommunist than his critics: House Committee on Post Office and Civil Service, Hearing on Proposals for Martin Luther King, Jr., National Holiday, 97th Cong., 2nd sess., Feb. 23, 1982, 11–12.

33. *Lee v. Kelley*, U.S. District Court for District of Columbia Circuit, No. 76-1185; and *SCLC v. Kelley*, No. 76-1186, in which, according to the court's ruling, Bernard Lee and SCLC had sued the FBI chief, Clarence Kelley, and former high officials in the FBI, claiming that recordings of King and his staff were leaked to the media and others outside the FBI. U.S. district judge John Lewis Smith, Jr., ordered that the FBI's tapes and transcripts be sealed and put in the custody of the National Archives until 2027. Jesse Helms attempted later, after the House passed the King holiday but before the Senate voted on it, to get a court order to unseal the records so that he and others in the Senate could be better informed for their vote on the holiday. Judge Smith denied Helms's request, and the U.S. Court of Appeals denied Helms's appeal on Oct. 19, 1983. 747 F.2d 777 and 241 U.S. App. D.C. 340, 40 Fed.R.Serv.2d 522.

34. McDonald testimony in House Committee on Post Office and Civil Service, Hearing on Proposals for Martin Luther King, Jr., National Holiday, 97th Cong., 2nd sess., Feb. 23, 1982, 20, 28, 32. The other congressional leader of what Coretta Scott King called the "traveling rightwing circus" of character assassination failed to appear: John Ashbrook did not even submit a statement to the February 1982 hearing, probably because he was busy with a quixotic campaign for the Senate. Ashbrook gave up his seat in 1982 to run for the Senate against incumbent Howard Metzenbaum. Soon enough—before the GOP primary, which Ashbrook was expected to win—Ashbrook died, nonviolently, on April 24. Only Larry McDonald, who retained some of Ashbrook's extragovernmental following, remained. No ideological opponent had yet appeared in the Senate. (Jesse Helms was still lying low.)

35. Stevie Wonder, quoting Reagan, in House Committee on Post Office and Civil Service, Hearing, "Proposals for Martin Luther King, Jr., National Holiday," 97th Cong., 2nd sess., Feb. 23, 1982, 46–47. The first time the holiday came up in Reagan's presidency, Reagan was noncommittal, though he echoed some of the views of holiday opponents. "I certainly can understand why the black community would like to do that. . . . But one of the problems from those who have preceded me in this office is . . . the discovery of how many—we're quite a mix in this country—how many other people there were with—people who just as sincerely want them also. We could have an awful lot of holidays if we start down that road. . . . [I]t might be that there's no way that we could afford all of the holidays that we would have with people who are also revered figures in the history of many of the groups that make up our population. . . . " "Remarks . . . Briefing in Chicago, Illinois," May 10, 1982, PPP, American Presidency Project, http://www.presidency.ucsb.edu/ws/index.php. In his next two statements on the subject, he clearly opposed the holiday but mildly praised King: Q&A, Jan. 21, 1983, and Q&A Roxbury, Oct. 26, 1983. In his notorious statement later that year, in which he joked that we will know "in about 35 years" (when the FBI tapes are un-

sealed) whether King had communist associations or sympathies, and defended Helms's efforts to unseal the tapes, Reagan also announced that although he would have preferred a mere day of recognition, he would sign the holiday bill because so many "seem bent on making it a holiday." News conference, Oct. 19, 1983. See also Remarks on Signing, Nov. 2, 1983, in ibid.

36. See Reagan quotations in PPP, 1982, Jan. 15, 1982; to Alabama legislature, March 15, 1982; to National Conference of Christians and Jews, March 23, 1982; Q&A Chicago, May 10, 1982.

37. Reagan's logic was more oblique, one might say milder, than other conservatives' at the time, who linked King more tightly to his violent end; see chapter 1. Reagan was somewhat obscure and confusing as he went on: "It seems possible that he was betrayed because he wasn't travelling fast enough." Asked if he was implying King's murderer was black, Reagan said no; he only meant that the crime might have originated among "those who want dissent and insurrection." *NYT,* April 10, 1968.

38. J. A. Parker, *Angela Davis: The Making of a Revolutionary* (New York: Arlington House, 1973).

39. Parker added that the Lincoln Institute had two hundred thousand responses—he did not say whether the black conservative institute included white respondents in its survey—and "more than 90%" voted against a national King holiday (he expressed an open mind about state or local recognitions, though he noted, as McDonald had done, that King's home state of Georgia did not have a King holiday). J. A. Parker in House Committee on Post Office and Civil Service, Hearing, 1982, 68–69.

40. Reagan, Remarks on the Anniversary of the Birth of Martin Luther King., Jr., PPP, Jan. 15, 1983.

41. Lugar and Lungren, in House Committee on Post Office and Civil Service, Hearings, "Martin Luther King, Jr., Holiday Bill," 98th Cong., 1st sess., June 7, 1983, 28–34, 59, 87. Lungren admitted he had taken the cost objection, and other objections, too far in his previous vote against the holiday. "I had to look within myself and ask whether I, as a fiscal conservative, got so hung up on the question of cost that I lost sight of what this occasion symbolizes."

42. Representative William Dannemeyer (R-California) said on the House floor that Reagan would veto the holiday: Aug. 2, 1983, 22209.

43. Roll call in CR-House, Aug. 2, 1983, 22243. Ashbrook was gone. Stockman and Quayle, who had voted on previous King holiday bills, were no longer in the House. By party affiliation, AP dispatch, Aug. 2, 1983.

44. Before entering the Senate in 1973, however, he had fought against civil rights as a TV commentator in North Carolina, and accused Martin Luther King of "holding himself above the law." Peter Ross Range in *New York Times Magazine,* Feb. 8, 1981. He once said that King "may have participated in the creation of an atmosphere of terrible tension in Memphis" that led to his assassination. *WSJ,* July 16, 1981. On Helms's extremist background, see Ernest Ferguson, *Hard Right: The Rise of Jesse Helms* (New York: Norton, 1986), and William Link, *Righteous Warrior: Jesse Helms and the Rise of Modern Conservatism* (New York: St. Martin's, 2008).

45. Helms began at CR-Senate, 98th Cong., 1st sess., Oct. 3, 1983, 26866, and continued with occasional brief interruptions to 26869, when Kennedy began. Helms picked up the story again on the next page, 26870, and continued until 26878. Along the way, he made such observations about King as "His own description of the civil rights movement as a liberation struggle suggests a Marxist perspective" (26872). Helms concluded by reaffirming Ashbrook's conclusion from the CR-House, Aug. 4, 1967, 13005, that by working with communists and making them respectable, King had "done more for the communist party than any other person of this decade" (26878). CR-Senate, Oct. 3, 1983, 26868–70, and East on 26881; Helms added that the vast

amount of material released by the FBI under the Freedom of Information Act—some sixty-five thousand documents, he said—had never been considered by the Senate Committee: Oct. 18, 1983, 28071.

46. CR-Senate, 98th Cong., 1st sess., Oct. 3, 1983, 26870; he again admitted no evidence King was a member then added, "but the pattern of his activities an[d] associations . . . show[s] clearly that he had no strong objections to working with or even relying on Communists or persons and groups whose relationships with the Communis[t] Party were, at the least, ambiguous" (26877).

47. Specter on Helms's accusations and insinuations: ibid., Oct. 3, 1983, 26880.

48. Dole on FBI: ibid., Oct. 18, 1983, 28110–11. Dole later took the interesting tack of defending King by putting him in the company of Washington, Jefferson, and Lincoln, who had been vilified and had their patriotism impugned publicly in their lifetimes: ibid., Oct. 18, 1983, 28113.

49. Pro-holiday votes from the Deep South included such ideological conservatives as Strom Thurmond of South Carolina, Mack Mattingly of Georgia, Jeremiah Denton of Alabama, Thad Cochran of Mississippi, and John Warner of Virginia. One had to stretch the meaning of "the South" to find the other three southern senators who voted (with Helms, East, and Stennis) against the holiday: West Virginia's Jennings Randolph, a relatively liberal Democrat (70 percent rating from Americans for Democratic Action); Oklahoma's Don Nickles; and Texas's John Tower—the last two being as much western as southern. Senators from the states that had initiated and led massive resistance to civil rights in the 1950s and 1960s—Arkansas and Virginia—voted unanimously for the holiday. See final roll-call vote on the holiday, CR-Senate, Oct. 19, 1983, 28380.

50. Reagan leaked his support for the holiday through aides: CR-House, Oct. 4, 1983, 27058.

51. Robert C. Smith in *San Francisco Chronicle*, Jan. 21, 2008, at http://www.sfgate.com.

52. Richard Gregg, *The Power of Nonviolence* (Philadelphia: Lippincott, 1934). King wrote the foreword to a later edition (Nyack, N.Y.: Fellowship, 1959).

53. Speakers at annual John M. Ashbrook Memorial Dinner: Ashbrook Center website, ashbrook.org.

CHAPTER FIVE: JESSE JACKSON'S REBIRTH

1. Hints that Jackson would run: *Amsterdam News*, Oct. 29, 1983, 3; *Atlanta Daily World*, Oct. 30, 1983, 1; *NYT*, Oct. 30, 1983, 28; *CT*, Oct. 31, 1983, 1; *LAT*, Oct. 31, 1983, 1; *NYT*, Oct. 31, 1983, 1; *WSJ*, Oct. 31, 1983, 1; *WP*, Oct. 31, 1983, 1; *Atlanta Daily World*, Nov. 1, 1983, 1; *LAT*, Nov. 1, 1983, 1; *NYT*, Nov. 1, 1983, 20; *WP*, Nov. 1, 1983, 1.

2. On Jackson's *60 Minutes* and Morehouse appearances, *Washington Informer*, Nov. 9, 1983; *NYT*, Oct. 31, 1983, 1. Reagan spoke at 11:06 A.M. on Nov. 2: PPP, Reagan, Nov. 2, 1983. Jackson was present at the signing, along with Coretta Scott King, and Mayors Andrew Young and Marion Barry: *NYT*, Nov. 3, 1983, and UPI, Nov. 2, 1983. The days of, before, and after the signing, the papers carried prominent stories about Jackson's historic announcement of his candidacy. The night before the signing, Jackson held a press conference and spoke at a dinner for the NAACP Legal Defense Fund in New York, setting out the aims of his candidacy, which he said he would formally announce at the convention center two days later, on Nov. 3. *NYT*, Nov. 2, 1983. Jackson on Reagan's high and low moments: AP, Nov. 2, 1983. Jackson on Reagan's showmanship: Facts on File, Nov. 4, 1983.

3. See Elizabeth Colton, *The Jackson Phenomenon* (New York: Doubleday, 1989), 7; Richard Levine, "Jesse Jackson: Heir to Dr. King?" *Harper's*, March 1969; "A Candid

Conversation with the Fiery Heir Apparent to Martin Luther King," *Playboy,* November 1969, 85–112, 188, 290–92.

4. Jackson's donors: Marshall Frady, *Jackson* (New York: Random House, 1996), 259–60, 288, 325.

5. Ford foundation, CBS, Merrill Lynch, and $6 million in federal grants and contracts: ibid., 325. More than $17 million in federal and private and corporate donations: Colton, *The Jackson Phenomenon,* 9.

6. Concessions after five-month boycott of Schlitz: *CD,* Aug. 21, 1972; *Amsterdam News,* Sept. 2, 1972. Breadbasket had earlier concluded agreements in Los Angeles with Royal Crown Cola, Better Foods Markets, ABC Markets, Food Giant Markets, and ITT-Continental Bakeries, to hire and promote more black workers and deposit funds in a black-owned bank: *LAT,* April 4, 1971.

7. A copy of PUSH's "covenant" with General Foods is in *Amsterdam News,* Sept. 30, 1972. See also PUSH's accord with Avon, *WSJ,* July 12, 1973.

8. "Covenants" with Burger King, 7-Eleven, 7-Up, Coca-Cola, Southland, Coors, and Heublein: Colton, *The Jackson Phenomenon,* 9. Kenneth R. Timmerman, *Shakedown: Exposing the Real Jesse Jackson* (Washington, D.C.: Regnery, 2002). Other coverage of boycotts by Breadbasket, in *WSJ,* Feb. 8, 1971.

9. See *NYT,* Oct. 31, 1976. Other emphasis of Jackson on Voter Registration: *CT,* April 21, 1974; McClory in *CT,* Jan. 21, 1975; *CT,* May 15, 1979; *NYT,* Nov. 4, 1980; *CT,* July 15, 1982; Aug. 31, 1982; *CT,* Feb. 27, 1983; *WP,* May 11, 1983; *WP,* May 17, 1983; *CT,* May 22, 1983; Raspberry in *WP,* June 20, 1983; PUSH's annual convention, in Atlanta, stressing Voting Rights Act enforcement, registration: *WP,* July 26, 1983; Romano in *WP,* July 31, 1983; *CT,* Aug. 12, 1983; *CT,* Aug. 18, 1983.

10. Eddie Williams of the Joint Center for Political Studies said "this is the first time in history that Blacks have played such a major role in the nomination of a presidential candidate and in the election of a president." The black vote provided the margin of victory, he observed, in Missouri, Pennsylvania, Ohio, Louisiana, Texas, Mississippi, and Maryland, without whose electoral votes Carter would have lost. *Amsterdam News,* Nov. 13, 1976.

11. The figure of 2 million black voters registered is from Colton, *The Jackson Phenomenon,* 6.

12. Preaching abstinence: *WP,* May 18, 1975.

13. Jesse Jackson on abortion: "It's murder no matter what you call it"; "We can't solve the problems of a degenerate society by killing babies. . . . Only He who makes life has a right to take it." Jackson cautioned that black people's political strength was in their numbers, and that they should therefore beware of abortion advocates. As the *Pittsburgh Courier* paraphrased him, "the medical profession is offering cash incentives to the poor who consent to abortions." Jackson added that Moses and Jesus might never have been born had abortion been in vogue in their day, and that his own mother had been counseled to terminate her pregnancy when she conceived him out of wedlock. But a minister persuaded her that "what's in your womb may be your salvation." All from "Rev. Jesse Jackson . . . Opens Abortion War," *Pittsburgh Courier,* March 31, 1973. "Abortion is genocide. . . . If you get the thrill to set the baby in motion and you don't have the will to protect it, you're dishonest." Jesse Jackson, quoted in Al Rutledge, "Is Abortion Black Genocide?" *Essence,* September 1973, 36. Referring to the possibility that abortion might "threaten the birth of another Martin Luther King," Rutledge added that Jackson endorsed the view that "abortion would possibly deprive our people of a savior" (70). Other sources who cite Jackson referring to abortion as "genocide" include: Mark Hatfield, "We Have Lost Respect for Human Life," *LAT,* Aug. 8, 1973, and Donald Baker, " 'The Great Right Hope' Stalks Abortion," *WP,* Sept. 24, 1979. Jackson set out his views on abortion in "How We Respect Life Is the

Moral Issue," in *Pittsburgh Courier*, Feb. 10, 1979, reprinted from the *National Right to Life News* of Jan. 1977.

14. On reasons for dismissal from SCLC: Colton, *The Jackson Phenomenon*, 7.

15. Lois Romano in *WP*, July 31, 1983.

16. Reynolds and Jackson in Mississippi: *NYT*, June 17, 1983; AP, July 31, 1983; UPI, Nov. 5, 1984; *Seattle Skanner*, June 29, 1983.

17. There were rumors of a split in the NAACP leadership, which burst into the open when board director Margaret Bush Wilson suspended President Benjamin Hooks in June 1983. *Time* noted the NAACP's "demoralizing decline" in its 400,000 membership. Tony Brown in *Washington Informer*, June 8, 1983. Hooks also discouraged support for Jackson's candidacy. Tony Brown in *Washington Informer*, Aug. 17, 1983.

18. Rustin and National Urban League (principal sponsor of the original march) refused to join "We Still Have a Dream," the twentieth-anniversary march for Jobs and Freedom: *NYT*, Aug. 10, 1983; UPI, Aug. 16 and 24, 1983. Coretta Scott King acknowledged a split in the civil rights movement. She, Lowery (SCLC), Hooks (NAACP), Judy Goldsmith (National Organization for Women), Asia Bennett (American Friends Service Committee), and Stevie Wonder were official cochairs of the 1983 march. The press made much of the refusal of Jewish groups to endorse the march, including ADL–B'nai B'rith and the American Jewish Committee, who were principal sponsors of the 1963 march. *WP*, Aug. 21, 1983. Rustin's main objection appeared to be that he thought mass marches had to send a simple, direct signal. The solutions to poverty could not be conveyed with such an instrument. *Christian Science Monitor*, Aug. 26, 1983. See William Schneider in *LAT*, Aug. 28, 1983; *NYT*, Aug. 27, 1983, 1, 27.

19. *WP*, Aug. 28, 1983. Crowd peaked at 200,000 present at any given moment; 250,000 total attended (National Park Service estimates). "Run Jesse run," *NYT*, Aug. 28, 1983.

20. Detroit mayor Coleman Young, for example, told the press in July 1983 that the much-predicted Jackson presidential candidacy would be "suicidal" to black interests. *WP*, July 16, 1983.

    Newsweek referred to Jackson as "a former aide to King whose controversial flirtation with a presidential candidacy has split the black community." *Newsweek*, Aug. 29, 1983.

    The National Conference of Black Mayors declined to endorse Jackson, a guest speaker at the conference, though individual members did endorse him. *Washington Informer*, Nov. 23, 1983. Defenders of Jackson's candidacy often led with the conflict among black leaders over it, and the belief that Jackson would only hurt the candidate (necessarily white) who could do the most for black America, and who could win if Jackson stayed out. See, e.g., Julian Bond in *Seattle Skanner*, July 20, 1983, and Calvin Rolark in *Washington Informer*, Nov. 16, 1983.

21. Headline, "Left Revives," over an article by John Herbers, *NYT*, Aug. 29, 1983.

22. Frady, *Jesse*, 192, 466.

23. Jackson said Reagan did not return his calls. Ibid., 336.

24. Before declaring his candidacy, Jackson often relied on Farrakhan's Fruit of Islam for security. *NYT*, Feb. 27, 1984. Wyatt Tee Walker, *Road to Damascus: A Journey of Faith* (New York: M. L. King Fellows Press, 1985).

25. *WP*, Feb. 13; Feb.. 18; Feb. 22; Feb. 24, 1983.

26. Farrakhan on Jackson's enemies: *WP*, Feb. 27, 1984. On Jackson at the New Hampshire synagogue, *WP*, Feb. 28, 1984 (3 stories); John Herbers and Howell Raines in *NYT*, Feb. 28, 1984; Gilliam in *WP*, March 1, 1984.

27. Bob Faw and Nancy Skelton, *Thunder in America: The Improbable Presidential Campaign of Jesse Jackson in 1984* (Austin: Texas Monthly Press, 1986), 103, 153, 123–24. Manning Marable in *Pittsburgh Courier*, April 28, 1984.

28. On Jackson's victories in Virginia, Louisiana, and South Carolina in 1984: Juan Wil-

liams in *WP,* May 9, 1984; AP, April 27, 1984; and http://www.uselectionatlas.org. Jackson won more votes (2,800, or 24.92 percent) than any of the other candidates in the South Carolina caucuses on March 17, 1984, but 5,937 were uncommitted. Jackson complained that unfair delegate selection rules deprived him of delegates and, in some states, victories. Jackson came in ahead of the other candidates in raw popular votes in Mississippi, for example, with 8,435 to Mondale's 4,176 and Hart's 1,155 (4,704 were uncommitted). But Mondale won: See editorial, *WP,* March 21, 1984; UPI in *NYT,* March 21, 1984; *WP,* April 26, 1984; and http://www.uselectionatlas.org.

29. Faw and Skelton, *Thunder in America,* 153.

30. A top GOP strategist summed up Jackson's position after the four Super Saturday caucuses on March 14, 1984: "I can see this guy splitting the Democratic coalition with his demands, . . . but I can also see him turning out the vote that beats us." Broder in *WP,* March 21, 1984. Tom Sherwood and George Lardner expand on this point in *WP,* March 28, 1984. Jackson suggested, quite plausibly, that he could get out his voters more reliably than the next biggest broker, AFL-CIO president Lane Kirkland: "Kirkland can't deliver his folks. I can." He spoke of himself in the third person, asking rhetorically, "Does Jesse Jackson speak for all blacks?" Then he answered, "No. But when you get 85 percent of the vote, you speak for a generous portion." Faw and Skelton, *Thunder in America,* 128–29.

31. Ibid., 126, 153.

32. King speech by Jackson, *WP,* April 16, 1984.

33. On Jackson's convention speech, see, for example, *LAT,* July 18, 1984. Democratic leaders fretted over the possibility of low black turnout in November: *WP,* Nov. 5, 1984; *NYT,* Nov. 6, 1984. On delegate rules—of which Nancy Pelosi was one of the architects—and the damage they did to Jackson, see also Skelton, *LAT,* April 13, 1984, and Robert Kaiser in *WP,* April 22, 1984; *WP,* editorial, May 2, 1984; *NYT,* May 3, 1984.

34. Black turnout from exit polls increased in key states over 1980 (except in South Carolina, where it decreased 3 percent). But that was not enough to offset the shift of white voters from Democratic to Republican, especially in the South: *WP,* Nov. 8, 1984. Exit polls show 90 percent of black voters going for Mondale: *WSJ,* Nov. 12, 1984; Gilliam in *WP,* Nov. 26, 1984.

35. Faw and Skelton, *Thunder in America,* 123.

36. Thus Jackson, who won Virginia, Georgia, Louisiana, Mississippi, and Alabama, split the South with Al Gore, who won North Carolina, Tennessee, Kentucky, Arkansas, and Oklahoma, and Dukakis, who won Florida and Texas, although Jackson went away with almost half of Texas's delegates. Jackson notably came in second in four of the southern states he didn't win. Until his post-Michigan losing streak, Jackson led the pack both in total popular votes and in delegates. Jackson also won the primaries in the District of Columbia, Puerto Rico, and the U.S. Virgin Islands. He won more than 29 percent of the popular votes in the primaries and caucuses, a total of nearly 7 million votes, 2 million of them white. On Vermont and Alaska caucuses, see http://www .uselectionatlas.org; and Elizabeth Drew, *New Yorker,* April 4, 1988, 82.

37. Elizabeth Drew pointed out that all the candidates except Jackson finished Super Tuesday in exactly the order of how much money they spent on TV ads. TV advertising totals from Drew, *New Yorker,* April 4, 1988, 80.

38. In July 1983, the *Post* quoted the *Defender* saying only this: "Jackson, whose face appeared drawn, talked briefly with newsmen about the moments just before and after the shooting occurred. He said he rushed to Dr. King's side immediately, but got no response when he asked, 'Doc, can you hear me?'" Strictly speaking, there is nothing in the record to contradict that quotation. The *Post* also cited Jackson's interview in *Playboy* twenty months after the assassination and an undated *Washington Post* story. *WP,* July 31, 1983. In fact, the *Post's* actual story on the assassination, published on

April 5, 1968, does not substantiate the generalizations in its July 1983 story. See below, n. 42.

39. The 1968 coverage is summarized in n. 42, below. For journalistic uses of the memory of Jackson's post-assassination behavior during the campaigns of 1983–88, see, for example, David Finkel, *St. Petersburg Times,* Jan. 24, 1988; Gail Sheehy, "Jesse Jackson: The Power or the Glory?" *Vanity Fair,* January 1988, reprinted in Sheehy, *Character: America's Search for Leadership* (New York: Morrow, 1988), 96; *Newsweek,* Nov. 14, 1983; AP, Dec. 31, 1983; *WSJ,* Jan. 4, 1984; *WP,* Jan. 19, 1984; AP, July 17, 1984; *WP Magazine,* Jan. 25, 1987; Jack Anderson and Joseph Spear col., in (e.g.) Ellensburg, WA, *Record,* June 26, 1987; *NYT,* Nov. 29, 1987; *Christian Science Monitor* editorial, reprinted in Annapolis *Capital,* Jan. 31, 1988; *NYT,* April 18, 1988; *Toronto Star,* May 7, 1988.

40. Williams quoted in Finkel, *St. Petersburg Times,* Jan. 24, 1988, and in Sheehy, *Character: America's Search for Leadership,* 96. Barbara Reynolds (see below) also relied heavily on Williams.

41. That surviving footage (see next note) was relevant to the story that the *Washington Post* and other national papers constructed about Jackson in the 1980s. The tapes were available all along in the library of Memphis State University (renamed University of Memphis in 1994). But none of the 1983–88 background stories on Jackson's manipulation of King's blood and death scene refer to or quote these tapes. As far as I know, no reporter in the 1980s even looked at them, and no biographer or scholar of Jackson's campaigns used them, either.

42. The journalistic effort in 1983–88 focused on getting other witnesses to refute or to question Jackson's alleged version of events. Nobody ever established that Jackson himself had ever actually given that version of events. Had they attempted to establish that, they would have found no confirmation in the eyewitness press accounts published in April 1968, in the only known photographs made of the scene, and in the only known film footage that has been preserved of the immediate aftermath of the scene. Some of Joseph Louw's photos of the assassination scene appeared in *Life,* April 12, 1968, and see editor George P. Hunt in *Life,* April 19, 1968, 3; his contact sheets are available today from Getty Images. Louw's photos begin only after the shooting, so they resolve nothing about where anybody was at the moment of the shooting. The contact sheets clearly show Jackson at the scene, and on the balcony near King's fallen body.

Film footage of the post-assassination scene in Memphis, preserved at the time and held by the University of Memphis Library, includes a little bit of Jackson talking to reporters, but saying nothing to the effect that he held the dying King or spoke with him. On the videotape, Jackson says nothing about holding or cradling the dying King. He simply describes hearing the shot, and that all "we" could see was police coming (Reel 47, 355–506). No blood (or other visible stain) shows on Jackson's shirt or hands. Nowhere does he say he was on the balcony at the moment of the shooting. Nowhere does he claim that King spoke to him after the bullet hit. Nor do any of the press accounts of the shooting in the *Memphis Press-Scimitar* or *Memphis Commercial Appeal* attribute any such claims to Jackson. Nor does the story by Earl Caldwell, the only reporter at the Lorraine Motel at the time of the shooting, in *The New York Times.* The *Commercial Appeal* does say Jackson "was with Dr. King on the balcony of the hotel," but it does not attribute that idea to Jackson, nor does it specify whether he was with Dr. King *at the time of the shooting,* as opposed to after he was shot (when Louw's photos clearly establish him as present on the balcony near King). Later in the same story, according to the *Commercial Appeal,* "Jackson said" that King "leaned over the green iron railing and started chatting with the Rev. Mr. Jackson who introduced him to Ben Branch." This language is consistent with all other accounts, that

King spoke to Branch and Jackson, who were in the parking lot below the balcony at the time of the shooting. *Commercial Appeal* (paraphrasing Jackson), April 5, 1968.

The *Commercial Appeal*'s photographer on the scene, Sam Melhorn, took a picture of Jackson talking to law enforcement officials shortly after the shooting. Jackson's shirt is partially visible and, as in the film footage from Memphis, shows no blood or other stain. That photo is available on the Landov Media website, image no. 5937440, http://lan.merlinone.net/scripts/foxisapi.dll/wmsql.wm.request?HIT_12005121_3VK0 MXVAC1P200090782.32, and at http://www.commercialappeal.com/photos/1968/apr/04/31599/.

One AP dispatch appears to put Jackson close to King before the shooting. It quotes Jackson referring to King after the shot, saying "I knocked him down" (for example, AP in Florence, South Carolina, *Morning News*, April 6, 1968). But in other renderings of the same AP dispatch, Jackson says, "It knocked him down," meaning the shot (for example, AP in Portsmouth, Ohio, *Times*, April 5, 1968). This could be a matter of mistranscription or misquotation.

The Washington Post, relying on "news dispatches" from Memphis for its account of the assassination scene, repeats the "I knocked him down" version of the Jackson quotation. But it does not place Jackson on the balcony. It says simply, "The Rev. Jesse Jackson, with Dr. King and Ben Branch of Chicago when King was shot, said they were getting ready to eat dinner. 'King was on the second floor balcony of the motel. He had just bent over,' Mr. Jackson said. 'If he had been standing up he wouldn't have been hit in the face.'" The story says nothing about cradling King, King's speaking to Jackson after the shot, or Jackson doing anything with King's blood. *WP*, April 5, 1968.

About Jackson's later getting close to the dying King, one thorough post-assassination account quotes not Jackson on that subject but King's attorney and confidant Chauncey Eskridge: "Jesse went and got a blanket and put it over him. If Dr. King ever said anything after he was shot he must have said it to Rev. Jackson. But I don't believe he did." Eskridge quoted in Wayne Chastain story in the *Memphis Press-Scimitar*, April 5, 1968. Chastain relied in this story on Eskridge and Solomon Jones, not on Jackson. Chastain reports, "Standing with King on the balcony several feet away was the Rev. Jesse Jackson." Again, there is no implication or suggestion that Chastain got this idea from Jackson. Other sources say that Abernathy brought the blanket and leaned over King with a towel. Others (such as Earl Caldwell) say that Billy Kyles put the blanket over King; that "someone" rushed with a towel to stem the flow of blood; and then that Abernathy "hurried up with a second larger towel." Caldwell clearly places Jackson with Ben Branch "standing just below [King] in a courtyard." Caldwell in *NYT*, April 5, 1968. These and other discrepancies in the initial published accounts of eyewitnesses to the shooting probably say more about the confusion on the scene than they do about any effort to aggrandize Jesse Jackson.

The closest to a corroboration of the idea that Jackson wanted people to think he communicated with the dying man actually contradicts the notion that Jackson heard King's last words: *The Chicago Defender*'s Betty Washington wrote of Jackson's return to O'Hare Airport with Ben Branch. "Both men were clearly shaken, and Jackson, whose face appeared drawn, talked briefly with newsmen about the moments just before and after the shooting occurred. He said he rushed to Dr. King's side immediately, but got no response when he asked, 'Doc, can you hear me?'" Washington said Jackson was "almost speechless," and "red-eyed and appeared very tired." She says nothing about any stain on Jackson's shirt, or about Jackson referring to blood. *CD*, April 8, 1968.

A photo of Jackson returning to Chicago appeared in the *Defender* of April 8, 1968; another photo of Jackson appeared in the *Chicago Tribune* of April 6, 1968, presumably taken around the time of his City Council appearance on April 5. (The

Tribune kept no morgue of negatives.) Neither shot shows Jackson's shirt fully. The quality of both shots, as printed in the surviving microfilm version, is low. But no stain appears on Jackson's shirt in either. The Chicago City Council does not provide a full record of its proceedings. Its *Journal of Proceedings* briefly noted Jackson's appearance as one of the clergymen who offered prayers for Dr. King in its session, but no quotations or summary of what he said. Chicago City Council, *Journal of Proceedings*, Special Meeting—Friday, April 5, 1968, 2565–67. (My thanks to Kathy Mikel of the City Council staff for her assistance in tracking down those records.) The only papers that covered the substance of Jackson's words to the council were the *Chicago Sun-Times* and the *Chicago Tribune.* In the *Sun-Times:* " 'The blood (Dr. King's) is on the chest and hands of those that would not have welcomed him here yesterday,' the Rev. Mr. Jackson told a packed council chamber. 'A fitting memorial to Dr. King would not be to sit here looking sad and pious and feeling bad, but to behave differently.' " That is the only reference to blood in the *Sun-Times.* Harry Golden quoting Jackson in *Sun-Times,* April 6, 1968.

The *Tribune* had a different version of Jackson's words: " 'I come here with a heavy heart,' the Rev. Mr. Jackson said to the council and audience, 'because on my chest is the stain of blood from Dr. King's head.' " No other paper that I know of carried that quotation. Clearly Jackson used the word "heart" metaphorically. Neither the *Tribune* nor any other paper, in Chicago or elsewhere, as far as I know, indicated whether Jackson was speaking literally, whether he referred to any factual stain. There is nothing in the *Tribune* to suggest Jackson emphasized this point or gestured toward any actual stain on his shirt. If anybody at the paper attempted to verify the claim, there is no record of that. As in the *Sun-Times,* the emphasis in the *Tribune* was on Jackson's calling for calm in the streets—not on any mystical connection or allegiance he may have been claiming with the dead man. *CT,* April 6, 1968. (The *Chicago Daily News, Chicago American,* and *Chicago Defender* did not quote from the City Council meeting. Neither did *The New York Times* or the *Los Angeles Times.*)

The first instance I can find of anybody saying Jackson cradled King was in Richard Levine's 1969 article, which does not attribute the idea to Jackson, but merely states in passing, "After three years of organizing Negroes in Chicago, bringing the largest chain stores in the city to heel with a series of boycotts, travelling around the country to set up other Breadbaskets, cradling Martin Luther King's head in his arms on the balcony of the Lorraine Motel in Memphis, gaining national prominence last June as manager of Resurrection City, finally landing in a hospital for 'sins against my finitude,' who could still think he was a crook?" Levine, "Jesse Jackson: Heir to Dr. King?" *Harper's,* March 1969, 59. Jackson's *Playboy* interview in November 1969 repeated the idea, but again did not attribute the line to Jackson. *Playboy* says on its own authority, rather, in an editorial headnote, which refers to Levine's article as a source, that Jackson "was talking to King on the porch of the Lorraine Motel in Memphis when the fatal shot was fired and cradled the dying man in his arms." In the interview, Jackson does not say he cradled King or heard words from him. He says simply that "I was with Dr. King when the assassin's bullet was fired," that they were talking with Ben Branch, and that Abernathy, Andrew Young, James Bevel, and Bernard Lee "were very near. When Dr. King was shot, I hit the ground, along with the others. We scrambled toward the steps where he was." He hit the "ground." The "ground" could mean the second-floor balcony floor, where King was, but it seems more likely to have meant the ground in the parking lot below. *Playboy,* November 1969, 85. *Time* repeated this idea a few months later on the second anniversary of King's murder. But the magazine did not attribute the idea to Jackson as a source: "Jackson was the last man King spoke to before he was shot in Memphis. Jesse ran to the balcony, held King's head, but it was too late." *Time,* April 6, 1968, 22. Barbara Reynolds used the *Playboy* headnote and *Time* statements, along with her own interviews with other eyewitnesses—and what she says were "at least 100 other articles"—to claim that Jackson himself was the source of Jackson's self-aggrandizing story "that Jackson cradled King, that he was the last man King spoke to before he died, or that Jackson later attended a Chicago City Council meeting with the blood of King on his shirt." She adds, "These accounts, of course, were accepted as fact by everyone—except King's staff, who had been eyewitnesses to the assassination." She also says of her own account, "This is the first time, according to King's aides whom I interviewed, that the view from their side has been sought or reported." Reynolds, *Jesse Jackson: The Man, the Movement, the Myth* (Chicago: Nelson-Hall, 1975), 82–84. In my reading of post-assassination coverage, however, if the press promotes or emphasizes any figure as King's anointed successor, it is not Jackson but Abernathy.

One of Reynolds's interviewees, Chauncey Eskridge, was quoted at the time (see above) contradicting what Reynolds attributes to him. She refers to the photographer on the scene, who "caught forever in his camera lens all those who were on the balcony seconds after the gun blast. They were pointing in the direction from where the shots were fired. . . . Jesse was not identified in photos as being among them" (88). She can only mean Louw, and she is clearly wrong on this. As noted above, Louw's contact sheets clearly show Jackson among those on the balcony with the fallen King.

In attributing the Jackson-aggrandizing story to *Time,* Reynolds overlooks the newsmagazine's actual editorial judgment of him, and what *Time* did attribute to Jackson: resentment of people who see him as King's heir or Abernathy's rival. Jackson "has a host of admirers as well as caustic critics. But he is still too young to assume a black leadership role on a national scale. He rightfully resents white journalists who portray him as the heir to King or the rival to Abernathy." *Time,* April 6, 1970, 21. Though scarcely any newspapers cite Reynolds in their 1984 and 1988 stories on Jackson's background, a lot of their stories about him seem to originate in her book.

The author attempted to track down Richard Levine, to ask whether he remembered Jackson himself saying he cradled King, et cetera, and his survivors, to see whether he left any notes of interviews. To date, these efforts have been fruitless.

43. The *St. Petersburg Times* undermined Jackson's clear denial when it introduced it this way: "To this day, Jackson has yet to clear up what happened." This after quoting Jackson saying, "I never said that I picked him up and held him in my arms. . . . That's not true. That's not what I said." "My story hasn't changed," he insisted. "Not a bit." David Finkel in *St. Petersburg Times,* Jan. 24, 1988. The only other story I know of that explored the ambiguities and discrepancies in the testimony was David Maraniss in the *WP,* April 3, 1988.

44. The percentage of eligible black voters who reported they were registered ran as follows:

1976: 58.5
1980: 60.0
1984: 66.3
1986: 64.0*
1988: 64.5
1992: 63.9
1996: 63.5
2000: 63.6
2004: 64.4
2008: 65.5

* This off-year election is significant for Jackson's campaign. He claimed credit for the Democrats' retaking the Senate that year. Black registration in previous off-years was: 57.1 in 1978 and 59.1 in 1982. In 1990, it went back down to 58.8.

White registration held pretty steady from 68.3 in 1976 to 67.9 in 1988. White registration was 67.7 in 1996, 65.6 in 2000, 67.9 in 2004, and 66.6 in 2008. Only in 2008, that is, did black and white registration approach equality. Actual percentage reporting they voted was another story. Sources: 1976–88: *Statistical Abstract of the United States,* 1992, table 435; 1992: *Statistical Abstract of the United States,* 2000, table 477; 1996–2008: *Statistical Abstract of the United States,* 2009, table 406. All-time high based also on figures back to 1964 (black registration in eleven southern states for 1964 was 35.5 and 1969 was 64.8): *Statistical Abstract of the United States,* 1970, table 555.

CHAPTER SIX: PUBLIC RECKONINGS WITH KING'S CHARACTER

1. By 1988, just two years after the national holiday went into effect, forty-three states had ratified the national holiday with matching state holidays—all but Arizona, Hawaii, Idaho, Montana, New Hampshire, South Dakota, and Wyoming. *NYT,* Jan. 15, 1988.
2. Abernathy's resentment of those who were getting the attention (and related funding) that he believed he and his organization deserved in King's name came through from time to time on the record. Abernathy drew attention to himself in the summer of 1973, for example, when he threatened to resign from the SCLC. He said the SCLC's troubles—the organization was "broke and aimless," in the words of *Chicago Tribune* columnist Nick Thimmesch—were the fault of black leaders who had benefited most from King's sacrifices. He may have been referring to Jesse Jackson (by then attracting a huge following, press coverage, and funds to his spinoff organization, PUSH) and Andrew Young, the former King aide by then serving his second term in Congress, when he said black people who hold "high positions made possible through our struggles" were not doing their part to keep King's organization solvent. Thimmesch, and Thimmesch quoting Abernathy, in *CT,* July 29, 1973.
3. Georgia Davis Powers, *I Shared the Dream: The Pride, Passion, and Politics of the First Black Woman Senator from Kentucky* (Far Hills, N.J.: New Horizon Press, 1995).
4. Abernathy, *And the Walls Came Tumbling Down* (New York: Harper & Row, 1989), 434–36.
5. Ibid., 470–75.
6. Mike Royko, in *Salt Lake Tribune,* June 23, 1969. I. F. Stone made a similarly indignant point: *I. F. Stone's Weekly,* June 30, 1969. *Newsweek* commented, "For years, it has been an open secret that the FBI maintained a tap on the telephone calls of Dr. Martin Luther King." The FBI admitted to the wiretaps, and to continuing them until King's death, during the draft-evasion trial of Muhammad Ali in June 1970. Ali's lawyers charged that the FBI had improperly used information from King's conversations with Ali to support the Justice Department's denial of conscientious objector status to Ali. Robert Kennedy had denied authorizing the wiretaps back when the subject came up in Drew Pearson and Jack Anderson, "Kennedy Ordered King Wiretap," *WP,* May 24, 1968. The FBI was insisting in June 1970 that Kennedy had in fact ordered them. *Newsweek,* June 16, 1970.
7. Coretta Scott King, *My Life with Martin Luther King* (1969; reprint, New York: Avon, 1970), both quotations, 99; cf. 192, 194.
8. Ibid., 134.
9. Stern and Harwood, " 'King Tape' Emerges from Legend to Underline a Danger to Liberties," *WP,* June 11, 1969.
10. "Person C" in John A. Williams, *The King God Didn't Save: Reflections on the Life and Death of Martin Luther King, Jr.* (New York: Coward-McCann, 1970), 150, 154–55, 161–62, 166, 170–71. Williams claimed that one of his six anonymous sources—identified as Person C—had been photographed in two compromising positions with

King: on a bed with King naked and next to a bathtub in which King was again naked. Person C claimed that she had no sex with King, however. She said she also helped to conceal a wild orgy in a hotel where King stayed on his Nobel Prize trip, involving prostitutes and groupies, several men in King's entourage, and probably King himself. Person C claimed to have slept through the action, however.

Another source, Person D, told Williams that an attractive white woman had insinuated that she had slept with King. A third source, "a reporter," told Williams that he knew several other reporters who had heard the FBI's tapes of King's extramarital sex. A fourth, "a newsmagazine reporter," had told Williams of one publication's decision to suppress a story in which King "had to leave a place in a hurry, his pants in his hands." The magazine reporter also alluded to the systematic purging of news files to keep King's secret from getting out.

11. Negative review of Williams, *Time,* Aug. 17, 1970, 12–13. Ralph Abernathy, Andrew Young, and Walter Fauntroy, statement quoted at length in *Oakland Post,* Aug. 20, 1970. Coretta King in AP in Bridgeport, Connecticut, *Telegram,* Aug. 11, 1970. Another denial of the truth of Williams's claims about King came from Rev. Charles Gordon in the *Bridgeport Telegram,* Aug. 11, 1970. In its review, *Time* confirmed that Williams was "basically correct" about the FBI's tapes: The bugs and taps had turned up no communist links but did turn up, as *Time* put it, "an astonishing amount of information about King's extensive and vigorous sexual activities. . . . Most newspapers ignored the rumors and leaks to them of King's extramarital activities, but their existence undermined King's effectiveness." *Time* added to Williams's account the revelation that when King met with Hoover in December 1964, Hoover had told King "just what damaging private detail he had on the tapes and lectured him that his morals should be those befitting a Nobel prizewinner."

A few months earlier, King's former aide Andrew Young had told an interviewer that he had heard rumors from "the press" that the FBI was leaking damaging information about King from bugs and wiretaps—about communist associations, financial improprieties, and "some kind of wild sexual activity." King, Young, and other staffers had met with Hoover about this, according to Young, but never asked him directly about the tapes. Young said that he and Abernathy and Fauntroy met later (without King and without Hoover) with Hoover's deputy director, Cartha "Deke" DeLoach, who denied the rumors of the bureau's eavesdropping on King. Young said he could not get any clear responses from the FBI or any of the relief they sought from the Justice Department about the damaging rumors. Young interview, LBJ Library, June 18, 1970, 16–18. DeLoach later lent credibility to the substance of the account in *Time,* saying that in the first meeting with King, Hoover had warned King to "be very careful of his associates . . . and very careful concerning any personal escapades. . . ." DeLoach interview, LBJ Library, Jan. 11, 1991, 44.

12. Jack Anderson, in *WP,* Aug. 15, 1970, and in Lumberton, North Carolina, *Robesonian,* Aug. 16, 1970. Pearson and Anderson in *WP,* May 24, 1968.

13. See Nikki Giovanni, *Gemini: An Extended Autobiographical Statement on the First 25 Years of Being a Black Poet* (New York: Bobbs-Merrill, 1972), 81–83; Jesse Owens, *I Have Changed* (New York: Morrow, 1972), 43–53; Carl Rowan, *Just Between Us Blacks* (New York: Random House, 1974), 16–18; Jesse Jackson and Alvin Poussaint, "For Closer Scrutiny of the F.B.I.," *NYT,* op-ed, Aug. 10, 1974; Harry Waters and Philip Cook in *Newsweek,* Feb. 17, 1975; Julian Bond column, *CD,* Dec. 6, 1975; Kenneth Clark, interview, May 10, 1976, in *Reminiscences of Kenneth B. Clark* (New York: American Psychological Association, 1989), 176–77; Abby Mann in *Toronto Globe and Mail,* Jan. 17, 1978.

14. *NYT,* Nov. 19, 1975. Soon FBI officials were dissociating themselves. And soon there were reports that individual agents might be liable to criminal prosecution for spying on King. See *WSJ,* Nov. 21, 1975. See Senate Select Committee to Study Governmental

Operations with Respect to Intelligence Activities, 94th Cong., 1st sess., vol. 6, November–December 1975; Supplementary Detailed Staff Reports on Intelligence Activities and the Rights of Americans, Book 3, 94th Cong., 2nd sess., April 23, 1976; and Final Report, Book II, Intelligence Activities and the Rights of Americans, 94th Cong., 2nd sess., April 26, 1976.

15. Rustin, interview with Ed Edwin, in *The Reminiscences of Bayard Rustin* (Alexandria, Va.: Alexander Street Press, 2003), 462–76.

16. Garrow, *Bearing the Cross,* and Garrow, *The FBI and Martin Luther King: From "SOLO" to Memphis* (New York: Norton, 1981). See also Victor Navasky, "The Government and Martin Luther King," *Atlantic,* November 1970, 43–62, and John Williams to editor, *Atlantic,* January 1971, 35–36.

17. Garrow, *Bearing the Cross,* 371. Garrow reported that, as early as May 1964, the FBI was shopping around what a former representative of Florida governor C. Farris Bryant called a "very lurid tape recording." The representative told Garrow that the FBI told state officials that they could use the tape "as a weapon if we wanted to run King out of St. Augustine by threatening to expose him." The officials rejected the offer. Garrow seems to identify the source of these quotations as Daniel R. Warren, then personal representative of Governor Bryant. Garrow, *Bearing the Cross,* 328, and see 373–76, and 689, n. 18. Warren later published a memoir, *If It Takes All Summer: Martin Luther King, the KKK, and States' Rights in St. Augustine, 1964* (Tuscaloosa, Ala.: University of Alabama Press, 2008).

    The earliest and most striking allusion to King's dalliances, surprisingly, was a public one, before the FBI began to eavesdrop systematically on him: See Garrow, *Bearing the Cross,* 96. Garrow refers to Robert Ratcliffe's "Behind the Headlines" column, *Pittsburgh Courier,* June 29, 1957, 7.

18. The last tryst Garrow records is on March 30, 1968, just five days before his murder. Garrow, *Bearing the Cross,* 617, and see 375.

19. Stoney Johnson in *USA Today,* Oct. 12, 1989. (Johnson was later killed in a motorcycle crash.) A month later, the Nashville *Tennessean* ran a story about Martin Luther King III, who confronted Abernathy, telling him, "I think your treatment of my father was unfair," and that it "embarrassed" his family. King spoke for himself and not other members of the family. Apparently alluding to the time when the FBI files are finally released, King told the paper, "When the truth is told, people will find out that the information in the book is not factual." Abernathy also told the paper that he had never said King *had sex* with any woman outside his marriage. (Abernathy said then that he did not know what King did with those women he was alone with in hotel rooms: "He may have counseled them. He may have prayed with them.") The AP story on this is one of the few that confirmed Abernathy had had a stroke in January 1983. AP dispatch on *Tennessean* story, in *LAS,* Nov. 16, 1989.

20. Abernathy on his "minor" strokes, the first in January 1983, and experimental surgery at Johns Hopkins to install a new carotid artery, in *And the Walls Came Tumbling Down,* 603–606, 610. Abernathy also named Hooks in his memoir. The standard story of King's last night alive, Abernathy reminded people, was that he spent much of the evening at Hooks's house. Ibid., 433–34. (Hooks was then a Memphis preacher and judge.)

21. All this was discussed in a press conference that Hill called. It took place at King's crypt, almost certainly with Mrs. King's approval.

22. Statement by Jesse Jackson et al. at Jesse Hill's press conference, in AP, Oct. 13, 1989; David Garrow pointed out that this high-profile reaction probably only provided more publicity and sales for Abernathy's book in his statement in the Portland *Oregonian,* Oct. 22, 1989. Mrs. King later indirectly confirmed that she endorsed the statement and would have no further comment, but hardly anybody picked up on that: "King Center Officials," AP, Oct. 12, 1989. The statement was also quoted at length and

endorsed by Benjamin Chavis in the *Muslim Journal,* Nov. 10, 1989, 3, 26, and in the New York *Daily News,* Oct. 13, 1989. Art Harris said this grew out of a "long simmering feud" between Abernathy and others who took "the reins of the movement." Harris in *WP,* Oct. 18, 1989.

Hosea Williams did not corroborate Abernathy's testimony as to King's affairs, though he took pains not to deny it: "I was there," Williams told columnist Earl Caldwell, "and I didn't see any such women. But then, I don't see everything that goes on." Caldwell in New York *Daily News,* Oct. 13, 1989. Caldwell defended Abernathy in his next column: ibid., Oct. 16, 1989.

23. AP dispatch on Colorado Springs, and Samuel Lewis to editor, in *LAS,* Oct. 26, 1989.
24. On Sharpton: Abiola Sinclair in *Amsterdam News,* Oct. 21, 1989, and J. Zamgba Browne in *Amsterdam News,* Oct. 21, 1989.
25. On Abernathy's death threats: Art Harris in *WP,* Oct. 18, 1989. It cannot have reassured Abernathy that his most prominent defender was the notorious Roy Innis, who had been such a great enemy of nonviolence and integration, and had taken up with Nixon, and later right-wing thugs and vigilantes. Innis praised Abernathy for his courage and said, "They're trying to make him the Black man's [Salman] Rushdie." Innis on Abernathy, *Amsterdam News,* Oct. 21, 1989, stories by Mel Tapley, 1, and by J. Zamgba Browne, 38.
26. Clarence Page, *CT,* Oct. 18, 1989; Milton Reid, *Norfolk Journal & Guide,* Oct. 18, 1989; William Raspberry, *WP,* Oct. 18, 1989; Jim Cleaver, *LAS,* Oct. 19, 1989; Doc Young, *LAS,* Oct. 26, 1989; Chuck Stone, *LAS,* Nov. 9, 1989; Don Wycliff, *NYT,* Nov. 14, 1989; Tony Brown, *Pittsburgh Courier,* Jan. 20, 1990. Henry Hampton— whose brilliant documentary *Eyes on the Prize* may have influenced more people's understanding of civil rights than any other figure—took out a review in *The New York Times.* He blamed Abernathy for the firestorm. Hampton in *NYT,* Oct. 29, 1989. Eric Bentley responded to Hampton: "One should not make Dr. King a role model in areas where he wasn't. To say this may be to pull him off a pedestal. But a pedestal is a bad place to be. A real great man, warts and all, is a far more interesting and sympathetic figure than a plaster saint." Bentley to editor, *NYT,* Nov. 26, 1989.
27. Juan Williams in *WP,* Oct. 15, 1989. Another of Abernathy's few defenders, a rather lukewarm one, was more emphatic on Jesse Jackson. According to Mary McGrory, Jackson "has a personal interest in discrediting the book. Abernathy tells us something else we knew, namely that Jackson, when King was killed, went about for several days wearing a shirt that was stained with blood that Jackson said was King's and claiming to have held the dying King in his arms." Mary McGrory in *St. Louis Post-Dispatch,* Oct. 24, 1989. Other defenses came later in black papers—notably a very thoughtful one by Almena Lomax in the *Kansas City Call*—but they were not widely reprinted or heard. See Lomax in *Kansas City Call,* Jan. 12, 1990.
28. Abernathy quoted in Art Harris in *WP,* Oct. 18, 1989.
29. Abernathy, interview in *Boston Herald,* in AP in *LAS,* Nov. 16, 1989.
30. UPI on Alabama State University dorm, Nov. 5, 1989; AP story on dorm, *LAS,* Nov. 9, 1989. Alabama State went ahead and named a dorm for male students—originally planned as half of a pair—after King. It was completed and named Martin Luther King Jr. Hall—along with a dorm for female students named Bessie Sears Estell Hall—in 1989. Sometime later, after the controversy died down, ASU inaugurated a lecture series in Abernathy's name. It also erected a Ralph D. Abernathy Museum on campus, next to the Nat King Cole House. In 2008, it announced a $30 million construction project, the Ralph D. Abernathy College of Education Building, scheduled for occupancy in April 2009. That building has since been completed and stands now as Ralph David Abernathy Hall. Alabama State University website (alasu.edu) as of Dec. 12, 2008; updated, as of May 22, 2013.
31. *Boston Globe,* Nov. 7, 1989; *LAS,* Nov. 16, 1989.

32. Abernathy's sales figures: Art Harris in *WP,* Oct. 18, 1989, and *WP,* Oct. 16, 1989.
33. Garrow in *Oregonian,* Oct. 22, 1989, and in Harris, *WP,* Oct. 18, 1989.
34. Cal Thomas in *St. Louis Post-Dispatch,* Oct. 24, 1989.
35. Poll: 63 percent of those who changed their vote to no in the last two days before the election said they did so because of CBS broadcaster Greg Gumbel's brief report on the NFL threat. That meant about 60,000 of the roughly 1 million voters who voted on the question. *Arizona Republic,* Nov. 14, 1990. (A different poll came up with a different result, taking this question of motive from an indirect angle. In *Arizona Republic,* Nov. 16, 1990.) Polls before the election found pro-holiday sentiment running higher than sentiment against it, and indeed the conservative *Arizona Republic,* which had endorsed the holiday, confidently predicted a victory before the election, and even a full day after polls had closed, while votes were being counted. *Arizona Republic,* Nov. 2, editorial and voters' guide Nov. 4, editorial Nov. 6, and a front-page banner headline story Nov. 7, 1990. Sportscaster Greg Gumbel took a lot of heat for reporting that the NFL planned to "take back" the Super Bowl if Arizona failed to enact the holiday on the CBS show *The NFL Today.* See *Arizona Republic,* Nov. 8, 1990 (two stories).
36. Charlotte was one of the few success stories of school desegregation. It was also supplanting Atlanta—which despite black mayors and black representation in Congress made conspicuously little racial progress—as the commercial capital of the New South. See Matthew Lassiter, *Silent Majority: Suburban Politics in the Sunbelt South* (Princeton, N.J.: Princeton University Press, 2007), and Kevin Kruse, *White Flight: Atlanta and the Making of Modern Conservatism* (Princeton, N.J.: Princeton University Press, 2007).
37. In challenging incumbent Democrat Bennett Johnston, Duke had no support from national Republicans—who had been on record opposing him before. Missouri's Republican senator John Danforth in fact endorsed Johnston. Though Johnston won, Duke managed to get an embarrassing 44 percent of the vote. Liberals—as well as some Republicans who were distinctly right of center—were deeply disturbed that a symbol of unrepentant racial hatred could get such a big vote, despite losing his party's support, and despite being vastly outspent. Figures from Michael W. Giles and Melanie Buckner, "David Duke and the Electoral Politics of Racial Threat," in John C. Kuzenski, Charles S. Bullock III, and Ronald Keith Gaddie, eds., *David Duke and the Politics of Race in the South* (Nashville, Tenn.: Vanderbilt University Press, 1995), 88–98. On Duke, see also, Douglas Rose, ed., *The Emergence of David Duke and the Politics of Race* (Chapel Hill: University of North Carolina Press, 1992); Tyler Bridges, *The Rise of David Duke* (Jackson, Miss.: University Press of Mississippi, 1994); and Michael Zatarain, *David Duke: Evolution of a Klansman* (Gretna, La.: Pelican, 1990).
    In 1992, Duke ran for governor—perhaps aided by all the media attention he had gotten against Johnston. Democrat Edwin Edwards—already widely believed to be corrupt—beat him handily, 61 percent to 39 percent, though Duke ran over 60 percent among middle-income white voters and white Protestants. *Almanac of American Politics 1994.*
38. This example is taken from Theodore Pappas, "A Dr. in Spite of Himself: The Strange Career of Martin Luther King, Jr.'s Dissertation," *Chronicles,* January 1991. It was widely repeated—along with several other examples that Pappas (and, earlier, John Shelton Reed) had found—in newspaper and magazine coverage of the controversy. Pappas reprinted his article in Pappas, ed., *The Martin Luther King, Jr., Plagiarism Story* (Rockford, Ill.: Rockford Institute, 1994), 48–61.
39. The calculations were made by the Martin Luther King Papers Project, under the direction of Professor Clayborne Carson at Stanford, and later quoted in Cartwright, Hardwick, Hart, and Neville, "Report of the Boston University Committee to Investigate Charges of Plagiarism in the Ph.D. Dissertation of Martin Luther King, Jr.," September 1991, in Gottlieb Archive, Boston University.

40. *WSJ*, Nov. 9, 1990. This article can also be found in Pappas, ed., *The Martin Luther King, Jr., Plagiarism Story*. In February 2008, the Online Computer Library Center found copies of this book in thirty libraries worldwide, all presumably accessible through interlibrary loan. In May 2008, I was able to find seven copies (all overpriced) on ABE.com. Many libraries still have *The Wall Street Journal* on microfilm. Some very rich, privileged institutions are able to afford the unconscionably overpriced version of the *Journal* available from ProQuest. See below for more on the double-standard question.

41. Frank Johnson in *Telegraph*, Dec. 3, 1989. This article is reprinted in Pappas, ed., *The Martin Luther King, Jr., Plagiarism Story*, 43–44.

42. Wieseltier quoted in Babington in ibid., 73. Babington reports that Dan Balz of *The Washington Post* had the story early on but failed to pursue it. Babington reports that *The Atlanta Journal-Constitution*, *The New York Times*, and *The New Republic* all similarly had much of the story in hand and decided to muzzle it, either actively and consciously or by an abnormal amount of indecision.

43. BU statement by "school officials" in AP, Nov. 9.

44. Mel King in *Boston Globe*, Nov. 13, 1990. The university's province was academic criteria. Its job was to decide what no one else was ever asked to decide: whether King measured up to those criteria. Of course its authority extended beyond rules of citation, but in this instance, it *alone* had the authority to judge the only question now raised about King: whether he violated BU's rules under BU's supervision—and thus whether BU officials were negligent or complicit. See also Statement of Jon Westling, Nov. 9, 1990, Appendix A to Cartwright, Hardwick, Hart, and Neville, "Report of the Boston University Committee to Investigate Charges of Plagiarism in the Ph.D. Dissertation of Martin Luther King, Jr.," in Gottlieb Archive, BU.

45. *The New York Times* reported this even as it reported BU officials indicating that they forbade their appointed experts from deciding that the plagiarism extended very far. *NYT*, Nov. 10, 1990.

46. The *Times* was evidently under great strain in trying to straddle this issue. The same editorial went on that King's plagiarism "cast a shadow on his memory; a shadow should not, however, be confused with a cloud." *NYT*, Nov. 13, 1990. A reader could have searched far and wide without finding clarity. Cf. *Newsweek*: plagiarism and adultery revelations are "[c]learly enough to tarnish a reputation, but not a life." *Newsweek*, Nov. 19, 1990. *The Boston Globe*'s editorial was typical: "The academic community is understandably alarmed by charges of King's plagiarism. . . . [R]evelations that someone of King's stature may have [plagiarized] threaten the integrity of all scholarly pursuits." Like many papers, the *Globe* ceded judgment about King's cheating to academics, who it assumed were—or should be?—stricter about such things than ordinary folk.

47. See scholars quoted in, for example, *WSJ*, Nov. 9, 1990; *WP*, Nov. 10, 1990; and *NYT*, Nov. 10, 1990.

48. Statement of Jon Westling, Nov. 9, 1990, Gottlieb Archive, BU. This line is quoted in *Boston Globe*, Nov. 10, 1990, and elsewhere. Yet BU had already made comments compromising the committee.

49. Indeed, Westling's charge to the committee—later attached to its final report as if to excuse the committee's failure to come to any independent conclusions—had a peremptory tone. After noting the committee was asked to provide a "prompt and careful" examination of the evidence, he concluded: "It must be noted, however, that the stature of Martin Luther King, Jr., as the preeminent leader of America's civil rights movement does not depend upon the truth or falsity of the charges now being raised. Boston University contributed to Dr. King's education and opened to him areas of philosophical and theological scholarship on which he drew throughout his public career. But his great and lasting contributions to American society and to humanity rest upon the life

he made after he left the University." He also appeared to offer them a way out: "[T]o investigate allegations against an individual who is no longer alive is, in some important respects, different from investigating similar allegations in a case involving a living person who, by contrast, is able to discuss his research methods . . . and who has the opportunity to justify any misleading appearances in the documentary record." Statement of Jon Westling, Nov. 9, 1990, Appendix A to Cartwright, Hardwick, Hart, and Neville, "Report of the Boston University Committee to Investigate Charges of Plagiarism in the Ph.D. Dissertation of Martin Luther King, Jr.," in Gottlieb Archive, BU.

50. Lowery in *San Francisco Chronicle*, Nov. 10, 1990.
51. Jackson in *USA Today*, Nov. 13, 1990; AP also quoted Jackson using footprint images: AP, Nov. 13, 1990.
52. Miller, "The Influence of a Liberal Homiletic Tradition on 'Strength to Love' by Martin Luther King, Jr." (Ph.D. diss., Texas Christian University, 1984).
53. Miller says King did "absolutely nothing wrong." *The Washington Post* published that statement on Nov. 10. Miller's 1986 and 1990 articles were also cited in the *WSJ*, Nov. 9, 1990.
54. Keith Miller in *WP*, Nov. 10, 1990. Jesse Jackson took the black oral tradition line, too, but then insisted this practice was not exclusively black: Presidents don't write their own speeches, he noted. *USA Today*, Nov. 13, 1990.
55. This point of view is explored further in James Cone, "Martin Luther King, Jr., Black Theology—Black Church," *Theology Today* 40 (Jan. 1984): 409–420, "The Theology of Martin Luther King," *Union Seminary Quarterly Review* 40 (January 1986): 21–39, "Martin Luther King, Jr., and the Third World," *Journal of American History* 74 (September 1987): 455–67, Paul Garber, "Black Theology: The Latter Day Legacy of Martin Luther King, Jr.," *Journal of the Interdenominational Theological Center* 2 (Spring 1975): 100–113, "King Was a Black Theologian," *Journal of Religious Thought* (Fall–Winter 1974–75): 16–32, "Too Much Taming of Martin Luther King," *Christian Century*, June 5, 1974, David Garrow, "The Intellectual Development of Martin Luther King, Jr.: Influences and Commentaries," *Union Seminary Quarterly Review* 40 (January 1986): 5–20, Keith Miller, "Martin Luther King, Jr., Borrows a Revolution: Argument, Audience, and Implications of a Secondhand Universe," *College English* 48 (March 1986): 249–65, "Composing Martin Luther King, Jr.," *Proceedings of the Modern Language Association* 105 (January 1990): 70–82, "Martin Luther King, Jr., and the Black Folk Pulpit," *Journal of American History* 78 (June 1991): 120–23, and review in the *NYT Book Review*, March 15, 1992.
56. Carson to Reynolds, in *USA Today*, Nov. 13, 1990.
57. Ralph Luker and Ralph Hill in *WP*, Nov. 10, 1990. It should be noted that the *Sunday Telegraph* article in December 1989—the first published claim that King had plagiarized his graduate school work—cited Luker as its main source, though the reporter only had word of Luker's discoveries secondhand, from an unnamed "informant" who worked with Luker.
58. *Boston Globe*, Nov. 13, 1990.
59. Editorial, *St. Louis Post-Dispatch*, Nov. 14, 1990. In developing the humanity defense, King's defenders conjured up a straw man, the typical fragile admirer of King who could not accept his imperfections. Carl McClendon's theme in the *St. Petersburg Times*: "The mistake many King supporters make is in trying to deify the man." *St. Petersburg Times*, Nov. 14, 1990. Along the same lines, Ellen Goodman suggested that "we have had too much of heroes manufactured and disassembled. . . . [I]t's time not just for a revisionist view of King, but of hero-worship itself." *Boston Globe*, Nov. 15, 1990.
60. Ralph Luker and Ralph Hill in *WP*, Nov. 10, 1990.
61. Carson elsewhere declined to estimate what percentage of King's work he and his colleagues thought was plagiarized. *NYT*, Nov. 10, 1990.

62. See below for Garrow's suggestion that King was too busy. Garrow elaborated on this in "King's Plagiarism: Imitation, Insecurity, and Transformation," *Journal of American History* 78 (June 1991): 87, n. 4.

63. Garrow in *WP*, Nov. 18, 1990. Neither Garrow nor anybody else asked the question that should have sprung from Garrow's observation that King got low grades at Morehouse. By the mid-twentieth century, had the standards of American divinity schools and seminaries dropped far lower—had their professors grown more inured to sloppy and unoriginal thinking, and more easily snowed by confidence and eloquence of white or black students—than secular institutions, academic and otherwise?

64. David Lewis, admitting that he had failed to grasp something quite significant— "who he was simply escaped me"—faulted King's "delinquent professors." Lewis speculated—carefully admitting it was only speculation—that "a vintage liberal" like Harold DeWolf might have been impressed that King could do anything resembling scholarship, and that he and others had had expectations of their few black students that were "demeaningly modest." He thought it possible that "smug professors" were "willfully indulging a bright enough degree candidate who, his studies completed, would return to the South to serve his people." And further that King would instantly have sensed the "racial double standard of his professors"; he "may well have decided to repay their condescension or contempt in like coin. After all, neither he nor they knew who Martin Luther King was then." Lewis in *Journal of American History* 78 (June 1991): 84–85.

   David Thelen put the question to S. Paul Schilling, second reader of King's dissertation at BU. Schilling absolutely and categorically denied any double standard. Thelen interview with Schilling in *Journal of American History* 78 (June 1991): 65. Thelen put the question to Cornish Rogers, a fellow black student of King's, who was active with King in the Dialectical Society when they were both at BU. Rogers had a very different view of race at BU from Schilling. Thelen asked: Did DeWolf and Schilling pass King saying, in effect, "Aw, he's black. Let him through"? Rogers replied, "That I can't buy because I knew the two folks and I knew how tough they were on me." Rogers did not give "any credence at all" to the idea that reverse racism governed the process (55–56). But asked why King's professors thought so highly of him, Rogers also said the reasons were: "One, he was quick and bright, and he was black, of course, and that helped to ease their anxiety about black students who were not as good as they should be." Rogers said black students were marked by inferior early education; most lacked "good verbal and written skills." And in that sense, King stood out, "but not just on academics but also in his manner. In class, I'm told he had a serious and a very accommodating manner." Rogers said there was some cynicism among many black students about just going through the motions to get the credentials that would validate them in black communities they were destined to preach to, saying the substance of their studies meant nothing to them. King was distinctly not like that, and his professors noticed that with approval (49–50). Rogers said that white faculty did not think very highly of Howard Thurman, the only black professor at BU, who had just gotten there and was dean of the chapel. They didn't like him because he was a mystic, rather than a true Christian (52). Rogers said that DeWolf "took on a lot of dissertations from, especially, black students or others whom other professors would not take on." DeWolf took on many "whose topics were not in his field. I got the impression that he helped a lot of folks who had difficulty getting someone to be their readers" (53). Rogers wasn't sure whether racism was the reason others wouldn't take them on, "but I know a lot of blacks tended to move toward him or Muelder in social ethics" (54). As for copying, Rogers thought King expected DeWolf to determine where he was too close to Boozer and where he wasn't: "I think that King generally expected DeWolf to go over it with a fine-tooth comb, and I think he was relieved when DeWolf passed it eventually. I think King didn't worry about anything after that because he knew that if DeWolf put his imprimatur on it, it must be OK. I think he trusted DeWolf to guide him through that, to flag anything he needed to redo, or anything he did wrong. . . . I think he really depended on DeWolf to do that . . ." (54).

65. AP, Oct. 11, 1991; Gregg Easterbrook in *Newsweek,* July 29, 1991. As though Destiny insisted that every university involved in brokering King's past scholarship get egg on its face, the nation's other major academic plagiarism case sullied the name of Stanford: A member of its famed business school faculty was caught stealing three whole pages, in a profit-making textbook, from a prominent journalist. Easterbrook in *Newsweek,* July 29, 1991.

Such distinguished writers as Wallace Stegner and John Hersey were accused (see Fradkin in *LAT,* Feb. 3, 2008). Gregg Easterbrook—plagiaree in the Stanford case— said that America appeared to be on its way to a "harmonic convergence of plagiarism." He wrote a hilarious column about the absurdities—he had the reaction common to victims: He felt flattered, but he wanted a percentage of the take. He pointed out that if an author paraphrases a universally known passage—from the Gettysburg Address or the first line of Dickens's *Tale of Two Cities,* for example—it cannot be plagiarism since everybody recognizes it and it doesn't need to be pointed out. But if someone paraphrases, or riffs satirically on, a more obscure passage, it might be plagiarism, provided that nobody gets the joke and people assume the satirist to be that eloquent. If in either case the original is so mangled by inept paraphrase as to be unrecognizable, then it is not plagiarism by anybody's definition, though it is no more original, only less good. He characterized a scandal over Conor Cruise O'Brien's selling the same prose passages to two magazines as "self-plagiarism." See also Thomas Mallon, *Stolen Words* (New York: Ticknor & Fields, 1989); Philip Martin, "Carefully Borrowed Lines a Disease of the Soul," *Arkansas Democrat-Gazette,* March 10, 1996; David Callahan, *The Cheating Culture* (New York: Harcourt, 2004); Marcus Boon, *In Praise of Copying* (Cambridge, Mass.: Harvard University Press, 2010).

66. Jack S. Boozer, "The Place of Reason in Paul Tillich's Concept of God" (Ph.D. diss., Boston University School of Theology, 1952).

67. *NYT,* Nov. 11, 1990.

68. See Ken Adelman in the *Syracuse Herald-Journal,* Nov. 14, 1990; Pat Buchanan in the Portland *Oregonian, Seattle Post-Intelligencer,* etc., Nov. 14, 1990; Jeffrey Hart in the Doyleston, Pennsylvania, *Intelligencer,* Nov. 20, 1990; Joseph Sobran in the *Arizona Republic,* Nov. 14, 1990; Cal Thomas in the *St. Louis Post-Dispatch,* Nov. 15, 1990; and Manchester *Union Leader,* editorials, Nov. 15, 18, and 21, 1990. The long-term holdouts that had kept company with Arizona for a while fell into line as follows: Wyoming's governor Mike Sullivan signed a state King holiday into law March 15, 1990; Idaho's Cecil Andrus signed one on April 10, 1990; Montana's governor Stan Stephens signed a state holiday into law on Feb. 8, 1991; North Dakota's governor George Sinner, rejecting a referendum, signed a paid state holiday into law on March 28, 1991. (In listing the holdouts before March 1991, some papers omitted North Dakota, since its holiday was unpaid. Also note: Louisiana's holiday was by proclamation—which had to be renewed every year, and fell on Jan. 19; Maryland's was on Jan. 15 whether that was a weekday or not; and some states gave state employees other holiday options to substitute for King Day. AP, April 10, 1990.)

69. The committee found "no evidence whatsoever" that King's professors "had a double standard that would let African American students off easy. On the contrary, students from that era as well as faculty report that standards were applied with equal strictness to black as well as to white students. Black as well as white students failed out of the program." Cartwright, Hardwick, Hart, and Neville, "Report of the Boston University Committee to Investigate Charges of Plagiarism in the Ph.D. Dissertation of Martin Luther King, Jr.," in Gottlieb Archive, Boston University. Appendix D to the report, a letter from S. Paul Schilling, the second reader of King's dissertation, to Clayborne

Carson, gives a somewhat different perspective. Schilling admits that "King is guilty of shoddy scholarship" and that Carson had "a right to ask how King could have gotten by with so many instances of shoddy scholarship." Schilling denied any racial motive on his own part. He said he was very exacting and required King to correct many kinds of errors. He explained his lack of vigilance on the narrow question of attributions by saying that he was "relatively inexperienced in dissertation evaluation" when he read King's work. "I have to admit that I was not sufficiently perceptive in regard to plagiarism." Speaking of King's motives, Schilling added, "I can hardly imagine his not knowing that his failures to cite sources were unacceptable." King's tight schedule as a pastor was "no justification of his failure to cite sources, but it could help explain how he might have regarded his omissions from and additions to unattributed quoted passages as sufficient to deliver him from the charge of failure to quote." Although Schilling attributed his own lapses in evaluating King to his inexperience, and said that he became more exacting in later years, he wrote later in the letter that "I judged King's work by exactly the same standards as those operable in my estimate of [white candidate Edward] Bauman's dissertation and those that followed in later years in judging other white candidates." Schilling to Carson, Nov. 5, 1990, appendix D to committee report, Gottlieb Archive, Boston University.

70. A copy of the committee's letter was indeed placed with the copy of King's dissertation deposited in the King Papers collection at the BU library—but nowhere else that anyone might find it. The letter does not say that King plagiarized, or even that instances of plagiarism appear in his work. It states only two facts the committee could not conceal: "this dissertation contains numerous passages that lack appropriate quotation marks and citations of sources consulted and used" and "King fully understood that dissertations are to be properly documented." The word "plagiarism" appears only once, in the name of the committee that signed the letter. Though the letter referred readers to the report deposited in BU's library, the report can only be obtained by someone persistent and informed enough to seek it out—and then, again, minus its substantive appendices. Boston University does not send copies of the five appendices to researchers and does not allow them to be photocopied. Appendix B is pages 23–40 from the *Journal of American History* of June 1991. Appendix E is the original of the committee's letter, a copy of which is included in the copy of King's dissertation kept in the BU Library's Special Collections. Letter from "the Committee to Investigate Charges of Plagiarism in the Dissertation of Martin Luther King, Jr., whose members we are," enclosed with the noncirculating copy of King, "A Comparison of the Conceptions of God in the Thinking of Paul Tillich and Henry Nelson Wieman," in Boston University, Mugar Library, Special Collections, Box 2. The official copy of King's dissertation is supposed to be shelved with all the other dissertations in the Mugar Library stacks. But during my visits to BU in April 2009, nobody on the library staff was able to locate that copy, or to tell me whether it contains a copy of the committee's letter. As of January 24, 2009, there were ninety-six copies of King's dissertation available from the major research libraries listed by the Online Computer Library Center (OCLC). It appears from my spot checks that none of these include the committee's letter, or any acknowledgment of the plagiarism charges.

71. The committee report stated, "Although the committee did not attempt to duplicate the exhaustive work of the King Papers Project, our spot checks, found below as Appendix C, indicate that the project's study is accurate." Interestingly, the committee did not share the King Papers Project director's view of King's motives, or his conclusion that carelessness was the cause of his many unattributed borrowings. Rather, the committee stated, "Dr. King is responsible for knowingly misappropriating the borrowed materials that he failed to cite or to cite adequately." On the other hand, the committee pulled its punch in the next paragraph, giving King a generous benefit of the doubt: "Although often theft of language cannot be distinguished from theft of ideas, the fact

that Dr. King did not try to represent the ideas of others as his own, only their language, mitigates the most serious kind of charge that might have been brought." A major part of the committee's reason for refusing to consider revocation of the degree was that the dead King could not explain his motives and methods. Yet the committee states as "fact" that King did not "try" to take credit for others' ideas. Appendix C, containing the "spot checks" by Professor Ray L. Hart of Boston University and Professor Charley D. Hardwick of American University, has numerous damning instances of unattributed quotations.

72. King's dissertation is reprinted in full in Clayborne Carson et al., eds., *The Papers of Martin Luther King,* vol. II (Berkeley and Los Angeles: University of California Press, 1994), 339–548. Though that copy does not include the committee's letter, it has extensive annotations identifying the portions King copied, and a headnote that depicts the extent and character of King's plagiarism far more frankly and thoroughly than the letter.

73. *New Yorker,* April 13, 1968, 35–37.

Index

Page numbers in *italics* refer to illustrations.